# vegetarian

## dishes FROM THE MIDDLE EAST

### arto der haroutunian

# vegetarian
## dishes FROM THE MIDDLE EAST

### arto der haroutunian

GRUB STREET | LONDON

Published in 2008 by
Grub Street, 4 Rainham Close, London SW11 6SS
email: food@grubstreet.co.uk
www.grubstreet.co.uk

Reprinted 2008

First published in Great Britain in 1983
by Century Publishing Co. Ltd

ISBN 9781902304816
A CIP catalogue for this book is available from the British Library

Printed and bound by MPG Ltd, Bodmin, Cornwall

This book is printed on FSC (Forest Stewardship Council) paper

Acknowledgements

Poems from the *Book of 1001 Nights* are taken from R.J. Burton's translation of 1885. For Sidgi Effendi, see *Mal-ja-ot-Tabahin* (Cairo, 1886). The lines from Mahmoud Darwish are from *The Music of Human Flesh*, translated by Denys Johnson-Davis (Heinemann, 1980); 'Armenian Folksong' from *Anthology of Armenian Poetry* ed. D.D. Hovanessian (CUP, New York, 1978); the anecdotes were translated and edited from various late 19th-century and early 20th-century Turkish and Armenian periodicals.

**Note: Unless otherwise stated, the recipes serve 4–6 people. Ideally, Middle Eastern dishes should be combined according to taste and the occasion.**

# contents

introduction
6

soups
11

appetisers
35

salads
61

egg and cheese dishes
85

pilavs
107

cold and warm dishes

139

stuffed vegetables 140 olive oil-based dishes 157

pastas and cereals 165 vegetables 179

savouries — pies and pastries 197

breads
213

pickles
223

sauces and dressings
241

desserts
251

index
284

*When frying an aubergine be gentle. Ask its permission first, then thank the Lord.*
**Armenian saying**

The Middle East, the 'cradle' of our Western civilisation, has not only been the centre of three major world religions, the foundation stone of great empires and the birthplace of many of history's greatest men, but also the major source of much of our Western culture. It was on the slopes of what is now Kurdistan that man first succeeded in cultivating wheat and barley 8–10,000 years ago. It was in Mesopotamia and Asia Minor (modern Turkey) where animals were first domesticated and where man built his first crude shelter, to be followed by fortified cities, communities, law, order and literature. One of the least-known and appreciated achievements of the Middle Eastern people has been in the field of food cultivation or, in present day technological jargon, 'food culture'.

Innumerable tribes, races and nations have appeared on the podia of history, acted out their roles and then returned into the void of time, only to be followed by others who have retrieved their predecessor's mantle and assured the evolution of history. Thus, down the ages have come (only to go in their turn) the peoples of the Pharaohs, Sumerians, Assyrians, Hebrews, Hittites, Babylonians, Urartians, Phoenicians, Greeks and Romans.

The people of the Middle East today, who regard themselves as Arabs, Armenians, Iranians, Kurds, Jews or Turks are, in essence, the descendants of those people of the past. They have retained the basic cultures of their ancestors almost intact although their own ancestry is often hidden in self-perpetuating shrouds of mystery and romance. A brief study of their cultures, be it of food, mythology, art or applied sciences, will illustrate clearly the contention that the people of the Middle East are virtually – with a very few exceptions – of the same ancestry and culture, and their food is part of that same culture.

Time was when a handful of daring and eccentric Europeans – one had to be eccentric to be daring in those days – dressed as Arabs or, acting as missionaries or archeologists, traversed the dunes of Arabia, plundered their way through Asia Minor or descended into the valleys of Kurdistan in search of knowledge and excitement – or in pursuit of personal achievement or enlightenment. On their return they brought with them smatterings of half-truths, hearsay and mumbo-jumbo; ideas picked from the corners of the souks or from the hot, sweaty chambers of partly ruined Turkish baths. To them, and to most other Westerners, the Middle East was – and in some ways still is – the 'mysterious Orient'.

Yet there was never anything mysterious about the Middle East. The mystery was in the eyes and minds of the foreign beholders! Little was – and still is – known about the food of this region; only in recent years has the average European or American heard of such Middle Eastern specialities as kebabs, yoghurt, stuffed vegetables and sheep's eyes! But one of the most interesting (dare one say *exciting*) contributions to the culinary culture of the world is still hardly known or appreciated: I refer, or course, to the Middle Eastern art of vegetable cooking.

The people of the Middle East are in essence vegetarians; meat, poultry or fish are really 'extras' to their basic diet of cereals, pulses, dairy produce and vegetables. Over the centuries, versatile, rich and often ritualistic methods of vegetable cooking have evolved; for both to the men of the desert and those on the hills, a little had to go a long way and this meant careful husbandry, clever use of what was available, relatively imperishable and even edible. There is such a thing as Middle Eastern cuisine, as there is Indian, Chinese or European cuisine, yet this can be subdivided by taking into account certain religious, geographic and ethnic differences. Nevertheless, there is an overall uniformity in approach, preparation and presentation.

The first obvious characteristic of the region's cooking in general – and vegetarian cooking in particular – is its innate simplicity. The nomadic tribesmen or the peasants in their mud-baked shelters were not interested in, nor could they afford to create, 'haute cuisine'. Theirs is a simple, honest type of food without pretensions or ornamentation. Simplicity, however, does not imply monotony – thanks to the many spices and herbs available to give flavour and character to the main ingredients used.

The Middle East is fortunate in these spices. Because of its geographical position, the people of the Middle East have for centuries been the middlemen in trade transactions between the Far Eastern lands and Europe. Through Arabia, Persia and Anatolia passed the caravans carrying carpets, silk, jewellery and spices; indeed virtually everything that came to Europe prior to the discovery of the route to India via the Cape of Good Hope, passed through the Middle East.

Another important characteristic is the method of preparing vegetables. No self-respecting housewife will just boil her vegetables; they will be fried in olive oil or butter first. If the vegetables are to be served cold, they will be cooked in oil as this does not congeal when cold. Vegetables prepared in this way make excellent appetisers, salads or side dishes. Cooking with olive oil is most common along the Mediterranean coastline and has been known there for millennia. Butter or ghee dishes are more popular in Iran, Iraq, the Caucasus and the desert lands, where olives are not readily available. Here, the vegetables are fried, stewed, grilled, baked or stuffed with other vegetables; they are pickled, used in salads and also made into delicious sweets and preserves.

Vegetables such as onions, leeks, spinach, beans, tomatoes and cucumbers are all well known and used by European and American housewives, but there are certain others which, although they have entered Western cuisines in recent years, are still best exploited by the people of the Middle East. For example:

a) **The aubergine** – originally from India, it appeared in the Middle East in the 7th and 8th centuries (much earlier in Persia). If there is such a thing as a 'Middle Eastern vegetable' then it is most certainly the aubergine. There are literally hundreds of ways of cooking this vegetable, several of which have been included in this book.

b) **The avocado** – this pear-shaped fruit is a recent addition to the cuisine of the Middle East, and to date is still only really popular in Israel, where it was introduced from the USA several decades ago.

c) **The courgette** – is a variety of narrow summer marrow and until recently was only popular in the Mediterranean region. It is perhaps, after the aubergine, the most-used vegetable and there are innumerable recipes for its use, too.

d) **Okra** – also known as ladies' fingers – is, as its name suggests, delicately finger-shaped. It is a hairy fruit pod of African origin and, while popular throughout the Middle East and India, it is still relatively unknown in the West, though it is becoming more readily available.

e) **The pumpkin** – the 'Cinderella of the vegetable kingdom' is very popular in Turkey, Armenia and Kurdistan. It was once also popular in Europe in pre-potato and tomato days.

Great use is also made of many fruits, such as apples, pears, apricots, peaches, grapes, cherries, oranges and many more. Some favourite ones are not so well known in the West, for example:

a) **Dates** – particularly popular with the Arabs who, as well as eating them fresh, use them in stews, sweets and even drinks.

b) **Figs** – these are grown throughout the region and are indigenous to Asia Minor. They are used fresh or dried in soups, salads and stews.

c) **Pomegranates** – a large, round many-celled fruit with seeds enclosed in an acidy rind of golden colour tinged with red. It was known in Europe merely as an ornament or decoration – as evidenced by a great number of late Renaissance and Dutch paintings of the 15th and 16th centuries. In the East, however, pomegranates were used for their unique flavour – not only as a fruit, but in stews, sweets and, especially with Armenians and Iranians, as the source of one of the most original syrups in the Middle Eastern cuisine.

d) **Quinces** – another fruit not unknown in Europe, but little used. It is a yellowish pear-shaped fruit that was once very popular in medieval Britain.

All the herbs and spices that are currently used in Middle Eastern cuisines are known in the West. However, in addition, there are a few which have not as yet acquired the recognition they deserve:

a) **Sumak** – the powdered seeds of the Mediterranean plant *Rhus coriaria* which is extensively used by the Armenians and, to a lesser extent, by the Turks and Iranians in flavouring and colouring a great number of their dishes.

b) **Cumin** – an ancient favourite of Egyptian origin, extensively used throughout the region, but particularly by the peoples living close to the Mediterranean coastline.

c) **Tarragon** – this is very popular with the Caucasians and appears in its fresh form throughout their cuisine as also do:

d) **Basil** – a fragrant herb with a subtle flavour, used in salads, pilavs, pickles and stuffings.

e) **Fenugreek** – known as 'Greek hay' to the Romans. It is an unusual Asiatic herb with reddish-brown seeds, aromatic and bitter. It is used by Armenians, Iranians and, at the other edge of the region, by the Yemenis who generously flavour their salads and relishes with it.

f) **Oregano and dill** – both very popular in Turkey, while the Iranians and Iraqis have a strong penchant for:

g) **Turmeric** – a dark yellow powder, which is indigenous to the Indian subcontinent.

h) **Saffron** – an orange-red product of the plant *Crocus sativus*, indigenous to India and Iran. In its powdered form it appears in pilav dishes, stews and desserts.

An outstanding ingredient that has now become almost a cult in the West is yoghurt. Unfortunately it is, as yet, not appreciated to the full, and it is used more as a sweet or a light finish to a meal than as a nourishing food and an aid to digestion which either accompanies a meal or is one of its essential components. Yoghurt goes extremely well with warm or cold vegetables and there are many recipes in this book which demonstrate its versatility.

The Mediterranean has produced two outstanding edible oils – olive oil and tahina oil:

a) **Olive oil** – has been known and used for centuries. The ancient Hittites, Capadocians and Greeks popularised the oil extracted from the fruit of the tree *Olea sativa* and they used both the oil and the fruit in cooking, thus creating a unique 'school' – that of the olive oil-based dishes of the Middle East. Incidentally it was not the Romans, but more the Arabs who encouraged and popularised the wide use of olives in Spain and Portugal.

b) **Tahina** – a nutty-flavoured paste made from crushed sesame seeds. It was known to the Hittites and Urartians of Asia Minor, where it most probably originated. Today it is widely used by the Arabs in salads and as a sauce for fish dishes. It also figures strongly in Armenian cuisine, not only in salads, but in soups and breads as well as in pilavs, vegetable dishes and cakes. During recent years it has acquired an almost 'mystical' appeal with the Israelis, who have created several new dishes using this unique and versatile oil.

The Middle East abounds in cereals, but the most popular ones are rice and burghul:

a) **Rice** – This is, of course, the staple cereal of the region. Arabs, Iranians and Turks use nothing but rice.

b) **Burghul (cracked wheat)** – is the staple cereal of the Armenians, most Kurds and the Anatolian Turks who no doubt acquired it from the Kurds several centuries ago. Other cereals such as whole wheat, barley, maize and kasha are also used. The latter appears only in Israel (brought over by the Russian immigrants) and in the Caucasus – again due to the Russian influence.

Pulses also play an important part in the cuisine and account for the fact that many of the dishes are cheap to prepare, wholesome and filling. Among the most commonly used are: chickpeas, lentils, 'ful' beans, red kidney beans, haricot beans and black-eyed beans. They are used in soups, salads, dips and main dishes.

Finally, some mention must be made of the extensive use of nuts. Almonds, especially by Armenians and Turks; hazelnuts by the Iraqis and the Turks; pistachios by the Syrians and Iranians; pine kernels by the Syrians and Lebanese, and walnuts by almost everyone.

So rich is the cuisine of the Middle East, so varied the use of ingredients and versatile their application and, above all, so tried and tested the dishes – for thousands of years – that anyone who approaches these recipes will find satisfaction and contentment. In addition, they will be in touch with the past when perhaps life was simpler, more leisurely and undeniably, if judged by the quality of the food offered, more healthy, wholesome and natural – and what was good for Methuselah should be good enough for you and me! In the words of the Arab poet I, too

*'will be silent now and eat*
*A meal which poets shall respect*
*In songs of cooking, sounds and sage*
*Down all the hungry roads of age'.*

**Bon appetit!**

# soups

The Middle Eastern cuisine abounds with soups made both with and without meat. The mainstay of most peasant cuisines throughout the world, soups have formed the basic subsistence of the people.

There are few consommé-type soups; most are rich and filling, and brilliant use is made of fruits and vegetables. It gives these soups a prominence which is lacking in other cuisines, e.g. those of India or China.

Other popular ingredients include nuts, cereals, pulses, yoghurt and tahina. From the simplest soup such as Spas (yoghurt and barley) to the richest – Ashe Lubi Kharvnez-ba-Esfanaj (red bean and spinach), they are often eaten as a main meal just with bread as an accompaniment – often broken up and added to the soup itself. Here are some recipes including some for cold soups, which are ideal on a hot summer's day. Others are cooked in large pans which simmer for hours, to nourish and warm the family on winter nights in mountainous Anatolia, the Caucasus and Iran.

# tahinov-abour

## chickpea soup with tahina

This is a rich and nourishing Armenian soup of chickpeas, lentils and spinach flavoured with tahina. It can be prepared well in advance, with the exception of the tahina – which must be added just before serving.

2 oz (50g) chickpeas, soaked overnight in cold water
2 oz (50g) dried white beans, soaked overnight in cold water
3 pints (1.8 litres) water
2 oz (50g) whole brown lentils
1 oz (25g) butter
1 large onion, finely chopped
4 oz (110g) fresh spinach, washed thoroughly, squeezed dry and chopped
1 teaspoon salt
1/2 teaspoon black pepper
4 fl oz (120ml) tahina paste

Drain the chickpeas and beans; rinse and place them in a large saucepan with 3 pints (1.8 litres) of water. Bring to the boil, then simmer until the beans are nearly tender. Much of the water will be absorbed or have evaporated, so keep topping-up with boiling water to maintain the original level. Remove any scum that appears on the surface. Add the lentils and cook for 40–50 minutes, or until all the ingredients are tender.

Melt the butter in a small saucepan. Add the onion and fry until it is soft and turning golden brown. Add the onion and butter to the soup together with the spinach, and cook for a further 10–15 minutes. Season with the salt and pepper.

When ready to serve, bring the soup to the boil. Place the tahina in a mixing bowl, add some of the stock and mix until the tahina is very liquid.

Remove the soup from the heat and stir in the tahina mixture. Serve immediately.

# çevisli nokhud çorbasi

## walnut and chickpea soup

This Anatolian soup from Southern Turkey is popular with Turks, Armenians, Kurds and the Alouites of Syria. The unusual combination of walnuts and chickpeas gives it a rich, earthy flavour. Any leftover soup will darken in colour because of the nuts, but this will not affect the taste.

3 oz (75g) chickpeas, soaked overnight in cold water
3 pints (1.8 litres) water
1 oz (25g) butter
1 medium onion, coarsely chopped
2 carrots, peeled and finely diced
2 large potatoes, peeled and finely diced
$1/2$ teaspoon chilli pepper
$1^1/2$ teaspoons salt
2 tablespoons finely chopped parsley
2 tablespoons lemon juice
3 oz (75g) chopped walnuts

Garnish
thinly sliced lemon rounds

Drain the chickpeas and place in a large saucepan with the water. Bring it to the boil and then simmer until the beans are tender, adding more boiling water if necessary.

Melt the butter in a small pan, add the onion and fry until soft and turning golden. Check that there is still about 3 pints (1.8 litres) of liquid in the pan with the chickpeas, then pour in the butter and onion.

Add the rest of the vegetables, chilli pepper and salt, and simmer for a further 15–20 minutes or until the vegetables are tender.

Stir in the parsley, lemon juice and nuts. Simmer for a further 1–2 minutes. Serve hot and garnish each bowl with a slice of lemon.

# kahtzer tzavabour

## wheat and nut soup

*A man can live without spices, but not without wheat.*
Jewish Wisdom

A most unusual sweet soup from the Caucasus which has a most exquisite flavour
and should be very popular, especially with children.
It can be served either hot or cold.

2 oz (50g) large burghul
1 oz (25g) butter
1/2 pint (300ml) red grape juice
1 1/2 pints (900ml) water
1 oz (25g) crushed walnuts
1 teaspoon cinnamon
2 teaspoons sugar

Wash the burghul several times in a bowl under cold water until the water poured away
is clear.

Melt the butter in a saucepan, add the burghul and fry for 2–3 minutes, stirring
constantly. Add the grape juice and water, bring to the boil; lower the heat and simmer
for about 15 minutes, or until the burghul is cooked.

Add the walnuts, cinnamon and sugar and stir well. Remove from the heat and serve
hot or cold.

# badem çorbasi

## almond soup

*As in their sea-green shell the pearls*
*In a triple green we hide, shy girls,*
*We care to pass the green of youth*
*In hauberks bitter and uncouth,*
*Until the waking comes and we*
*Wanton white hearts from out our tree.*
1001 Nights

An extremely delightful soup from Turkey, this is a speciality of Istanbul making use of almonds – 'the pride of Anatolia'. It is rich and sophisticated.

6 hard-boiled eggs, shelled
2 oz (50g) ground almonds
6 bitter almonds
1 teaspoon lemon rind
1 teaspoon coriander seeds
2 pints (1.2 litres) water
1 teaspoon salt
1/4 teaspoon dried sweet basil
1/4 teaspoon thyme
1/2 pint (300ml) single cream

Halve the eggs and remove the yolks. Put the yolks, ground and bitter almonds, lemon rind and coriander seeds in a liquidiser and blend to a paste.

Scrape the paste out into a saucepan and stir in the water slowly so that the liquid stays smooth and lump-free. Bring to the boil, season with the salt, basil and thyme, then lower the heat and simmer for about 10 minutes.

Remove from the heat and pour into a soup tureen. Stir the cream through the soup and serve immediately.

# herishde

## pasta and tahina soup

This is a thick, filling soup from Armenia. The tahina stock gives it a distinctive flavour. You can substitute bought, dried pasta for the home-made pasta. Tahina paste can be bought from most Middle Eastern stores.

4 oz (110g) chickpeas, soaked in cold water overnight
3 pints (1.8 litres) water
8 oz (225g) plain flour
1 egg
2 teaspoons salt
4 oz (110g) rice, washed thoroughly under cold running water
1/2 teaspoon black pepper
8 fl oz (250ml) tahina paste

Rinse the chickpeas and put into a large saucepan with the water. Bring to the boil and cook until the chickpeas are tender. You may need to top up with boiling water from time to time.

Meanwhile, sieve the flour into a large bowl, add the egg and 1 teaspoon of the salt and knead, with a little water, until it forms a smooth dough. Divide this dough into 2 balls.

Roll each ball out until it is very thin, then cut into strips 2in x 1/2in (5cm x 1cm), spread out and leave to dry.

When the chickpeas are cooked, add the rice and the pasta strips. Stir in the remaining salt and the black pepper and continue to cook. You will probably need to top up the water again to maintain a level of about 3 pints (1.8 litres).

When all the ingredients are cooked, remove the soup from the heat.

Put the tahina paste into a bowl and thin it down by stirring in some of the hot stock, a little at a time.

When ready to serve, pour the tahina mixture into the soup and stir well. Do not bring to the boil again or the soup will curdle.

# makhlouta

## rice and lentil soup

A traditional Syrian soup which is simple, delicious and wholesome.
It is also popular with Turks and Armenians, who use burghul instead of rice.

4 tablespoons olive oil
1 onion, finely chopped
3 oz (75g) long-grain rice, washed thoroughly under cold water and drained
3 pints (1.8 litres) water
1 teaspoon salt
1/2 teaspoon black pepper
1 teaspoon ground cumin
1/4 teaspoon cinnamon
pinch ground cloves
6 oz (175g) red lentils
pinch cayenne pepper

Heat the oil in a large saucepan, add the onion and fry, stirring frequently, until soft. Now add the rice and fry for 2–3 minutes, stirring frequently. Stir in the water, salt, pepper, cumin, cinnamon and cloves. Bring quickly to the boil, then simmer for 5 minutes.

Add the red lentils and continue simmering until the rice and lentils are tender but not mushy – about 15–20 minutes depending on the quality of the lentils.

Garnish with a pinch of cayenne pepper and serve immediately.

# spas

## yoghurt and barley soup

A classic yoghurt soup from Armenia; easy to prepare and tastes delicious.
It is ideal on cold winter nights served with a warm bread, e.g. pita;
it can also be served cold.

3 oz (75g) pearl barley, soaked in cold water overnight
4 pints (2.4 litres) water
3/4 pint (450ml) plain yoghurt
4 eggs
1/2 oz (15g) flour
1 oz (25g) butter
1 small onion, finely chopped
2 teaspoons salt
1 level teaspoon black pepper
2 teaspoons finely chopped mint
2 teaspoons finely chopped parsley or coriander

Drain the barley and put in a large saucepan with about half the water; bring to the boil and simmer for about 1/2 an hour or until tender. Drain through a fine sieve.

Put the yoghurt into a large bowl and add the rest of the water. Mix until well blended.

Break the eggs into a saucepan and whisk in the flour, a little at a time. Stir in the yoghurt mixture and put over a moderate heat. Whisking constantly, bring the mixture almost to the boil, then quickly lower the heat, and allow just to simmer very gently for 2–3 minutes until the mixture thickens slightly.

Meanwhile, melt the butter in a small pan and fry the onion until soft and just beginning to brown.

Stir the barley, cooked onion with the butter, salt and black pepper into the soup and simmer for another minute. When ready to serve, sprinkle with finely chopped fresh herbs.

*vospabour*

## lentil soup

Lentil soup is perhaps the most popular and most ancient of all Middle Eastern soups: Esau sold his inheritance for a bowl of it. There are several variations and every nationality has its favourite version.

This recipe is slightly unusual since it also makes use of chickpeas and burghul. It is an Armenian favourite.

2 oz (50g) chickpeas, soaked overnight in cold water
2 carrots, peeled and diced
4 sticks celery, washed and diced
3 pints (1.8 litres) water
4 oz (110g) brown lentils
2 oz (50g) large burghul, rinsed
2 oz (50g) butter
1 onion, finely chopped
1 tablespoon finely chopped fresh mint or 2 teaspoons dried mint
1 tablespoon finely chopped parsley
2 teaspoons salt
1 teaspoon black pepper
1 teaspoon ground cumin

Place the chickpeas in a saucepan of lightly salted water, bring to the boil and simmer until tender. Top up with a little more boiling water if necessary and remove any scum that appears on the surface. Drain and set aside.

Place the carrots, celery and water in a large saucepan, bring to the boil and simmer for 15 minutes. Add the lentils and chickpeas and simmer for a further 20–30 minutes. Now add the burghul and cook for a further 15–20 minutes, by which time the vegetables, lentils and burghul should all be cooked.

Meanwhile, melt the butter in a small saucepan, add the onion and fry until golden brown. Stir in the mint, parsley, salt, pepper and cumin.

Pour the onion mixture into the soup and mix well. Taste and adjust seasoning if necessary, and serve sprinkled with a little extra cumin.

# chourba adas wa isbanekh

## lentil and spinach soup

Cheap, simple and economical, this is a traditional peasant soup from Mesopotamia (Syria and Iraq). It has been passed down unaltered through the centuries and is a favourite of all – rich and poor, nomad and village dweller alike.

2<sup>1</sup>/2 fl oz (75ml) oil
1 large onion, thickly sliced
2<sup>1</sup>/2 pints (1.5 litres) water
3 oz (75g) brown lentils, picked over and rinsed well
8 oz (225g) fresh spinach
1<sup>1</sup>/2 teaspoons salt
1/2 teaspoon chilli pepper
juice of 1 lemon

Heat the oil in a large saucepan, add the onion and fry until soft. Add the water and lentils, bring to the boil, cover and simmer for about 30 minutes, or until the lentils are just tender.

Meanwhile, trim and thoroughly wash the spinach and then chop coarsely.

When the lentils are just tender add the spinach, salt, pepper and lemon juice. Stir well, simmer for a further 10 minutes and adjust seasoning if necessary.

Serve hot with fresh bread.

# ashe lubi kharmez-ba-esfanaj

## red bean and spinach soup

A nourishing soup from Iran, this is often eaten, with bread, as a main meal.

4 oz (110g) red kidney beans, soaked overnight in cold water
2¹/2 pints (1.5 litres) water
2 tablespoons oil
1 onion, finely chopped
1 teaspoon turmeric
1 teaspoon salt
¹/4 teaspoon chilli pepper
¹/2 teaspoon black pepper
4 oz (110g) lentils, washed and drained
2 oz (50g) long-grain rice, washed thoroughly under cold water and drained
¹/2 lb (225g) fresh spinach, washed very thoroughly, drained and chopped
juice of 1 large lemon

Drain the beans and place in a saucepan with 1 pint (600ml) of the water. Bring to the boil, lower the heat and simmer until the beans are tender. Add a little more boiling water if necessary. Set aside.

Heat the oil in a large saucepan, add the onion and fry, stirring frequently, until soft and golden. Stir in the turmeric, salt, chilli, black pepper and the lentils, and fry for 1–2 minutes. Add the remaining 1¹/2 pints (900ml) water and the contents of the bean pan and bring to the boil. Simmer for a further 30 minutes.

Stir in the rice and spinach and cook for a further 20 minutes. Test to see if the lentils are tender; if not, cook them a little longer.

Stir in the lemon juice; taste and adjust the seasoning, if necessary, before serving.

## leek and tahina soup

Although delicious hot, this soup is usually served at room temperature. Do not reheat any leftover soup as it has a tendency to curdle. Simply remove it from the refrigerator and leave it to come to room temperature. A regional speciality from Southern Turkey (Cilician Armenia) whence most tahina-based dishes originate, and one of the famed Lenten dishes of the Armenian Apostolic Church.

4 oz (110g) chickpeas, soaked overnight in cold water
2$^1$/$_2$ pints (1.5 litres) water
3 leeks
4 spring onions
1$^1$/$_2$ teaspoons salt
$^1$/$_4$ pint (150ml) tahina paste
2 fl oz (60ml) olive oil
1 tablespoon dried mint

Drain the chickpeas, place in a large saucepan, cover with the water and bring to the boil. Simmer until tender, adding more boiling water if necessary.

Meanwhile, trim the roots and any bruised leaves from the leeks and spring onions. Chop the vegetables into $^1$/$_2$in (1cm) pieces, place in a colander and rinse very thoroughly under cold water to remove all the sand and grit.

When the chickpeas are tender, check that there is still about 2$^1$/$_2$ pints (1.5 litres) of liquid in the pan. Add the vegetables and salt; stir well and simmer, covered, for about 15 minutes or until the vegetables are tender.

Place the tahina in a bowl and stir until smooth. Add a tablespoon of the soup and stir briskly.

Gradually stir in several more spoonfuls of the soup, then stir the tahina mixture back into the soup. Remove it from the heat.

Place the oil in a small pan and heat well. Add the mint to the oil, then pour the mixture into the soup. Stir once to swirl the mint through the soup, then set aside until it reaches room temperature before serving.

# dabanabour

## vegetable soup

This is a famed Armenian soup also known as 'Noah's Ark Soup'. It hails, as the name suggests, from the region of Ararat in Western Armenia. The vegetables listed below are really only suggestions. You can use whatever is available and include your own personal favourites.

2 potatoes, peeled
2 carrots, peeled
1 leek, trimmed
2 sticks celery, trimmed
2 tomatoes, blanched and peeled
2 courgettes, trimmed
1 turnip, peeled
3 pints (1.8 litres) water
2 bay leaves
1$^1$/2 teaspoons salt
1 teaspoon black pepper
1 teaspoon thyme
1 oz (25g) butter
1 onion, finely chopped

Dice all the vegetables, wash and put in a large saucepan with the water. Bring to the boil, lower the heat and simmer for about 20 minutes until the vegetables are almost cooked. Add the bay leaves, salt, pepper and thyme and cook for a further 10–15 minutes.

Meanwhile, melt the butter in a small saucepan and fry the chopped onion until golden. Add the onion and butter to the soup, stir well, taste and adjust the seasoning if necessary.

# armyanski borsch

## armenian borsch

Borsch in the Middle East! Yes indeed; this great soup of Eastern Europe also appears in certain regions of the Middle East that have had social or political intercourse with 'Mother Russia'. There are borsch-type dishes in Eastern Turkey, Northern Iran, Israel and, of course, the Caucasus.

I have included 2 recipes, one from Armenia and the other from Israel. Although both make use of beetroot, the basic ingredient of any such dish, they are quite different and regional in approach.
The Armenian version uses yoghurt instead of the traditional smetana (soured cream).

1 medium beetroot, unpeeled, but washed
2 oz (50g) butter
1/2 onion, finely chopped
1 carrot, peeled and chopped
1 stick celery, chopped
4 oz (110g) finely shredded cabbage
2 oz (50g) mushrooms, thinly sliced
1 small turnip, peeled and finely chopped
2 1/2–3 pints (1.5–1.8 litres) water
1 lemon
1 teaspoon salt
1/2 teaspoon black pepper

Garnish
1/2 pint (300ml) yoghurt

Place the whole beetroot in a saucepan, cover with water, bring to the boil, then simmer until cooked – about 30 minutes. Drain and leave to cool.

Melt the butter in a large pan, add prepared vegetables and sauté for a few minutes. Add the water, bring to the boil and then simmer until vegetables are just tender.

Remove the skin from the beetroot, then chop the beetroot and add it to the soup. By cooking the beetroot in its skin and adding it at this stage you should get a rich red soup.

Poke holes in the lemon and drop it into the soup. This will give a tartness to counteract the sweetness of the beetroot. Add the seasoning and simmer for a further 10–15 minutes.

Taste and adjust the seasoning, if necessary, and remove and discard the lemon before serving. To serve, spoon the soup into individual bowls and place 2 tablespoons of yoghurt in the centre of each.

# milchik borsch

## beetroot soup

Borsch is an equally popular soup in Israel due mainly
to the Jews who have, for a century now, been emigrating to settle
'in the lands of their fathers'.

Milchik Borsch is eaten cold and is therefore ideal during
the hot summer months in Israel.
If you wish you can use yoghurt instead of smetana – soured cream.

1 carrot, peeled and coarsely grated
1 small onion, thinly sliced
1¹/2 lb (675g) beetroot, peeled and coarsely grated
2 pints (1.2 litres) water
2 tablespoons sugar
2 teaspoons salt
¹/2 teaspoon white pepper
2 eggs
juice of 1 lemon

Garnish
¹/4 pint (150ml) smetana or yoghurt

Place all the vegetables in a large saucepan, add the water, sugar, salt and pepper and bring slowly to the boil. Lower the heat, cover and simmer for about 1 hour.

Pour the contents of the pan through a coarse sieve into a large bowl. Return the liquid to the pan and discard the vegetables.

Beat the 2 eggs in a small bowl, add some of the beetroot soup and mix thoroughly. Stir the lemon juice and the egg mixture into the soup, then bring it to the boil and simmer for 10 minutes. Remove from the heat, leave to cool and then refrigerate.

Before serving, transfer to a glass bowl and lightly stir in the yoghurt or soured cream to produce a marbled effect. Serve chilled.

# marak tiras

## corn soup

*This is an Israeli soup of Californian origin and has an unusual flavour, creamy texture and light golden colour.*

1/2 lb (225g) corn kernels, frozen or canned
1/2 pint (300ml) water
1 pint (600ml) milk
1 teaspoon salt
1/2 teaspoon black pepper
1 teaspoon sugar
1 teaspoon fennel, coarsely ground in a mortar and pestle
1 tablespoon cornflour
2 tablespoons water
1 tablespoon mayonnaise
1 tablespoon chopped chives

Thaw out frozen corn or strain canned corn. Place in a blender with 1/4 pint (150ml) of the water and blend to a smooth paste. Transfer the paste to a saucepan and stir in the remaining water and the milk. Season with the salt, pepper, sugar and fennel.

Place the cornflour in a small bowl and mix to a paste with the 2 tablespoons of water. Stir the mayonnaise into this paste, then stir this mixture into the soup.

Bring the soup to the boil and simmer for about 10 minutes, stirring frequently. Taste and adjust the seasoning if necessary.

Add a little more water if the soup is too thick for your taste. Sprinkle with the chives and serve immediately.

# chourba-bi-kousa

## courgette and milk soup

A rich and creamy Lebanese soup: it is the wonderful balance of courgettes and milk which gives this soup a sophistication often lacking in Middle Eastern dishes, which are basically of peasant, often nomadic origin.

The lemony spice known as sumak powder can be purchased from many continental and Middle Eastern shops.

3/4 lb (350g) courgettes
1 oz (25g) butter
1 tablespoon flour
1 pint (600ml) milk
1 teaspoon salt
1/4 teaspoon white pepper
1/2 teaspoon ground cumin
2 tablespoons finely chopped parsley

Garnish
1 tablespoon sumak

Wash the courgettes and cut into 1in (2.5cm) chunks. Half-fill a large saucepan with lightly salted water, add the courgettes and simmer until soft, then drain. Put the courgettes into a liquidiser and blend until smooth. Set aside.

Melt the butter in a saucepan, remove from the heat and stir in the flour. Slowly add the milk and stir constantly until you have a thin, smooth paste. Stir in the remaining milk and return to the heat, stirring constantly until the mixture thickens.

Add the courgette purée and season with the salt, pepper and cumin. If the soup is a little too thick for your liking, add a little water and adjust the seasoning if necessary.

Just before serving stir in the parsley. Serve in individual bowls with a little sumak sprinkled over the top.

# melokhia

## melokhia leaf soup

This is an Egyptian speciality; in fact, it is the traditional soup of Egypt –
well-loved, even by the Pharaohs.

Melokhia is a spinach-like vegetable – *Corchorus olitorius* – and its leaves
can be eaten fresh or dried for the winter months.
You should be able to purchase dried melokhia from Middle Eastern grocery stores.
There really is no substitute – don't use spinach.

### Stock
3 pints (1.8 litres) water
1 onion, quartered
2 tomatoes, blanched, skinned and quartered
2 cloves garlic, roughly chopped
1 teaspoon salt
1/2 teaspoon black pepper

### Soup
2 oz (50g) dried melokhia leaves or 1lb (450g) fresh leaves – if you can find them
2 cloves garlic
2 tablespoons butter or oil
1 teaspoon cayenne pepper
1 tablespoon ground coriander

Place all the stock ingredients in a large saucepan; cover and simmer for about
30 minutes. Strain the stock into another large saucepan.

Crush the dried melokhia leaves. (If they are not brittle enough to crush, dry them out
in a warm oven for a few minutes.) Place the crushed leaves in a bowl and moisten with
a little hot water until they double in bulk. Add them to the stock and simmer for
20 minutes.

Crush the garlic with a little salt.

Heat the butter or oil in a small saucepan and fry the garlic until golden. Stir in the
cayenne pepper and coriander to form a smooth paste and cook for 2–3 minutes, then
stir this mixture into the soup; cover and simmer for a few more minutes.

Taste, and adjust the seasoning if necessary before serving.

# labaneya

## yoghurt and spinach soup

An Egyptian soup usually made from the leaves of a plant of the spinach family called 'silg' (beet). As it is rather difficult to find in the West, I suggest you use spinach instead.

1 lb (450g) silg or fresh spinach, or 1/2 lb (225g) frozen leaf spinach
3 tablespoons samna, (clarified butter) or vegetable oil
1 large onion, coarsely chopped
4 spring onions, finely chopped, including heads
4 oz (110g) long-grain rice, washed under cold running water and drained
2 pints (1.2 litres) water
1 teaspoon salt
1/2 teaspoon black pepper
1/2 teaspoon ground cumin
1/2 teaspoon paprika
3/4 pint (450ml) yoghurt
1 clove garlic, crushed

Wash the silg or fresh spinach thoroughly, drain and cut into large pieces.

Heat the samna, (clarified butter) or oil in a large saucepan, add the onion and fry for a few minutes until soft. Add the silg or spinach and spring onions, and sauté for 2 minutes, stirring constantly. Add the rice, water, salt, pepper, cumin and paprika. Stir well and bring to the boil, then lower the heat and simmer for 15–20 minutes, or until the rice is cooked.

Meanwhile, mix together the yoghurt and garlic in a bowl. Remove the soup from the heat and stir in the yoghurt. Serve immediately.

# marak tapouzim im limon

## orange and lemon soup

A most unusual fragrant and refreshing soup from Israel. Make sure that the juices you use are pure fruit juices.

2 tablespoons margarine
1 onion, finely chopped
3/4 pint (450ml) tomato juice
3/4 pint (450ml) orange juice
8 fl oz (250ml) lemon juice
1/2 teaspoon sweet basil
1/2 teaspoon dried oregano

Melt the margarine in a large saucepan, add the onion and fry until soft. Add the tomato, orange and lemon juices and bring to the boil. Lower the heat and simmer for 5 minutes.

Stir in the basil and oregano and serve immediately.

# ab dough khiar

## cold yoghurt soup

A cold soup from Iran similar to Jajig salad (page 73), but enriched with onions, raisins and sometimes walnuts. The people of Tabriz, in northern Iran, often include one or more chopped hard-boiled eggs.

1 large cucumber
1 pint (600ml) yoghurt
1 tablespoon mint, finely chopped or 2 teaspoons dried mint
2 spring onions, finely chopped, including green heads
1 pint (600ml) water
2 teaspoons salt
1/2 teaspoon black pepper
1–2 oz (25–50g) raisins

Peel the cucumber and chop it finely. Mix all the ingredients together in a large bowl and stir well. Refrigerate for a few hours. Serve with a few ice cubes added.

**Note:** Shredded chicken breast is often added to this soup (Ab Dough Khiar ba Goosht-e-Morgh).

Use 1 breast of poached or grilled chicken, bone it, cut into shreds and add to the soup, mixing well. Also stir in 1 tablespoon of chopped walnuts, 1 teaspoon of thyme and 1 teaspoon of tarragon. Finally, melt 1 oz (25g) butter in a small pan, sauté 1 tablespoon dried mint and pour into the soup. Serve cold.

# mirkov soongabour

## mushroom and fruit soup

An Armenian soup which makes use of mushrooms and dried fruit. It has a very dark, almost black appearance and a very distinctive flavour. It is one of the most typical of Middle Eastern soups.

2 pints (1.2 litres) water
2 oz (50g) mushrooms, washed and sliced
1 oz (25g) butter
1 oz (25g) spring onions, sliced
1 teaspoon flour
1¹/2 oz (40g) raisins
1¹/2 oz (40g) prunes, halved and stoned
1 teaspoon salt
¹/2 teaspoon black pepper

Bring the water to the boil in a large saucepan, add the mushrooms and simmer for 5 minutes.

Meanwhile, melt the butter in a small saucepan, add the onion and fry until golden brown. Stir in the flour and then a few tablespoons of the soup.

Now add the onion-flour mixture to the mushroom soup. Stir in the raisins and prunes and simmer for 30 minutes.

Season with the salt and pepper, taste and adjust if necessary.

Serve hot.

# marak yerakot ou perot

## fruit and vegetable soup

An Israeli soup making clever use of fruits and vegetables; it can be served hot or cold and you can use yoghurt instead of soured cream (smetana) if you wish.

4 oz (110g) grapes, cut in half and seeded
2 lb (900g) ripe tomatoes, sliced
1 large apple, cored and sliced
1 carrot, peeled and thinly sliced
1 stick celery, chopped
1 small green pepper
1/2 onion, thinly sliced
1 pint (600ml) water
2 teaspoons salt
1 teaspoon ground cumin
1 teaspoon dried mint
2 tablespoons lemon juice
2 egg yolks, beaten
8 fl oz (250ml) soured cream or yoghurt

Garnish
1 tablespoon fresh tarragon leaves, finely chopped

Place the grapes, tomatoes, apple, carrot, celery, green pepper and onion in a saucepan with the water and bring to the boil. Stir in 1 teaspoon of the salt, the cumin and the mint. Lower the heat and simmer for about 45 minutes or until the carrots are very tender.

Pour the soup through a sieve into another saucepan, pressing through as much of the pulp as possible. Stir in the remaining salt and the lemon juice.

Mix together the beaten eggs and soured cream or yoghurt in a small bowl. Stir a few tablespoons of the soup stock into the egg mixture and then pour this back into the soup, mixing thoroughly.

Serve hot or cold in individual bowls, garnished with the chopped tarragon.

# marak anavim

## grape soup

An Israeli soup that is fast becoming popular throughout Europe and the USA.
It is ideal for a summer's day as it is served cold and is very refreshing.

1 pint (600ml) water
1/2 pint (300ml) grapefruit juice
1/4 pint (150ml) dry white wine
2-3 oz (50-75g) sugar, depending on taste
1/2 teaspoon cinnamon
3 cloves
1 tablespoon chopped fresh mint or 1 teaspoon dried mint
1 oz (25g) cornflour
1 egg yolk
4 oz (110g) grapes, washed

Place the water, grapefruit juice, wine and sugar in a saucepan and bring to the boil. Add the cinnamon, cloves and mint.

Place the cornflour in a small bowl, add a few tablespoons of the hot liquid and stir to a smooth paste about the consistency of double cream. Slowly add the paste to the saucepan, stirring constantly.

Remove the pan from the heat. Add the egg yolk and mix well. Finally, add the grapes, pour into a large serving bowl and chill for several hours.

# ab-goosht-e sib

## apple and cherry soup

This is a sweet-sour soup from Iran. If fresh, sour cherries are not available use Morello cherries, or – better – dried ones which can be bought from many health food shops.

It is best to soak these for 3 hours. Do not attempt to stone them as this will be too difficult.

1¹/2 pints (900ml) water
2 oz (50g) yellow split peas, soaked overnight in cold water
1 teaspoon salt
¹/2 teaspoon black pepper
1 onion, thinly sliced
2 large cooking apples, peeled, cored and cut into ¹/2in (1cm) pieces
8–10 sour cherries
1 tablespoon lemon juice
1 teaspoon sugar

Bring the water to the boil in a saucepan. Add the drained split peas, salt, pepper and onion. Cover and simmer for 20 minutes.

Add the remaining ingredients, mix well, cover the pan and simmer for 25–30 minutes or until the split peas are tender.

Serve immediately.

# appetisers

Appetisers (*mezzeh* in Arabic) are the glory of the Syrian–Lebanese cuisine. Nowhere is an array of rich dips made of fruits, vegetables, nuts, pulses and cereals of varying colours and textures better presented than in the small restaurants on the foothills of Mount Lebanon.

They are a way of life with nomads who, for centuries, have traversed the deserts and mountains carrying small leather bags of wheat, rice, lentils and other dried vegetables which they turned into such delightful dishes as Falafel, Pooreh-Ye-Adas or Peynir Kagiti, served with huge quantities of freshly baked bread, pickles, herbs and fresh or dried vegetables.

They lived well, those nomads – contrary to accepted notions. Their diet, though frugal, was nevertheless well balanced.

Middle Eastern appetisers are excellent on their own or as part of a large buffet table, and they are also often eaten as an accompaniment to main dishes. There is no set rule. Do not impose the rigid Western codes of eating on them; in short, eat them when and with whatever course you like.

# yazarf sabzi

## a bowl of herbs

*Even the tiny worm inside the rocks dreams of fresh herbs.*
Persian Proverb

The Caucasians and Iranians, and particularly the latter, have a beautiful custom of offering fresh herbs and vegetables with cheese at the beginning of a meal. The platter would include many of the following:

mint sprigs
spring onions
garlic chives
tarragon
coriander leaves
watercress
fenugreek
flat-leaf parsley
dill
radishes
cos lettuce leaves
garlic cloves
onions
Feta-type cheese
pita bread or lavash
a jug or two of Ayran (or Tan – see page 243)

Choose a variety of herbs and vegetables from those listed and wash well under cold running water. Remove discoloured leaves and shake off excess water. Chill for 2–3 hours.

Arrange the selection in a large bowl or on a platter.

To eat yazarf Sabzi, wrap a selection of herbs and thin slices of cheese in pita or lavash bread and drink ice cold Tan.

# zahtar

## a nuts and spices dip

Served at breakfast time, or on the buffet table as an appetiser,
Zahtar is a mixture of the following ingredients – wild marjoram, sesame seeds,
cinnamon, chickpeas and coriander seeds.

The ingredients are mixed together, then a piece of bread is first dipped
into a bowl of olive oil, then into a plate of Zahtar and eaten. Hazelnuts and walnuts
are also used, particularly in Iraq. Try it for breakfast with a cup of tea or coffee.
(I spent most of my early life smelling of olive oil and sesame seeds!)

There is no fixed recipe. The one given below is a family favourite.

Known as Dukkah in Egypt it makes a considerable amount, but it can be stored
for some months in an airtight container.

8 oz (225g) sesame seeds
8 oz (225g) coriander seeds
4 oz (110g) walnuts
4 oz (110g) chickpeas – the most suitable are those which are pre-cooked,
salted and dried. You can buy in many delicatessens
3 tablespoons ground cumin
1 teaspoon salt
1/2 teaspoon black pepper
1 tablespoon cinnamon
2 tablespoons crushed, dried wild marjoram
1 tablespoon sumak powder

Roast or grill the sesame seeds, coriander seeds, walnuts and chickpeas separately in
a warm oven – or under the grill.

Pound them together until finely crushed, but do not pulverise them or the oils from
the nuts and seeds will be released and the mixture will start to form a paste. The
essence of this dip is that it is a mixture of dry ingredients.

Mix the pounded ingredients with the herbs and seasonings in a large bowl, taste and
adjust the seasoning if necessary.

Arrange a little of the Zahtar on a plate and pour a little olive oil on to another. Dip a
piece of bread first into the olive oil and then into the Zahtar – and eat.

# chickpea paste with tahina

This is a traditional dip – a must on any *mezzeh* table; it is one of the most popular and best-known of all Syrian dishes, and in recent years has become equally popular throughout Europe and in America. It is normally eaten with pita bread or other Middle Eastern flat breads.

1 lb (450g) chickpeas, soaked overnight in cold water
3 cloves garlic, peeled
1/2 pint (300ml) tahina paste
1 teaspoon chilli pepper
3 teaspoons salt
2 teaspoons ground cumin
juice of 2 lemons

Garnish
a little paprika, cumin, olive oil, lemon juice and chopped parsley

Rinse the chickpeas under cold running water, then place them in a large saucepan threequarters-full of cold water. Bring to the boil, then lower the heat and simmer until the chickpeas are tender. From time to time, remove the scum which appears on the surface and add more boiling water if, and when, necessary.

Drain the chickpeas into a sieve and rinse very thoroughly under cold running water. Reserve 2–3 tablespoons of chickpeas for the garnish.

Reduce the chickpeas in a liquidiser to a thick paste or purée. You can add a little water to aid the liquidisation, but don't add too much or the purée will be too thin.

While liquidising, add the cloves of garlic to the chickpeas – this will ensure that they are properly ground and evenly distributed.

Empty the purée into a large bowl, add the tahina, chilli pepper, salt, cumin and lemon juice and mix in very thoroughly. Taste and adjust the seasoning.

To serve, use either individual bowls or a large serving dish. Smooth the Hummus with the back of a soup spoon from the centre out to the edges so that there is a slight hollow in the centre.

Decorate in a star pattern with alternating trickles of paprika and cumin. Pour a little olive oil and lemon juice into the centre and garnish with a little chopped parsley and the whole chickpeas. **Serves 8–10.**

# ta'amia or falafel

## spicy fried chickpea balls

This is another Egyptian favourite which in recent years has caught the imagination of other Middle Eastern countries; so much so that it has become as much the favourite of the Lebanese. Basically, it consists of chickpeas, tahina, breadcrumbs and spices, shaped into small round rissoles and fried in oil.

1 lb (450g) cooked chickpeas
3 fl oz (90ml) water
1 egg, lightly beaten
1 teaspoon salt
1/2 teaspoon black pepper
1/2 teaspoon turmeric
2 tablespoons chopped fresh coriander leaves
1/4 teaspoon ground cumin
1/4 teaspoon cayenne pepper
1 garlic clove, crushed
1 tablespoon tahina paste or olive oil
2 oz (50g) fresh white breadcrumbs
2 oz (50g) flour
vegetable oil for deep frying

Mince chickpeas twice into a large mixing bowl. Add the water, egg, salt and pepper, turmeric, coriander leaves, cumin, cayenne pepper, garlic, tahina paste or olive oil and breadcrumbs.

With your hands, combine all the ingredients into a soft, but firm mixture. Form the mixture into 1in (2.5cm) balls, flatten slightly between your palms and coat them with the flour.

Heat the oil in a large pan until it reaches 360F (185C) on a deep-frying thermometer, or until a small piece of stale bread dropped into the oil browns in about 50 seconds.

Put the balls, about six at a time, in a deep-frying basket and fry them in the oil for 2–3 minutes, or until they are lightly browned. Remove them from the oil as they are cooked, and drain well on kitchen paper while you fry the remainder.

Drain well and serve hot.

# el ful (ful medames)

## egyptian brown beans

This is an Egyptian speciality though extremely popular in Syria, Lebanon and Israel. In Egypt it is often eaten for breakfast, lunch or dinner but, in essence it should be treated as an appetiser. Sometimes hard-boiled eggs are added to give it substance. Serve with pita bread.

1¹/2 lb (675g) Egyptian brown beans, soaked overnight and drained
3 cloves garlic, crushed
2 tablespoons olive oil
juice of 2 lemons
1 teaspoon salt
¹/2 teaspoon black pepper
4 hard-boiled eggs, shelled
2 tablespoons finely chopped parsley

Preheat the oven to 250F (120C) gas ¹/2.

Put the beans in an ovenproof casserole and cover them with water. Place in the oven and cook for 4–7 hours, depending on the quality of the beans. At the end of the cooking time, the beans should be soft but still whole – and not have disintegrated. Drain the cooking liquid from the beans and discard it.

Stir in the garlic, olive oil, lemon juice, salt and pepper. Spoon the mixture into 4 soup bowls and place a hard-boiled egg on top of each. Sprinkle the parsley thickly over the top and serve immediately.

# mutabbal

## aubergine purée with tahina

This is a dip, similar in principle to Hummus-Bi-Tahina but using
grilled aubergines instead of chickpeas. Easy to make and traditionally eaten
with flat bread, it is of Syrian–Lebanese origin.

2 large aubergines
3 cloves garlic, crushed
1 teaspoon salt
2–3 fl oz (60–90ml) tahina paste
juice of 2 lemons
1 teaspoon chilli pepper
1 teaspoon ground cumin
1 tablespoon olive oil

Garnish
2 tablespoons chopped parsley
a few black olives

Wipe each aubergine and make 2 or 3 slits in each with a sharp knife and cook them
over charcoal, or in a hot oven (450F/230C/gas 8), until the skins are black and the
flesh feels soft when poked with a finger. Allow to cool, then peel off the skin, scraping
off any flesh that gets stripped off with the skin.

Put the flesh into a large bowl and mash with a fork. Add the crushed garlic and salt
and continue to mash or pound the mixture until it is reduced to a pulp.

Add the tahina, lemon juice and chilli pepper. Stir in thoroughly.

Spoon the mixture on to a large plate, smooth it over and sprinkle with the cumin. Pour
the olive oil over the top and garnish with the chopped parsley and black olives.

## tahina sauce

This is a cream made from tahina paste. It hails from the Lebanon, but is also popular in Syria, Jordan and other countries in the Middle East. It is eaten as an hors d'oeuvre by dipping hot pita bread into it, or as a side dish to the main course – especially kebabs, which are dipped into the cream and then eaten.

This sauce will keep for several days in the refrigerator.

1/4 pint (150ml) tahina paste
juice of 2–3 lemons
approximately 1/2 pint (300ml) milk
2 cloves garlic, crushed
1 teaspoon salt
1/2 teaspoon chilli pepper
1 teaspoon ground cumin
1 tablespoon chopped parsley

Pour the tahina into a large bowl, add the lemon juice and stir. The mixture will become very stiff. Slowly add the milk, stirring until it becomes thick and creamy in texture.

Season with the garlic, salt, chilli pepper and cumin. Add half the parsley and stir.

Taste and adjust the seasoning, if necessary; pour into a serving dish and sprinkle with the remaining parsley.

# pooreh-ye adas

## lentil dip

An Iranian recipe from the region of Khorassan; similar to Arab dips,
this recipe is very simple and extremely easy to make.

Some people like to garnish this dish with cayenne pepper as well as parsley,
but this I leave to you.

Serve with warm pita bread.

1 onion, peeled and quartered
6 oz (175g) whole brown lentils, washed
1 teaspoon salt
1/2 teaspoon black pepper
2 tablespoons lemon juice

Garnish
1 tablespoon finely chopped parsley
1 tablespoon finely chopped tarragon – optional
1 teaspoon cayenne pepper – optional

Put the onion and lentils into a saucepan, cover with water to a depth of about 2in (5cm) and bring to the boil. Add the salt and pepper and simmer until the lentils are tender – about 30 minutes. Add more water if necessary.

When the lentils are cooked, strain them into a sieve, retaining any of the cooking liquid which is left over.

Place the vegetables in a blender with just enough of the cooking liquid, or water, to form a smooth purée. Stir in the lemon juice. Pour the purée into a serving dish and sprinkle with the garnishes.

# toureto

## cucumber and bread dip

This is a version of the famed Syrian Fattoush. It is a simple peasant dish that can be quickly prepared and makes use of stale, leftover bread – and cucumbers which are found in abundance in the region.

This dip should be eaten with lettuce leaves, bread or crisp, savoury biscuits.

6 slices dry bread
1 cucumber, peeled and chopped
2 cloves garlic, crushed
6–7 tablespoons olive oil
juice of 1 lemon
1/2 tablespoon salt
1/2 teaspoon white pepper
1 teaspoon paprika
1 teaspoon ground cumin
water for soaking bread

Cut off the bread crusts and discard. Soak the bread and then squeeze dry. Place it in a bowl and mix in the chopped cucumber, garlic and 5 tablespoons of the oil, the lemon juice and the salt and pepper.

Purée this mixture in a blender. Add a few drops of water, if necessary, to help it blend to a smooth mixture.

Pour this into a shallow serving dish and chill for a few hours.

Just before serving, mix the remaining oil with the paprika and cumin in a small cup. Trickle this mixture over the Toureto and serve.

# labna

## yoghurt dip

This is a dip made of concentrated yoghurt, and is one of the most popular and widespread recipes throughout the region. It is as popular with the Iranians as with the Turks, Arabs, Armenians and Kurds. Lebanese and Jordanians often shape this dip into little balls the size of a walnut, then sprinkle them with a little olive oil and paprika and then make a hearty breakfast of them.

Labna can be kept in the refrigerator for several days. It is at its best when eaten with a pita or lavash bread.

Prepare the yoghurt – see page 242. Pour or spoon into either a colander lined with damp muslin, fine cheesecloth or fine cotton cloth, or into a drawstring bag about 12 x 12in (30 x 30cm) which can be made from a piece of muslin or fine cotton cloth.

Leave the colander in the sink, or hang the bag above the sink to allow the whey to drain away.

What remains in the bag 5–6 hours later is a light, soft, creamy yoghurt which is more like a cheese.

# chatzilim im avocado amol

## aubergine and avocado dip

An Israeli recipe similar to several other Arab aubergine-based dips such as Mutabbal – poor man's caviar.

This recipe has avocados and curry powder which gives it that unusual flavour. Eat it with pita bread.

❧

2 aubergines
2 medium-sized, ripe avocados
3 hard-boiled eggs, shelled and roughly chopped
2 teaspoons vegetable or olive oil
2 teaspoons lemon juice
2 tablespoons finely chopped onion
1 teaspoon salt
1 tablespoon curry powder
1/2 teaspoon paprika
2 tablespoons raisins
6–8 black olives

Make 2 or 3 slits in each aubergine with a sharp knife and cook in a hot oven (450F/230C/gas 8), until the skins are black and the flesh soft when poked with a finger.

When cool enough to handle, peel off the skin, scraping off any flesh that gets stripped off with the skin. Put the aubergine flesh in a bowl.

Peel the avocados, remove the stones and chop the flesh coarsely.

Put the avocado flesh into the bowl with the aubergine and add the eggs. Add the oil, lemon juice and onion and mash to a purée with a fork. Stir in the salt and curry powder and mix well.

Spoon the purée on to a serving plate. Sprinkle with the paprika, raisins and black olives and serve.

# peynir kagiti

## fried and grilled cheese

The 19th-century Turkish writer Sidgi Effendi, who compiled a manual on 'Ottoman' food, describes many dishes that are either imaginary or (let's be polite) forgotten. Some have nevertheless remained in the Middle Eastern repertoire. One such recipe is the frying and grilling of cheese. This is how he describes Peynir Kagiti:

'Put a slice of cheese in parchment paper, wrap it and put it over a charcoal fire. When the paper begins to glow the cheese should be ready. . . . Eat it. A good food which should help all married men sexually.'

The recipe below, however, is not his: it is the one nowadays served in restaurants in Istanbul and Ankara.

Frying and grilling cheese is not a Turkish monopoly, however. It is general throughout the Middle East and forms an integral part of the *mezzeh* table, especially with Greeks, Cypriots and the Lebanese.

I have included two typical recipes, one for frying and one for grilling. The traditional cheeses are Haloumi, Kasseri and Kashkaval – all available in Greek and Middle Eastern shops. However, you can also use Gruyère or a hard Cheddar.

## peynir kagiti

### grilled cheese

**10 oz (275g) Haloumi, Kasseri or Kashkaval cheese**
**lemon juice**
**1 teaspoon paprika**
**1/2 teaspoon ground cumin**

Garnish
**lemon wedges, radishes, pickles and slices of cucumber and tomato**

Cut the cheese into 1/4in (1/2cm) thick slices. Arrange the slices side by side on a sheet of foil and squeeze a little lemon juice over them. Cover with more foil.

Place over charcoal or under a grill and cook until soft and beginning to melt. Remove the covering of foil and turn them once.

Open the foil and sprinkle the melting cheese with the paprika and cumin. Serve immediately with the suggested garnishes.

# saganaki haloumi

## fried cheese

**10 oz (275g) Haloumi, Kasseri or Kashkaval**
**flour**
**oil**
**lemon juice**

Garnishes
**lemon wedges, radishes and olives**

Cut the cheese into 1/4in (1/2cm) thick slices. Coat the slices in flour, shaking off any excess.

Put enough oil in a frying pan to cover the base to a depth of 1/4–1/2in (1/2–1cm) and heat.

Add the cheese slices, a few at a time, and fry for about 1 minute on each side. Remove them with a slotted spoon, place on a plate and squeeze a little lemon juice over them. Keep them warm while you fry the remaining slices in the same way.

Squeeze a little lemon juice over the remaining slices and serve immediately with suggested garnishes and hot pita bread.

# lubyi msallat

## black-eyed bean salad

This is a Syrian–Lebanese favourite and a must on any self-respecting *mezzeh* table. It can be eaten hot or cold, although the cold version is the more popular.

6 oz (175g) black-eyed beans, soaked overnight in cold water
1 clove garlic
1 teaspoon salt
juice of 1/2 lemon
1 small onion, finely chopped
3 tablespoons finely chopped parsley
1 teaspoon ground cumin
21/2 fl oz (75ml) olive oil
1/2 teaspoon paprika

Garnish
lemon wedges

Rinse the soaked beans in cold water. Half-fill a saucepan with water, add the beans and bring to the boil. Simmer until the beans are tender, adding more boiling water if necessary.

Crush the garlic and salt together and stir in the lemon juice. Strain the beans and place in a salad bowl with the onion and parsley.

Add the garlic-lemon mixture and the cumin, and mix the salad thoroughly. Pour the oil over the top and garnish with the paprika.

Serve hot or cold accompanied by lemon wedges.

# lobou kuntig

## spicy red bean balls

Walnuts, beans and garlic combine to create this delightful appetiser.
It's a regional favourite from Armenia,
which is also popular with Kurdish-speaking people in the area.

Excellent as part of a buffet.

6 oz (175g) dried red kidney beans, soaked in cold water overnight
1 small onion, finely chopped
1 large clove garlic, crushed
4 oz (110g) ground walnuts
1 teaspoon salt
1 teaspoon ground coriander
juice of 1 lemon
2 tablespoons chopped parsley

Garnish
olive oil
1 tablespoon chopped parsley

Drain the beans, place them in a large saucepan with plenty of water and bring to the boil. Simmer for about an hour, or until the beans are tender. Drain them and place in a large bowl.

Lightly mash the beans with a fork or potato masher. There should be small pieces of bean and red skin, so do not reduce to a smooth paste. Add all the remaining ingredients and blend thoroughly.

Keeping your hands damp with cold water or lemon juice, take lumps of the mixture and shape into small balls. Chill until ready to serve.

Arrange on a plate, drizzle olive oil over them and sprinkle them with the parsley.

# gaghamp shoushmayov

## cabbage with sesame seeds and walnuts

An appetising Armenian starter which incorporates that favourite lemony spice of mine – sumak, available from many Continental and Middle Eastern shops. Serve with warm bread, e.g. pita bread.

1 small head of cabbage
2 oz (50g) walnuts, finely chopped
2 tablespoons sesame seeds
1 clove garlic, finely chopped
1 teaspoon salt
1 tablespoon sumak powder

Bring a large saucepan, half-filled with lightly salted water, to the boil. Quarter the cabbage, place in the water and cook until tender. Drain and cool.

Cut away the stem and thinly slice the quarters.

Put the shredded cabbage into a salad bowl and add the walnuts, sesame seeds, garlic, salt and sumak.

Mix thoroughly and chill for 2–3 hours.

# tsitblig

## olive and walnut salad

A classic Anatolian appetiser making use of 2 major regional fruits;
serve with pita or thin lavash bread. Scoop a little of the salad on to a piece of
bread and eat. Alternatively, scoop a little up with lettuce leaves.

4 oz (110g) green olives, stoned
2 oz (50g) chopped walnuts
1 small onion, finely chopped
4 spring onions, finely chopped
2 tablespoons finely chopped parsley

Dressing
4 tablespoons olive oil
2 tablespoons lemon juice
2 tablespoons pomegranate juice or 2 more tablespoons lemon juice
1/2 teaspoon chilli pepper

Garnish
finely shredded lettuce leaves
3–4 thinly sliced radishes

Quarter the olives and place in a bowl with the walnuts, onions and parsley. Mix the salad carefully.

Place the dressing ingredients in a small bowl and whisk vigorously. Pour the dressing over the salad and then chill until ready to serve.

Arrange the shredded lettuce around a serving dish and spoon the salad into the centre. Arrange the sliced radishes decoratively around the salad and serve.

# aginares oma

## raw artichokes

Although this recipe has a Greek name, raw artichokes are equally popular in Lebanon and Turkey. In Cypriot and Lebanese tavernas globe artichokes are served with spring onions, small cucumbers, celery sticks and lemon wedges as part of the *mezzeh* table, accompanied by a glass of ouzo or arak.

**3 young globe artichokes**
**juice of two lemons**

Garnishes
**lemon wedges, celery sticks, slices of cucumber, spring onions**

Remove 3 or 4 layers of artichoke leaves. Trim off the top section of each leaf and cut around the base. Now cut each one into quarters and scoop out the chokes with a spoon.

Pour water into a large bowl, stir in the lemon juice and then drop in the quartered artichokes. After 10 minutes, drain the quarters thoroughly and transfer to a serving plate.

Garnish, squeeze a little extra lemon juice over them and serve.

# kharapaki lobi

## green beans in a yoghurt and tomato sauce

An Armenian speciality from the Caucasus, often made with soured cream
(smetana), but yoghurt is a fine substitute.

It makes an excellent hors d'oeuvre, but it can also be served as a side salad.

1 lb (450g) French beans, fresh or frozen, trimmed and halved
2 oz (50g) butter
1 onion, thinly sliced
1 green pepper, seeded and thinly sliced
3 tomatoes, blanched, peeled and coarsely chopped
1¹/2 teaspoons dried basil
1 egg
1/2 pint (300ml) yoghurt or smetana (soured cream)
1 teaspoon salt
1/2 teaspoon black pepper

Garnish
1 tablespoon chopped parsley or tarragon leaves

Half-fill a large saucepan with water, add a teaspoon of salt and bring to the boil. Add the beans and simmer vigorously for 8–10 minutes, or until the beans are just tender. Drain the beans into a colander, rinse under cold water and set aside.

Melt the butter in a large saucepan. Add the onion and green pepper and cook, stirring frequently until the vegetables are tender. Add the tomatoes and basil and cook for a further 5 minutes, stirring frequently.

Now add the beans, stir well to mix thoroughly and simmer for another 5 minutes.

Meanwhile, beat together the egg and yoghurt or smetana and season it with the salt and pepper. Stir the yoghurt mixture into the vegetables. Heat through and serve immediately, garnished with the chopped parsley or tarragon leaves.

# borani-ye-gharch

## yoghurt with mushrooms

A simple and charming treatment of mushrooms from Iran,
where great use is made of yoghurt. This, one of countless Borani, i.e. yoghurt-
based recipes, is typical of peasant sophistication.

Incidentally, mushrooms are not all that popular in the Middle East,
but I hasten to add that this particular recipe comes from the Caspian coast where
there is more than a hint of Caucasian and Russian influence.
A similar Georgian dish makes use of soured cream – smetana.

1 lb (450g) mushrooms
2 oz (50g) butter
8 fl oz (250ml) water
3/4 pint (450ml) yoghurt
1 teaspoon salt
1 clove garlic, very finely chopped

Wash the mushrooms and pat dry with kitchen paper. Slice them.

Melt the butter in a saucepan and sauté the mushrooms for a few minutes. Add the water and simmer for 15–20 minutes.

Remove from the heat and leave to cool a little. Add the yoghurt and salt and stir well.

Sprinkle the garlic over the top and serve warm.

# kharnabit emforakeh

## cauliflower in tomato sauce

This is an Arab speciality, a regional speciality from north-west Syria, and a delicious way of preparing cauliflower.

The Egyptians have a somewhat similar dish where, after boiling and draining, the florets are dipped in beaten egg and then in breadcrumbs and fried.

Serve with tahina sauce, yoghurt and a rice pilav of your choice.

1 large cauliflower
6–8 tablespoons oil
2 cloves garlic, crushed
3 spring onions, thinly sliced
2 tablespoons tomato purée
1 teaspoon salt
1/2 teaspoon black pepper
2–3 tablespoons water
juice of 1 lemon
3 tablespoons finely chopped parsley

Break the cauliflower into florets and wash. Bring a large saucepan half-filled with lightly salted water to the boil, add the florets and cook until only just tender. Drain and allow to dry.

Heat the oil in a large frying pan, add the florets and fry, turning carefully, for 4–5 minutes. Remove with a slotted spoon and reserve.

Add the garlic and spring onions to the oil in the pan and fry for 2–3 minutes. Stir in the tomato purée, salt, pepper and water and heat through. Add the florets and turn carefully to coat with the sauce. Fry for a few minutes and just before removing from the heat, stir in the lemon juice. Transfer to a serving dish and sprinkle with the parsley.

# chatzilim im gvina

## aubergines with cheese

This is a spicy aubergine and cheese recipe from Israel which makes a very fine starter when served chilled.

2 large aubergines
8 oz (225g) cheese, Feta, Cheddar, cream or cottage cheese
2 spring onions, finely sliced
2 cloves garlic, crushed
2 pimento peppers, seeded and finely chopped
8 black olives, seeded and chopped
3 tablespoons olive oil
pinch of salt
1/4 teaspoon black pepper
2 tablespoons lemon juice

Garnish
finely shredded lettuce leaves
1 teaspoon dried mint

Make 2–3 slits in each aubergine with a sharp knife and cook under the grill or in a hot oven (450F/230C/gas 8) until the skins are black and the flesh feels soft when poked with a finger. Leave to cool and then peel off the skin, reserving any flesh which gets stripped off with the skin. Put the flesh into a large bowl and mash with a fork.

Grate the Feta or Cheddar cheese, or mash the cream or cottage cheese. Add the cheese to the aubergine together with the onion, garlic, pimentoes and olives and mix.

Add the oil, salt and pepper and lemon juice – add a very little first, then taste because a cheese such as Feta is very salty to begin with – and mix thoroughly.

Garnish small individual salad bowls with a little of the shredded lettuce, arrange the salad in the middle and sprinkle with a little dried mint. Chill and serve with hot pita bread.

# patates köftesi

## potato fingers

These are delightful rissoles from Turkey, beloved of children and grown-ups alike.
Simple to make, they are ideal either as a starter or as part of a main meal,
and are usually served with sliced peppers or pickled cucumbers and cabbage.

3 large potatoes, peeled
8 oz (225g) white cheese, e.g. Feta, Haloumi or Cheshire
1 oz (25g) flour
1 egg
1 tablespoon finely chopped parsley
1 teaspoon salt
1/2 teaspoon black pepper
1/2 teaspoon dill
about 3 fl oz (90ml) oil for frying

Garnish
2 tablespoons chopped parsley
1 tablespoon paprika

Boil the potatoes in lightly salted water until cooked. Drain, mash until smooth and leave to cool.

Grate the cheese and add to the potatoes. Add the remaining ingredients except the oil and mix or knead thoroughly until smooth. Taking a tablespoon of the mixture at a time, form it into fingers about 2 1/2in (6cm) long and 1/2in (1cm) thick.

Heat the oil in a frying pan, add a few of the fingers and fry, turning once, until golden. Remove with a slotted spoon, drain on kitchen paper and keep warm while cooking the remaining fingers.

Sprinkle with parsley and paprika and serve.

## stuffed tomatoes

An Israeli recipe in the same style as the famed stuffed Middle Eastern dishes,
but with distinct European overtones;
it is very light and delicate and makes an excellent appetiser.

These tomatoes can be served either hot or cold.

❧

4 large tomatoes, halved horizontally
3 oz (75g) grated cheese, e.g. Cheddar, Gruyère, Edam or Feta
2 cloves garlic, crushed
4 tablespoons finely chopped parsley
1 tablespoon onion, finely chopped
1 tablespoon finely chopped fresh mint or 1 teaspoon dried mint
$1/2$ teaspoon salt
$1/4$ teaspoon dry mustard
1 tablespoon lemon juice

Garnish
finely chopped lettuce leaves
thinly sliced radishes

Scoop the flesh from the tomato halves and discard. In a small bowl, mix together the cheese, garlic, parsley, onion, mint, salt, pepper, mustard and lemon juice.

Fill the tomato halves with the cheese mixture. Lightly grease a shallow baking dish and place the halved tomatoes in it. Place in an oven preheated to 375F (190C) gas 5 and bake for 15 minutes.

Arrange the shredded lettuce and sliced radishes around either a large serving dish or on individual plates and place the tomatoes in the centre. Allow 2 halves per person.
**Serves 4**

# avocado in yin

## avocados in wine

An Israeli recipe that makes use of avocados which have but recently (during the last 30 years) been introduced to the Middle East and are already making significant inroads into the regional cuisine.

There are several avocado-based appetisers and no doubt with time and experiment, others will follow.

❧

2 ripe avocados
4 fl oz (120ml) dry red wine
2 oz (50g) sugar
1 teaspoon lemon juice

Garnish
fresh mint leaves and crushed ice

Cut the avocados in half and remove their stones. Mix together the wine, sugar and lemon juice in a small bowl. Pour into the prepared avocado halves.

Garnish with mint leaves and serve over crushed ice.

# salads

God has bestowed on the Middle East most of the fruits and vegetables daily consumed. Nothing need be imported. All, with their luxuriant colours, odours and tastes, are available. With such bounteousness the Middle Easterners have, through the centuries, developed a rich repertoire of salads as well as appetisers. 'There is no difference between an appetiser and a salad,' my late mother often remarked. 'The distinction is a European one. With us, everything is *mezzeh*.'

Indeed, there is no difference – well, hardly any. Every dish in this chapter of salads can easily claim to be also in that of appetisers, and vice versa. The 'hardly any' remark applies to such salads as Gardofilov Aghtsan, Jajig or Pançar Salatasi, which usually accompany main dishes; but there is no reason why even they cannot also be eaten on their own as appetisers – well, hardly any!

## chickpea salad with tahina dressing

A tasty and filling chickpea recipe from Egypt. Serve it with bread
and home-made pickles.

4 oz (110g) chickpeas, soaked overnight in cold water
1 large onion, sliced into thin crescents
2 teaspoons salt
2 tablespoons finely chopped parsley

### Dressing
4 fl oz (120ml) tahina paste
about 4-6 tablespoons water
4 tablespoons lemon juice
1 large clove garlic, crushed
1/4 teaspoon black pepper
1/2 teaspoon ground cumin

### Garnish
pinch of chilli pepper

Drain the chickpeas, place in a large saucepan with plenty of water and bring to the boil. Simmer until tender. Remove any scum that appears on the surface, and add more boiling water if necessary. Drain and leave to cool.

Mix the onion and salt together in a bowl, squeezing softly. Gently rinse the onion under cold water; drain, then squeeze out as much water as possible. Place the onion in a large bowl, add the cooked chickpeas and the parsley and mix well.

To prepare the dressing, pour the tahina into a bowl and stir in a little of the water. Gradually add enough water to make a thin paste, then mix in the lemon juice, garlic, pepper and cumin.

Pour all but about 2 tablespoons of this sauce over the salad, mix well and then chill until needed.

Stir the salad, spoon it into a shallow dish and trickle the remaining dressing over the top. Sprinkle with the chilli pepper and serve.

# portakal salatasi

## orange salad

An unusual Turkish combination of oranges, onions and olives, it makes a colourful and tasty salad to serve with all types of roasts.

2 large oranges
1 small head lettuce
1/4 head curly endive
3 tablespoons caster sugar
2 tablespoons filfar or sabra or curaçao
1/4 pint (150ml) yoghurt

Peel the oranges and slice them very thinly crossways. Wash the lettuce leaves and endive, pat dry with kitchen paper and arrange in a salad bowl. Now arrange the orange slices decoratively around the centre of the bowl.

Sprinkle the oranges with the sugar and liqueur and place the salad in the refrigerator for at least 2 hours.

When ready to serve, beat the yoghurt until smooth, then pour over the salad.

# salat gezer-hai

## orange and carrot salad

An Israeli salad that makes use of the carrot – beloved of the Ashkenazim (European) Jews – and the orange – the most outstanding fruit of the land. It is light and refreshing.

1 lb (450g) carrots
juice of 2–3 oranges
juice of 1 lemon
1 teaspoon salt
pinch of black pepper

Garnish
sprigs of fresh tarragon, or mint leaves

Wash and scrape the carrots, then grate them coarsely. Put the grated carrots into a bowl and pour the orange and lemon juices over them. Add the salt and pepper and mix well. Refrigerate for a few hours to allow the carrots to absorb some of the juices.

Chop the tarragon or mint leaves coarsely, sprinkle them over the salad and serve.

# tapooz im salat-zeytim

## a variation of orange salad

This is an Israeli salad which omits the onion, but incorporates a local Israeli liqueur, kirsch or filfar (or use any other orange-based liqueur). This salad is good with beef, veal or poultry dishes.

2 oranges, peeled and segmented
2 oz (50g) black olives, stoned and sliced
2 oz (50g) green olives, stoned and sliced
1/4 teaspoon salt
1/4 teaspoon cayenne pepper
1 tablespoon olive oil
1/4 teaspoon ground cumin
2 tablespoons kirsch or filfar, or other orange-based liqueur

Cut each orange segment into 3 pieces. Put them into a large bowl with the olives, salt, pepper, olive oil and cumin. Mix well, sprinkle the liqueur over the top and stir. Place in the refrigerator to chill.

Spoon into a serving dish and serve.

## avocado im egozim

### avocado with walnuts

An avocado recipe from Israel where they seem to have fallen in love with this rather bland-tasting fruit. Strangely enough, this salad tastes delicious and makes an excellent appetiser as well as a side salad.

1 large ripe avocado, stoned and peeled
2 tablespoons lemon juice
1 small onion, finely chopped
3 pickled cucumbers, thinly sliced
1 stick celery, chopped
3 oz (75g) walnuts, quartered
1 teaspoon salt
1/2 teaspoon black pepper
1/2 teaspoon ground cumin
1/2 small red pepper, thinly sliced
1 oz (25g) black olives, stoned

Cube the avocado flesh, place in a bowl and sprinkle with the lemon juice. Add the onion, cucumbers, celery and walnuts. Season with the salt and pepper, toss and chill for 30 minutes.

Before serving, sprinkle with the cumin and garnish with the strips of red pepper and the black olives.

# salata-al-khadar

## mixed vegetable salad

This is a typical recipe from Syria and Lebanon, but this type of salad (olive oil and lemon juice-based) appears throughout the Middle East, particularly in Turkey, Armenia and the Arab lands.

Any kind of fresh vegetables can be used.

2 spring onions, finely chopped
1 small onion, finely chopped
1 green pepper, seeded and finely sliced
1 Cos lettuce
1/2 cucumber, thinly sliced
2–3 tomatoes, thinly sliced

Dressing
1 clove garlic, crushed
1 teaspoon salt
1/2 teaspoon black pepper
1/2 teaspoon cayenne pepper
juice of 1 lemon
3 tablespoons olive oil

Garnish
2 tablespoons finely chopped parsley
1 tablespoon finely chopped fresh mint, or 2 teaspoons dried mint

Place all the vegetables in a salad bowl.

Mix the dressing ingredients together in a small bowl and pour over the vegetables. Toss the salad until well coated with the dressing. Sprinkle with the parsley and mint and serve.

# çoban salatasi

## shepherd's salad

This is by far the most popular salad in the whole of the Middle East.
The choice of ingredients and the quantities are up to the individual.
The basic vegetables are exact: green peppers, onions, tomatoes, radishes,
cucumber and lettuce. However, there is no reason why some – or all – of the
following should not be used: chicory, celery, carrot, pickled capers – and so on.

Greeks often add black olives and crumbled Feta cheese. This recipe is
from Anatolia and is aptly called 'Shepherd's salad'.

1 green pepper, thinly sliced
1 onion, thinly sliced
3 tomatoes, cut into thin wedges
4 radishes, thinly sliced
1/2 cucumber, thinly sliced
1 clove garlic, finely chopped
2 tablespoons finely chopped parsley

Dressing
4–5 coriander seeds, crushed, or 1/2 teaspoon ground coriander
1 teaspoon salt
1 teaspoon dried mint
1/2 teaspoon dried dillweed
3 tablespoons olive oil
juice of 1 lemon

In a large salad bowl, mix together the green pepper, onion, tomatoes, radishes,
cucumber, garlic and parsley.

Mix the remaining ingredients together in a small bowl and pour over the salad. Toss
gently and serve immediately.

**Here are two other popular ways of serving this salad.**

With tahina Use the same ingredients as above, except for the oil and lemon juice.

Make a tahina sauce by mixing the juice of 1 lemon with 4 tablespoons of tahina paste
and 1/4 pint (150ml) water until smooth. Pour this dressing over the vegetables, toss
gently and serve immediately.

With yoghurt In a large bowl, mix together the pepper, onion, tomatoes, radishes,
cucumber, garlic and parsley.

Mix the remaining ingredients together in a bowl with 1/2 pint (300ml) yoghurt. Pour
this dressing over the vegetables, toss gently and serve immediately.

# salad-e-havij

## carrot salad

Carrots make excellent salads. The simplest of all – and my personal favourite –
is grated carrots with chopped spring onions and parsley tossed in
an olive oil-lemon juice dressing. The recipe below is from Iran, and is also popular
in Israel. It includes fresh orange juice and seedless raisins and goes
very well with poultry dishes and roast meats.

1 lb (450g) carrots, coarsely grated
juice of 2 oranges
juice of 1 lemon
2 oz (50g) seedless raisins
1/2 teaspoon salt
1/4 teaspoon black pepper
2 tablespoons olive oil

Garnish
1 tablespoon finely chopped tarragon, mint or parsley

Put the grated carrots in a large salad bowl and pour the orange and lemon juices over
the top. Add the raisins, salt, pepper and oil and mix well. Chill for an hour to allow the
carrots to absorb some of the juices.

Sprinkle with chopped tarragon, mint or parsley and serve.

# salad-e-sabz

## potatoes, peas and pickles

This is an Iranian salad with very definite Russian overtones. Most Iranian salads are of Western origin, but have been modified to suit local tastes.

3 medium-sized potatoes
2 medium-sized carrots, peeled and grated
2 dill pickles, chopped
1 stick celery, chopped
2 spring onions, chopped
4 tablespoons green peas, cooked

Dressing
1/2 teaspoon dry mustard
1 teaspoon salt
3 tablespoons olive oil
1 1/2 tablespoons lemon or lime juice
1/4 pint (150ml) double cream or 1/4 pint (150ml) made up of 1/2 mayonnaise and 1/2 smetana (soured cream)

Peel and boil the potatoes in lightly salted water. Drain, leave to cool, then cut into 1/2in (1cm) cubes. Place the cubed potatoes in a large salad bowl with the carrots, dill pickles, celery, spring onions and peas.

Mix the dressing ingredients together in a small bowl and pour over the salad. Toss gently but thoroughly, then chill until ready to serve.

### patates salatasi

## potato and tomato salad

This salad is typical of the Turkish–Armenian cuisine.
It is simple to prepare and very tasty.

4 medium-sized potatoes, peeled
3 medium-sized tomatoes

Dressing
1 clove garlic, crushed
2 tablespoons olive oil
juice of 1 lemon
1 teaspoon salt
1/2 teaspoon black pepper

Garnish
1 tablespoon finely chopped parsley

Boil the potatoes in lightly salted water until just cooked, then drain. When cool enough to handle, cut into 1/2in (1cm) cubes.

Cut each tomato into quarters and then halve each quarter. Place the potato cubes and chopped tomatoes in a salad bowl. Mix together the garlic, oil, lemon juice, salt and pepper in a small bowl. Pour the dressing over the vegetables and toss well. Taste and adjust the seasoning if necessary, then chill for at least 1 hour.

Just before serving, sprinkle with parsley.

### gardofilov aghtsan

## potato and soured cream salad

A recipe from the Caucasus, popular with Armenians and Georgians, this is traditionally served with soured cream, but yoghurt is a good substitute.

It makes a fine appetiser or side salad.

11/2 lb (675g) even sized potatoes
1/2 cucumber, peeled and thinly sliced

2 shallots, finely chopped, or 2 spring onions, finely sliced
1 teaspoon salt
1/2 teaspoon black pepper
1/4 pint (150ml) yoghurt or soured cream
2 tablespoons finely chopped parsley

Wash the potatoes and cook in boiling water. When tender, drain, cool and peel.

Cut the potatoes into 1/2in (1cm) cubes and place in a large salad bowl. Add the cucumber slices and chopped onion. Gently stir in the salt, pepper and yoghurt or soured cream. Chill for an hour.

Serve sprinkled with the chopped parsley.

## salata al-banadora

### tomato salad

A typical tomato and olive oil-based salad from the Lebanon.

1 clove garlic, finely chopped
1 teaspoon salt
juice of 1 lemon
1/2 cucumber, thinly sliced
4 tomatoes, thinly sliced
1 small onion, thinly sliced
6–8 black olives (optional)
3 tablespoons olive oil
1 tablespoon finely chopped parsley
1/2 teaspoon paprika

Mix the garlic, salt and lemon juice together in a salad bowl. Add the cucumber, tomatoes, onion, olives and olive oil and toss well.

Sprinkle with the parsley and paprika and serve.

# spanak salatasi

## spinach salad with cream

This is an Azerbaijani salad popular throughout the Caucasus,
Iran and Eastern Turkey.

For this recipe you have to use fresh spinach; frozen spinach will not do.

1 lb (450g) fresh spinach, washed thoroughly and drained
1/4 pint (150ml) double cream
1 teaspoon salt
1/2 teaspoon black pepper
juice of 11/2 lemons
1/2 teaspoon dillweed
2 hard-boiled eggs
1 teaspoon paprika

Shred the spinach leaves thinly.

In a salad bowl, mix together the cream, salt, pepper, lemon juice and dill. Add the spinach and toss well.

Slice the eggs thinly, remove the pieces of yolk, chop them and sprinkle over the salad. Use the rings of egg white to decorate the salad. Sprinkle with the paprika and serve.

# jajig

## yoghurt and cucumber salad

A classic of the Armenian cuisine, this salad has spread throughout the Middle East. There are several versions, but it is basically yoghurt, cucumber and dried mint.

It is an excellent accompaniment to all dishes and ideal with grills and pilavs.

1 pint (600ml) yoghurt
1/2 teaspoon salt
1 clove garlic, crushed
1 cucumber, peeled, quartered lengthways and finely chopped
2 tablespoons finely chopped fresh mint, or 1 teaspoon dried mint
a little red pepper as a garnish

Pour the yoghurt into a mixing bowl. Stir in the salt, garlic, cucumber and mint and mix well. Place in the refrigerator to chill until needed.

Pour into individual dishes and sprinkle with a little red pepper for serving.

# cacik

## yoghurt and cucumber salad

This is the Turkish version.

1/2 pint (300ml) yoghurt
1/2 teaspoon salt
a few drops of vinegar
a few drops of olive oil
1 cucumber, peeled and sliced into 1/2in (1cm) pieces

In a bowl, beat the yoghurt with a little salt and a few drops of vinegar and olive oil. Add the cucumber and mix thoroughly. Chill for 1–2 hours, then serve.

# pancar salatasi

## beetroot and yoghurt salad

This Turkish beetroot salad is popular throughout the Caucasus and Northern Iran. It makes good use of yoghurt – one very important ingredient in the staple diet of the Anatolian villages.

**1 lb (450g) cooked beetroot**
**1 oz (25g) butter**
**1 onion, finely chopped**
**1/2 pint (300ml) garlic-yoghurt sauce (see page 245)**

Rub the skins off the beetroot; dice the beetroot.

Melt the butter in a saucepan and sauté the onion until golden brown. Add the beetroot, stir well and keep warm until ready to serve.

Pile the beetroot into a serving dish, pour the garlic-yoghurt sauce over the top and serve immediately.

## beetroot salad with dill

Turks love dill and use it generously in their cuisine.
This simple salad from Adana in southern Turkey is equally beloved by Kurds,
Armenians, Maronites and the Alouites of the region.

1 lb (450g) beetroot, scrubbed clean
1 small onion, coarsely chopped
2 tablespoons chopped fresh dill, or 2 teaspoons dried dillweed

Dressing
1 large clove garlic, crushed
1/2 teaspoon salt
4 tablespoons olive oil
3 tablespoons vinegar

Garnish
lettuce leaves

Trim the beetroot, but do not cut into them or they will 'bleed' during cooking. Place in a large saucepan, cover with water and bring to the boil; cook until tender and then drain.

When cool enough to handle, peel the beetroot and cut into small cubes. Place the chopped beetroot in a bowl with the onion and mix gently.

Put the garlic, salt, oil and vinegar in a small bowl and whisk until well blended. Pour the dressing over the salad, mix well and chill until ready to serve.

Stir the dill into the salad, then spoon into a serving dish lined with lettuce leaves.

# salata min shawandar

## spicy beetroot salad

A speciality of the Alouite people of Syria and southern Turkey,
who have a penchant for hot, spicy food.

1 lb (450g) beetroot, scrubbed clean
3 fl oz (90ml) vinegar
2 tablespoons fresh breadcrumbs
1 large clove garlic, crushed
2 tablespoons lemon juice
3 fl oz (90ml) olive oil
1/4 teaspoon chilli pepper
1/2 teaspoon salt

### Garnish
1 tablespoon finely chopped parsley
2 tablespoons finely chopped spring onions, white parts only

Prepare and cook the beetroot as described in the previous recipe. When cool enough to handle, peel the beetroot and slice it into thin rounds. Place in a bowl, add half the vinegar, stir gently, cover and set aside for a few hours.

Mix the remaining ingredients together in a small bowl to form a thick dressing. Turn the beetroot into a serving dish, pour the dressing over the top and refrigerate for at least an hour.

Garnish with the contrasting parsley and onion and serve.

# salat-e panir ve khiar

## cucumber and cheese salad

This salad is a speciality of Kurdistan – a region that stretches into Turkey, Iraq and Iran. The Kurds are famed for their excellent cheeses – as well as their bravery.

This is a dazzlingly simple recipe that is also popular in Turkey and Armenia. Feta or Haloumi cheese can be purchased from most Continental shops.

1/2 cucumber, peeled
1 1/2 tablespoons lemon juice
1 teaspoon olive oil
1/2 teaspoon salt
1 1/2 teaspoons dried mint
10 black olives, stoned and thinly sliced
2 oz (50g) Feta cheese (or grated Haloumi or Cheshire cheese)

Slice the cucumber thinly and place in a bowl.

In a small bowl, mix the lemon juice, olive oil, salt and mint. Add this dressing to the cucumber. Now add the olives and mix everything together.

Transfer the salad to a serving bowl. Sprinkle with the crumbled cheese and serve.

# fattoush

## bread salad

*When your hand is floured don't meddle in men's business.*
Said to women to put them in their place!

This is a much-loved Syrian peasant salad with an unusual texture.

1 large cucumber, chopped
1 lettuce heart, shredded
5 tomatoes, chopped
10 spring onions, chopped
1 small green pepper, chopped
1 tablespoon chopped fresh coriander leaves
1 tablespoon finely chopped parsley
1/2 tablespoon finely chopped fresh mint
1 clove garlic, crushed
6 tablespoons olive oil
juice of 2 lemons
1/2 teaspoon salt
1/4 teaspoon black pepper
5 thin slices bread, lightly toasted and cut into small cubes

Place all the ingredients, except the toast, in a large mixing bowl. Toss the salad so that all the ingredients are well coated with the oil and lemon juice. Chill until ready to serve.

When ready to serve, stir in the toast cubes and eat immediately.

# tabouleh

## burghul with salad vegetables

This salad is popular throughout Syria, Lebanon and parts of Jordan.
It is a mixture of burghul and finely chopped vegetables,
flavoured with lemon and mint. It is traditionally eaten with lettuce leaves
and/or pita bread, and the traditional way of eating it
is to make a parcel of the Tabouleh by folding a little of it up in a lettuce leaf,
or spooning a little of it into the 'pouch' of a pita bread.

3 oz (75g) fine burghul
1/2 cucumber, finely chopped
4 tomatoes, finely chopped
1 green pepper, seeded and finely chopped
1/2 onion, finely chopped
4 tablespoons finely chopped parsley
2 tablespoons dried mint, or finely chopped fresh mint
1 teaspoon salt
juice of 2–3 lemons
4 tablespoons olive oil
1 lettuce, preferably Cos, leaves separated and washed

Rinse the burghul in a bowl several times until the water runs clean. Squeeze out any excess.

Put the chopped vegetables, parsley and mint into a large mixing bowl and add the burghul. Stir in the salt, lemon juice and olive oil. Mix well, leave for 15 minutes, then taste and adjust the seasoning if necessary.

Arrange the lettuce leaves around the edge of a serving plate and pile the salad in the centre.

# spinach and chickpea salad

An Armenian speciality that can be served either as an appetiser or a side-salad. Traditionally eaten in the 40 days of Lent.

4 oz (110g) chickpeas, soaked in cold water overnight
(you can use a 425g can of cooked chickpeas instead)
1½ pints (900ml) water
1 lb (450g) fresh spinach, washed and chopped (if you use frozen spinach,
buy the leaf spinach and chop it, as the ready-chopped spinach is too fine)
4 tablespoons tomato purée
2 oz (50g) butter
1 teaspoon salt
1 teaspoon sugar
½ teaspoon black pepper
1 tablespoon ground cumin

If you are using canned chickpeas, drain them and then follow the recipe from paragraph three.

Wash the chickpeas and place them in a pan with 1 pint (600ml) of the water. Bring to the boil and simmer for 45 minutes, or until the chickpeas are tender. Add a little more boiling water if necessary. Strain and leave until cool enough to handle.

Now remove the skins from the chickpeas. The easiest way to do this is to hold a pea between thumb and forefinger and squeeze the pea from the skin.

Put the spinach and chickpeas into a saucepan and add the remaining ½ pint (300ml) water with the tomato purée, butter, salt, sugar, black pepper and cumin. Stir the mixture, bring to the boil and simmer for 30–40 minutes until the spinach and chickpeas are cooked and the water has evaporated.

Chill for 30 minutes before serving.

# lobi aghtsan

## white bean salad

This makes an excellent appetiser or side-salad to main courses.
It keeps well in the refrigerator for several days.

6 oz (175g) dried white haricot beans, soaked in cold water overnight
2 small carrots, peeled and diced
1 small green pepper, seeded and thinly sliced
1 stick celery, diced
1 clove garlic, finely chopped
2 tomatoes, finely chopped
2 tablespoons finely chopped parsley
1 teaspoon salt
1/2 teaspoon cayenne pepper
2 1/2 fl oz (75ml) olive oil
1 lemon, cut into wedges for a garnish

Rinse the soaked beans under cold water. Half-fill a large saucepan with cold water, add the beans, bring to the boil and then simmer until the beans are just tender. The cooking time will depend on the age and quality of the beans.

Add the carrots, green pepper, celery, garlic, tomatoes, parsley, salt and cayenne pepper. Cover and continue cooking for about 30 minutes, or until the vegetables are tender. Drain and transfer the beans and vegetables immediately to a serving bowl.

Add the olive oil and mix well. Leave to cool, then chill for 2–3 hours. When serving, garnish with the lemon wedges.

# mushosh

## lentil salad

An Armenian salad, and a fascinating mixture of lentils, walnuts and apricots –
the national fruit of Armenia, *Prunus armenicus*.

It is simply delightful.

6 oz (175g) brown lentils
1 small onion, chopped
3 oz (75g) dried apricots, chopped
2 oz (50g) walnuts, chopped

Dressing
3 tablespoons olive oil
1$^1/_2$ tablespoons lemon juice
1 teaspoon salt
$^1/_2$ teaspoon black pepper
2 tablespoons chopped parsley

Wash the lentils and cook in lightly salted water until almost tender. Add a little more water if necessary. Make sure you do not overcook the lentils. Stir in the onion, apricots and walnuts and cook for a further 15 minutes. Strain the mixture and leave to cool. Transfer to a serving bowl.

In a small bowl, mix together the oil, lemon juice, salt and pepper. Add the dressing to the lentils together with the parsley.

Toss and serve.

# salata bil adas wa jazar

## lentil salad with carrots

A Palestinian speciality which is also popular with Jordanians and Syrians. It is a typical falahine or peasant dish which makes a simple and delicious salad.

3/4 pint (450ml) water
6 oz (175g) brown lentils, rinsed thoroughly
3 medium-sized carrots, peeled and finely chopped
1 teaspoon salt
1/2 teaspoon ground cumin
1/2 teaspoon chilli pepper
6 tablespoons olive oil
4 tablespoons lemon juice

### Topping
1 small onion, finely chopped
2 tablespoons finely chopped parsley
2 spring onions, finely chopped
1 ripe tomato, finely diced

Place the water and lentils in a large saucepan, bring to the boil and simmer for 10 minutes. Add the carrots, seasonings and 4 tablespoons of the oil. Cover the pan and simmer for 20–30 minutes, or until the lentils are tender. The water should be absorbed.

If the lentils are not quite cooked, add a little more boiling water and continue to simmer, covered, until the lentils are tender. Spread the lentil mixture out over a large plate to cool quickly.

Meanwhile, prepare the topping by mixing the ingredients together. Cover and chill until ready to serve.

When the lentil mixture is cold, gently stir in the lemon juice. Arrange the mixture in a serving dish, spread the topping over the surface and then drizzle the remaining oil over the top.

# salad-e-nokhod

## chickpea salad

This is a Kurdish–Armenian salad which is very popular in Eastern Turkey.
It uses chickpeas in the typical 'olive-oil-and-lemon-juice' style
of many Middle Eastern salads.

It is possible to buy cans of ready-cooked chickpeas and you can use these
for convenience if you prefer.

8 oz (225g) chickpeas, soaked overnight in cold water
2 tablespoons finely chopped parsley
1/2 small onion, finely chopped
2 spring onions, finely sliced
1 clove garlic, crushed
2 tablespoons lemon juice
2 tablespoons olive oil
1 teaspoon salt
1/4 teaspoon cayenne pepper
1/2 teaspoon ground cumin

Rinse the chickpeas and place in a large saucepan half-filled with cold water. Bring to the boil and simmer until tender. It may be necessary to add more boiling water. Pour the chickpeas into a colander, rinse under cold water and set aside.

Mix the remaining ingredients together in a small bowl. Place the chickpeas in a salad bowl, add the dressing and mix thoroughly.

# egg and cheese dishes

Nasretin Hoça, who lived in the 14th century and whose wit and guile was a legend even in his own lifetime, was often subjected to every possible form of trickery and one-upmanship by friend and foe alike. A famed incident was when, on a Friday, a few friends invited him to go to the local Turkish baths. The baths – a sumptuous edifice of Byzantine origin as most buildings worthy of note in Turkey still are – was situated in the town centre behind the souk and turquoise-domed mosque.

Now the friends had so arranged that each took an egg with him except, of course, for our Hoça who, unbeknown, found himself eggless in the steam room. 'Well brothers,' said one, 'whoever cannot – or does not – lay an egg will have to pay all our expenses, both here and for dinner and drinks afterwards – agreed?'

'Naturally, we agree,' they all clucked.

So, one by one, they jumped up to the highest part of the baths near the gargoyles whence steaming water poured down, and clucked simultaneously.

'Cluck, cluck, cluck!'

Then each in turn produced an egg from where eggs are meant to be produced! Nasretin Hoça, stark naked, stood below in utter amazement, mouth agape.

'Well Hoça, how about you?' they all asked.

Nasretin gazed at these featherless specimens of human flesh for a few moments, grinned, shook his head gently and then climbed up to join them. He raised his arms and head and crowed aloud.

'Hey Hoça, what's the idea?' one asked.

'Nothing, except that with all you hens about there must be a cockerel around. Cock-a-doodle-doo!'

One laughed, the others joined in. 'Hoça, you are too cocky by half!'

He had made his point.

Eggeh or Kookoo is an interesting way of preparing omelettes. These are not omelettes in the true European sense, but more meals in their own right. They are usually prepared in specially made copper pans similar to heavy-based frying pans.

The Iranian cuisine is famed for Kookoo dishes. Serve them with fresh salads, pickles and bread.

The most popular cheeses used are Feta, Haloumi and Kashkaval. All are available in most Continental and Indian grocery stores. However, in many recipes I have suggested suitable alternatives.

# beid bil khal

## scrambled eggs with vinegar

This Arab recipe makes an excellent breakfast, especially when accompanied by warm pita bread.

2 tablespoons butter
2 cloves garlic, crushed
6 eggs
1 teaspoon salt
1/2 teaspoon black pepper
1/4 teaspoon ground cumin
3 tablespoons vinegar

Garnish
1 tablespoon finely chopped parsley
1 spring onion, finely sliced

Melt the butter in a frying pan. Add the garlic and fry for 3–4 minutes until it starts to turn golden.

Break the eggs into a bowl, add the salt, pepper and cumin and beat until well blended. Pour the egg mixture into the frying pan and cook on a low heat, stirring constantly.

As the eggs begin to thicken, slowly add the vinegar, stirring all the time. Remove from the heat.

Cut into 4 portions, sprinkle with the parsley and spring onion and serve immediately.
**Serves 4**

# vorpi jash

## yoghurt omelette

A very descriptive name for a very simple dish. Vorpi Jash means
'the orphan's meal', referring to its simple ingredients.
For centuries the Anatolian peasants lived, and still do, on such dishes.

If you are feeling rich, use cream instead of milk!

8 eggs
8 tablespoons milk
1 teaspoon salt
1/2 teaspoon black pepper
4 tablespoons butter
1/2 pint (300ml) garlic-yoghurt sauce (see page 245)

Break the eggs into a bowl. Add the milk, salt and pepper and beat lightly until just blended.

Melt the butter in a large frying pan over a moderate heat. Carefully pour in the egg mixture, stir and leave to cook for a few minutes until the surface is just set but not dry.

Transfer to a serving plate, pour the garlic-yoghurt sauce over and serve immediately.
**Serves 3–4**

# shertzazoon

## easter omelette

*In the shadow of our fathers we grow,*
*In the soul of our fathers we are.*
*In spirit,*
*In mind and body*
*We are the shadows of our fathers.*
*They did not know.*
Armenian Wisdom

This was my father's favourite omelette and, in the spirit of the poem above, it is mine. A speciality of the Armenians from Kilis (southern Turkey), these are 6in (15cm) round wafer-thin omelettes, prepared for Easter Sunday lunch. They are rolled up like pancakes and eaten in the hand.

6 eggs
3 tablespoons finely chopped parsley
1 clove garlic, finely chopped
1 teaspoon salt
1/2 teaspoon black pepper
pinch of paprika
about 4 tablespoons butter

Crack the eggs into a bowl and beat well. Add the parsley, garlic, salt, pepper and paprika and mix thoroughly.

Melt just sufficient butter in a 6–7in (15–18cm) non-stick frying pan to coat the bottom and sides. Pour a little of the egg mixture into the pan and swirl it around so that it is spread evenly and very thinly over the bottom. Cook for about 2 minutes or until it is golden underneath (lift edge with a spatula).

Remove from the pan, allowing any excess butter to drip back into the pan, and keep in a warm place.

Cook the remaining mixture in the same way, greasing the pan with a little more butter when needed. Serve immediately with a salad of your choice.

# eggeh bi sabanah

## spinach eggeh

This is a Syrian recipe, but it is popular throughout Southern Turkey, Armenia and other Arab lands.

Spinach has a great affinity with eggs and yoghurt and traditionally this eggeh is eaten with bread and a bowl of fresh yoghurt.

1 lb (450g) fresh leaf spinach or frozen leaf spinach
4 tablespoons butter
1 teaspoon salt
1/4 teaspoon black pepper
6 eggs

Wash the spinach very thoroughly and drain well. Place in a saucepan and cook in its own juices over a moderate heat until tender. Pour into a colander and, when cool enough to handle, squeeze out all the water and chop coarsely.

Melt 1/2 tablespoon of the butter in the saucepan, add the spinach, salt and pepper and stir well. Keep hot.

Melt 2 tablespoons of the butter in a frying pan, crack 3 of the eggs into the pan and cook over a low heat until just set. Place half the spinach on top of the eggs and carefully smooth it out with the back of a spoon to spread it evenly. Cook for about 5 minutes.

Place a large plate over the frying pan and carefully turn the eggeh out on to the plate.

Melt the remaining butter in the frying pan and break the remaining 3 eggs into it. When the eggs are cooked, spread the remaining spinach over the top in the same way and cook for about 5 minutes.

Now carefully slide the first eggeh back into the pan on top of the other one. Cook for a further 2–3 minutes to heat through and then slide the whole eggeh on to a serving plate.

Cut into wedges and serve.

# kookoo-ye baghala

## broad bean eggeh

An Iranian speciality in which the broad beans are mashed,
then mixed with the remaining ingredients. Use fresh or frozen beans if possible –
shelling them first and then removing their transparent skins.
You can also use dried broad beans, but if you do, soak them for 3 hours
in cold water before cooking.

Serve with a rice pilav or a salad of your choice.

1 lb (450g) broad beans – if dried, soak for 3 hours first
3 tablespoons butter
1 large onion, thinly sliced
4 tablespoons fresh dillweed or 2 tablespoons dried dillweed
6 eggs
2 teaspoons salt
1/2 teaspoon black pepper
2 tablespoons finely chopped parsley

Place the beans in a saucepan, add sufficient lightly salted water to cover by about 2in (5cm) and bring to the boil. Simmer until tender, strain and mash.

Heat 2 tablespoons of the butter in a frying pan, add the onion and fry until soft. Stir in the dill.

Break the eggs into a large bowl and thoroughly mix in the salt, black pepper, parsley, the onion mixture and the mashed beans.

Melt the remaining tablespoon of butter in an ovenproof baking dish, making sure that the sides are well coated. Pour the egg mixture into the dish and bake in the centre of an oven preheated to 350F (180C) gas 4, for about 45 minutes, or until the edges of the Kookoo are crisp and the top is golden brown.

Remove from the oven, place a serving plate over the dish and invert.

Serve immediately cut into wedges.

# kookoo-ye loobia

## bean eggeh

An Iranian recipe that makes a wholesome meal.

Serve with a rice pilav and/or a salad of your choice.

❦

3/4 lb (350g) string beans, washed, drained and cut into 1/2in (1cm) long pieces
2 oz (50g) butter
1 small onion, finely chopped
1/2 teaspoon saffron
6 eggs
1 teaspoon salt
1/4 teaspoon black pepper

Place the beans in a large saucepan with some lightly salted water and bring to the boil. Simmer until tender and then drain.

Meanwhile, melt half the butter in a large frying pan, add the onion and sauté until golden. Stir in the saffron and the beans and fry for 2–3 minutes.

Break the eggs into a mixing bowl, add the salt and pepper and beat thoroughly. Add the onions and beans and mix well.

Either melt the remaining butter in an ovenproof dish, add the egg mixture and bake in an oven preheated to 350F (180C) gas 4, for 30–45 minutes until firm and golden.

Or melt the remaining butter in a large frying pan, and the egg mixture and cook over a low heat. When the centre is almost firm, very carefully place a large plate over the pan and invert, dropping the omelette onto the plate.

Very carefully slide the omelette back into the pan and cook for another 3–4 minutes on the other side.

Cut the Kookoo into wedges and serve.

# Yumourtali Batrijan

## aubergines topped with scrambled eggs and tomatoes

This filling dish is from Azerbaijan in the USSR, and is typical
of the Caucasian region.

Serve it with fresh yoghurt or Jajig, bread and some home-made pickles.

4 medium-sized aubergines, about 1¹/₂ lb (675g)
2 large cloves garlic, crushed
2 oz (50g) butter
1 large onion, thinly sliced
1 red pepper, thinly sliced
4 large ripe tomatoes, blanched, peeled and chopped
6 eggs
1 teaspoon salt
¹/₂ teaspoon black pepper

Make 2 or 3 slits in each aubergine with a sharp knife and place in a hot oven
(450F/230C/gas 8) or under a hot grill. When the skins are black and the flesh soft
when poked with a finger, remove.

When cool enough to handle, peel off the skin, scraping off and reserving any pulp
that comes away with the skin. Place the pulp in a bowl and mash with a fork. Add the
garlic and blend well. Arrange in a shallow serving dish and keep warm.

Melt the butter in a large frying pan, add the onion and pepper and fry for about
10 minutes or until the vegetables are soft. Add the tomatoes and fry for a further
5 minutes, stirring frequently.

Beat the eggs in a small bowl together with the salt and pepper. Pour them into the
frying pan, stir to mix well and then leave over a low heat for a few minutes until the
eggs are set.

Spoon the egg mixture over the aubergines and serve immediately.

# bamia-bil-beid

## okra with eggs

Okra is a popular vegetable throughout the Middle East, particularly with the Egyptians, Iraqis and Kurds. This is a typical Coptic recipe from Egypt.

Choose fresh small okra, but if these are unobtainable,
you can use canned ones instead. If you do, drain the okra thoroughly before using.

1 lb (450g) small okra
2 tablespoons lemon juice
2 oz (50g) butter
1 small onion, thinly sliced
1 small red pepper, thinly sliced
2 large, ripe tomatoes, blanched, peeled and chopped
3 eggs
1³/4 teaspoons salt
1/4 teaspoon black pepper

Rinse the okra and trim the stems to a cone shape, taking care not to cut into the okra.

Half-fill a large saucepan with water and bring to the boil.

Add the okra and lemon juice and simmer for 5 minutes. Drain.

Melt half the butter in a large frying pan, add the onion and red pepper and fry for about 10 minutes or until the vegetables are soft. Lay the okra over the onion and pepper, then sprinkle the chopped tomatoes over the top.

Melt the remaining butter and pour it evenly over the vegetables. Cover the pan and simmer for about 10 minutes, or until the okra are tender.

Beat the eggs with the salt and pepper in a small bowl. Pour the eggs slowly and evenly over the vegetables and continue to cook until the eggs are set.

Serve from the pan or slide on to a serving plate.

# yumurtali lahana

## cabbage with milk and eggs

A favourite recipe from Turkey, this makes a wonderful change to plain boiled cabbage! It's a substantial meal in its own right.

Serve with a salad.

1 lb (450g) white cabbage, shredded
1¹/2 teaspoons salt
4 fl oz (120ml) milk
4 eggs
¹/4 teaspoon black pepper
2 tablespoons fresh breadcrumbs

Garnish
1 teaspoon paprika

Rinse and drain the cabbage and place in a large frying pan brushed with oil. Sprinkle with 1 teaspoon of the salt and add the milk. Cover the pan and cook, stirring occasionally, until the cabbage is soft.

Beat the eggs in a small bowl with the remaining salt, the pepper and breadcrumbs. Stir this mixture carefully into the cabbage. Cover the pan and cook over a low heat for 2–3 minutes, or until the eggs are just set.

Place under a hot grill for about 1 minute to brown the top and serve straight from the pan, or slide onto a serving dish. Sprinkle with the paprika and serve immediately.

# ougat agas

## cauliflower and pear pie

From Israel, this dish makes a fine accompaniment
to all types of roasts and kebabs.

1 large cauliflower
3 unripe pears, peeled, cored and sliced
4 eggs, beaten
1 teaspoon salt
1/2 teaspoon black pepper
1/2 teaspoon nutmeg
4 tablespoons breadcrumbs
2 red peppers, seeded and cut into 1/2in (1cm) slices
6 black olives, stoned and sliced
6 mushroom caps, wiped clean and thinly sliced
1 tablespoon finely chopped onion

Garnish
1 tablespoon finely chopped parsley

Remove any leaves and break the cauliflower into florets and wash. Drop them into a large pan of boiling water. After 10 minutes, add the pear slices and cook until just tender. Drain and put the cauliflower, pears, eggs, salt, pepper, nutmeg and breadcrumbs into a liquidiser and blend.

Lightly grease a baking dish large enough to take the mixture comfortably. Pour a quarter of the cauliflower mixture into the dish. Cover with half of the red pepper and olive slices.

Now pour in another quarter of the cauliflower mixture and cover it with the mushrooms and onion.

Repeat a cauliflower layer and then add the remaining red pepper and olive slices. Top with the remaining cauliflower.

Place in an oven preheated to 350F (180C) gas 4, and bake for 30–45 minutes until the top is golden.

Sprinkle with the parsley and serve.

A touch of Jewish humour:
*'Why is it, a nice-looking man like you, you're not married?'*
*'Because every time I meet a girl who cooks like Mamma, she looks like Papa!'*

# tzibbele kugel

## onion cake

This is a Jewish speciality popular in Israel – especially amongst European Jews.
There are several variations of this cake, pie, or baked pudding
using other vegetables and ingredients such as potatoes and noodles.
It is usually eaten as an accompaniment to meat dishes
but there is no reason why it cannot be eaten as a main course in itself
with a salad of your choice.

2 oz (50g) melted butter
4 eggs, separated
2 large or 3 medium-sized onions, finely chopped
3 oz (75g) matzo meal
1¹/₂ teaspoons salt
¹/₂ teaspoon white pepper

Use a little of the melted butter to grease a small ovenproof casserole dish.

In a large mixing bowl, beat the egg yolks until they are pale and thick. Stir in the onions, matzo meal, remaining melted butter, salt and pepper and set aside.

In another bowl, whisk the egg whites until they form stiff peaks. Fold the egg whites gently and carefully into the onion mixture.

Spoon the mixture into the prepared casserole dish and place in the centre of an oven preheated to 350F (180C) gas 4.

Bake for 30–40 minutes or until the top is lightly browned and the mixture is firm. Serve immediately.

# eggeh bi khubz wa kousa

## bread and courgette eggeh

An Arab recipe using bread to give the dish more substance, it is usually served with yoghurt or salad as a main dish.

1/2 lb (225g) courgettes, washed and cut into 1/4in (1/2cm) slices crossways
4 tablespoons butter
1 onion, finely chopped
3 slices bread, crusts removed and soaked in a little milk
6 eggs, well beaten
4 tablespoons chopped parsley
1 teaspoon salt
1/2 teaspoon black pepper
1/2 teaspoon cinnamon
1/2 teaspoon paprika

Arrange the courgette slices on a large plate, sprinkle with a little salt and leave for 30 minutes. Rinse under cold water and dry on kitchen paper.

Melt half the butter in a frying pan, add the onion and fry for a few minutes until soft. Now add the courgettes and fry, turning carefully, until coated all over with butter and turning a light golden colour. Remove the courgettes and onion with a slotted spoon and drain on kitchen paper.

Squeeze out the slices of bread, then crumble it into the beaten eggs. Now add the courgette and onion mixture with the parsley, salt, pepper and cinnamon and mix thoroughly.

Melt the remaining butter in the frying pan. Pour the egg mixture into the pan and cook over a low heat for about 20 minutes or until well set. Place a large plate over the pan and carefully invert, dropping the eggeh on to the plate. Carefully slide the eggeh back into the frying pan and cook for a further 10 minutes.

Remove from the heat and slide the eggeh on to a serving plate. Sprinkle with paprika, cut into wedges and serve.

# kookoo sibzamini

## potato eggeh

There are several recipes for potato omelettes throughout the Middle East, particularly in Iran and Iraq, and this recipe is from Iran. It is deliciously light and goes well with a vegetable dish and/or bowl of yoghurt.

2 large potatoes
3 tablespoons butter
6 eggs, well beaten
4 spring onions, finely chopped
2 tablespoons finely chopped parsley
1 teaspoon dried dillweed
1 teaspoon salt
1/2 teaspoon black pepper
1 teaspoon paprika

Peel and boil the potatoes in lightly salted water until tender, then drain and mash them. Add 2 tablespoons of the butter, the beaten eggs, onion, parsley, dill, salt and pepper and beat until smooth.

Melt the remaining butter in a baking dish and swirl it around to coat the sides. Pour the potato mixture into the dish, place in an oven preheated to 350F (180C) gas 4, and bake for about 45 minutes or until set and a light golden brown.

Sprinkle with the paprika and serve warm.

# kookoo-ye tareh ba gerdoo

## leek and walnut eggeh

This is a fine omelette which is traditionally served with yoghurt and/or a salad of your choice.

3 tablespoons butter
3/4 lb (350g) leeks, washed carefully and finely chopped
5 tablespoons walnuts, finely chopped
1 tablespoon flour
1/2 tablespoon turmeric
1 teaspoon salt
1/4 teaspoon black pepper
6 eggs, well beaten
2 tablespoons finely chopped parsley

Melt 2 tablespoons of the butter in a frying pan. Remove from the heat, and stir in the leeks, walnuts, flour, turmeric, salt and pepper. Now add the beaten eggs and parsley and stir thoroughly.

Melt the remaining butter in a baking dish or ovenproof casserole and pour in the egg mixture. Spread the mixture out evenly with the back of a spoon. Place in the centre of an oven preheated to 350F (180C) gas 4, and bake for about 45 minutes or until the Kookoo is set and golden.

Remove from the oven, cut into squares and serve with yoghurt.

# tfihat kishurim

## courgettes with egg and cheese

An Israeli dish similar to many other Sephardic egg dishes: this, too,
is of Spanish–Moorish origin. It makes a substantial omelette. I wouldn't call it
an Eggeh or Kookoo although it is almost there.

Serve it hot as a savoury with salads or cold, either as a side-dish
to cold meats and salads or cut into 1in (2.5cm) squares and served as a 'bite'
on cocktail sticks.

1/2 lb (225g) courgettes
2 oz (50g) clarified butter or ghee
1 small onion, finely chopped
1/4 lb (110g) mushrooms, wiped clean and sliced
1 oz (25g) plain flour
1/2 pint (300ml) milk
3 tablespoons crumbled cheese, e.g. Feta or Cheddar
1 teaspoon salt
1/2 teaspoon black pepper
2 tablespoons finely chopped parsley
4 eggs, separated
1 tablespoon grated Parmesan cheese

Wash the courgettes and grate them coarsely.

Melt the butter or ghee in a large, deep frying pan; add the onion and fry until soft.
Add the sliced mushrooms and fry for 1 minute. Stir in the flour and cook for 2 minutes.
Gradually add the milk and stir constantly over a low heat until the sauce thickens. Add
the cheese and continue to cook for a further 2 minutes.

Add the courgettes, salt, pepper and parsley and stir well. Blend in the egg yolks and
remove from the heat.

Whisk the egg whites until stiff and fold immediately into the mixture. Pour into a
lightly greased shallow ovenproof dish about 9–10in (22.5–25cm) in diameter. Sprinkle
with the Parmesan cheese and bake in an oven preheated to 350F (180C) gas 4, for
40–45 minutes or until well risen and golden.

If eating hot, serve immediately.

# nor bayazidi lobi

## green beans with eggs and cheese

A regional speciality from Nakhichevan in the Caucasus, this is one of the many similar dishes that abound in the region.

You can substitute peas, carrots, or broad beans for the green beans.

❦

1 lb (450g) green beans, trimmed, rinsed and cut into 1in (2.5cm) pieces
1$^1$/$_2$ oz (40g) butter
2 oz (50g) cheese – Cheddar or Haloumi, grated
4 eggs
1 teaspoon salt
$^1$/$_2$ teaspoon black pepper

Garnish
a little extra grated cheese (optional)

Place the prepared beans in a large saucepan, cover with lightly salted water and bring to the boil. Simmer for 7–10 minutes, or until the beans are just tender. Drain.

Melt the butter in a large frying pan, swirling it around to coat the sides. Add the beans and cook for a few minutes, turning frequently until they are all coated with butter. Sprinkle the cheese over the beans, cover the pan and cook for 1 minute.

Beat the eggs in a small bowl together with the salt and pepper. Pour them into the pan and stir until evenly mixed with the beans. Cover and cook for a few minutes over a low heat until the eggs are set and the bottom of the omelette is golden.

Invert the omelette on to a warm plate and serve immediately, garnished with extra grated cheese if you wish.

# prasifuci

## sephardic omelette

This is an Israeli recipe of Sephardic origin – oriental Jewish. Israeli omelettes are, on the whole, of oriental origin and similar to the Arab eggeh.

This omelette can be served hot or cold although I prefer the former; often served as a starter, there is no reason at all why it cannot be a main meal. If you wish to serve it in this way, accompany it with a salad of your choice.

1 oz (25g) butter
1 small onion, chopped
1/4 lb (110g) mushrooms, wiped clean and sliced
4 eggs
4 tablespoons milk
1/4 lb (110g) fresh or thawed frozen spinach, chopped coarsely
6 oz (175g) grated cheese, eg. Cheddar or Leicester
1 teaspoon salt
1/2 teaspoon black pepper
1 tablespoon finely chopped parsley
1 tablespoon chopped chives

Heat the butter in a large frying pan and sauté the onion until golden brown. Add the sliced mushrooms and cook for 3 minutes, stirring frequently.

Meanwhile, beat the eggs and milk together in a large bowl. Add the spinach, cheese, salt, pepper, parsley, chives and onion-mushroom mixture to the eggs.

Turn this mixture into a lightly buttered casserole dish, place in an oven preheated to 375F (190C) gas 5, and cook for about 30 minutes or until set and golden.

# menemen

## egg and cheese omelette

*'Madam,' insisted the shopkeeper, 'these are the best eggs
we have had for over a month.'*

*'Then keep them, my good man,' retorted the customer angrily. 'Who needs eggs
you've had that long?'*

A Turkish speciality which is excellent with fresh salad. Do not add salt if you are
using Feta cheese as this cheese is salty enough on its own. However, if using any
other type of cheese, add 1/2 teaspoon of salt.

2 tablespoons oil or butter
1 onion, thinly sliced
2 green peppers, seeded and thinly sliced
4 large tomatoes, chopped
pinch black pepper
8 eggs
4 oz (110g) cheese – Feta, Cheddar or Gruyère, grated
2 tablespoons finely chopped parsley
1/2 teaspoon paprika

Heat the oil in a large frying pan. Add the onion and green peppers and fry for a few
minutes until soft. Add the tomatoes and black pepper and fry for 3–4 minutes, stirring
occasionally.

Break the eggs into a bowl and beat in the grated cheese and parsley. Pour the egg
mixture over the vegetables and cook gently until set.

Sprinkle with the paprika and serve immediately.

# banirov tzvazegh

## cheese omelette

A wholesome meal which is tasty and filling. It is often accompanied by bread and garnished with tomatoes, pickles, olives and so on.

8 eggs
1 teaspoon salt
1/2 teaspoon black pepper
4 fl oz (120ml) milk
3 tablespoons finely chopped parsley
1 tablespoon finely chopped fresh mint or 1 teaspoon dried mint
1 tablespoon finely chopped fresh basil or 1 teaspoon dried basil
2 spring onions, finely chopped
4 oz (110g) grated cheese – Gruyère, Haloumi or Cheddar
2–3 tablespoons butter
1 teaspoon paprika

Garnish
olives, sliced radishes, sliced tomatoes, pickles

Break the eggs into a bowl, add the salt, pepper and milk and whisk until frothy. Add the parsley, mint, basil, spring onions and cheese and whisk in thoroughly.

Melt the butter in a large frying pan, pour in the egg mixture and tilt the pan to spread it evenly. Reduce the heat and cook until the edges of the omelette begin to set.

When the centre of the omelette is almost set, very carefully place a large plate over the pan and invert, dropping the omelette on to the plate. Now carefully slide the omelette back into the pan and cook for 2–3 more minutes.

Slide the omelette on to a serving plate, cut into wedges and serve accompanied by your choice of garnishes.

# gvina pancake

## cheese pancakes

This is an Israeli Ashkenazim recipe. It makes 4 tasty pancakes – an ideal lunch when served with a salad of your choice.

৵৵✦৵৵

4 oz (110g) cottage cheese
4 oz (110g) grated Feta or other white cheese, e.g. Lancashire
1 egg
2 tablespoons very finely chopped onion
3 tablespoons finely chopped parsley
1/2 teaspoon chopped chives
1/2 teaspoon black pepper
matzo meal
oil for shallow-frying

Put the cheeses, egg, onion, parsley, chives and pepper into a bowl and mix thoroughly. Divide the mixture into 4 portions and shape each portion into a circle about 1/4–1/2in (6–12 mm) thick.

Spread some matzo meal on a plate and coat each pancake generously with the meal.

Heat some oil in a frying pan and fry the pancakes until golden brown on each side. Serve immediately with a fresh salad.

# burghul with eggs

Another of my father's favourites, this kind of quick and simple meal was –
I am sure – served in *meyhanes* or drinking houses throughout Turkey
and Armenia early in this century.

Serve with a glass of tan or ayran (or, dare I say, raki or ouzo)
and a bowl of fresh salad.

4 tablespoons oil
1 onion, finely chopped
1 lb (450g) ripe tomatoes, blanched, peeled and chopped
1½ teaspoons salt
4 oz (110g) fine burghul
1 oz (25g) butter
6 eggs
¼ teaspoon black pepper
¼ teaspoon chilli pepper

Garnish
4 spring onions, finely chopped
1 tablespoon parsley, finely chopped

Heat the oil in a large frying pan, add the onion and fry until soft. Add the tomatoes and 1 teaspoon of the salt and simmer for about 10 minutes, stirring occasionally until the mixture has thickened a little.

Place the burghul in a bowl and wash with cold water until the water you pour away is clear. Drain well. Add the contents of the frying pan and mix until the burghul is thoroughly moistened. Cover and set aside for 10–15 minutes.

Meanwhile, heat the butter in the same frying pan.

Beat the eggs in a small bowl with the remaining salt and the black and red peppers.

Pour the eggs into the pan and cook over a low heat, stirring frequently, until just set. Stir the eggs into the burghul mixture and transfer to a serving dish.

Sprinkle with the chopped onion and parsley and serve immediately.

# pilavs

Pilavs, in their many and diverse forms, are a major component of the basic diet of most Middle Easterners. Rice is the main grain used, but burghul (cracked wheat) is extremely popular in many areas.

The masters of pilav cooking are the Iranians, closely followed by the Turks and Armenians. The Iranian pollo-type dishes are similar to the Italian risotto and the Spanish paella – but, I hasten to add, much more elaborate and colourful. Try, for example, Miveh Pollo-bo-Sabz (vegetable and fruit pollo).

Even the simplest of pilavs are never just boiled. First, the rice is fried and then it is simmered in water or stock. Traditionally the fat of a lamb's tail (alya) was used. This, although still popular in the villages, is usually replaced nowadays by saltless butter or clarified butter such as ghee.

Burghul is fast becoming available in the West. It is wholesome and tasty with an 'earthy' flavour. I have included several of the numerous burghul recipes, which particularly occur in the Armenian cuisine.

# roz

## plain rice pilav

A general rule when cooking rice is to use 2 cups of liquid for the first cup of rice and 1¹/₂ cups of liquid for every following cup of rice. This is a fairly standard recipe used throughout the Middle East.

**2 oz (50g) butter or ghee**
**9 oz (250g) long-grain rice, washed thoroughly under cold water and drained**
**1 pint (600ml) water, boiling**
**1 teaspoon salt**

Melt the butter or ghee in a medium-sized saucepan. Add the rice and fry, stirring frequently, for 2–3 minutes.

Pour in the boiling water, add the salt and stir. Allow the mixture to boil vigorously for 3 minutes, then cover the pan, lower the heat as far as possible and simmer for about 20 minutes, or until all the liquid has been absorbed.

The grains should be tender and separate and there should be small holes in the surface of the rice. Turn off the heat and leave the rice to 'rest' for at least 10 minutes.

Fluff up the rice with a long-pronged fork and serve.

# chelo

## iranian plain rice with butter

Iranians are the past masters of preparing rice. No other cuisine,
including the Indian and Chinese, can match its wealth in colour, content and taste.
Chelo is the great rice pilav of Iran. As well as being the most popular,
Chelo is also one of the simplest to make. It's often eaten 'as it comes' with a little
yoghurt spooned over the top.

12 oz (350g) long-grain rice, washed thoroughly under cold water and drained
2 tablespoons salt
2³/4 pints (1.65 litres) water
2 oz (50g) butter, melted
4–6 individual pats of butter and
4–6 raw egg yolks (the exact number depends on the number of servings)
1 large onion, sliced into 4–6 rings
a sprinkling of sumak – a lemony spice

Place the rice in a deep pan, add half the salt and enough cold water to cover it by about 1in (2.5cm) and leave it to soak for 2 hours.

Bring 2¹/2 pints (1.5 litres) of the water to the boil in a heavy saucepan with a close-fitting lid. Drain the rice thoroughly in a sieve, then pour it slowly into the boiling water and add the remaining salt. Stir it a few times and then boil, uncovered, for 5 minutes.

Drain the rice into a sieve. Pour 1/4 pint (150ml) water and half the melted butter into the saucepan; add the rice. Pour the remaining melted butter over the top.

Cover the pan with a teatowel, then fit the lid on and lift the ends of the cloth on to the lid so that there is no danger of them burning or catching fire.

Steam the rice over a very low heat for about 25–30 minutes until the grains have become tender and the liquid has been absorbed.

To serve, place a pat of butter and an egg yolk on top of each individual portion and sprinkle with sumak. The whole lot is then mixed together and usually eaten with a spoon.

# zaffron pollo

## saffron rice

Aromatic saffron rice is an Indian dish which is also popular in Southern Iran, especially among the fierce Baluchi and Afghan tribes. Magnificent in appearance, glowing, golden and exquisitely delicate in flavour. Often a meal on its own, accompanied by vegetables and yoghurt.

2 oz (50g) butter
seeds of 4 whole cardamom pods
4 whole cloves
3 x 1in (2.5cm) pieces cinnamon stick
1 medium-sized onion, finely chopped
12 oz (350g) long-grained rice, washed,
soaked for 30 minutes in cold water and drained
1 1/4 pints (750ml) water, boiling
1 teaspoon salt
1/4 teaspoon crushed saffron threads,
soaked in 2 tablespoons boiling water for 20 minutes

In a medium-sized saucepan, melt the butter over a moderate heat and when the foam subsides, add the cardamom seeds, cloves and cinnamon sticks and fry, stirring constantly, for 2 minutes.

Add the onion and fry, stirring occasionally, for 8–10 minutes, or until it is golden brown.

Add the rice, reduce the heat to moderately low and fry gently, stirring constantly, for 5 minutes. Pour the boiling water over the rice, add the salt and stir in the saffron mixture. Cover the pan, reduce the heat to low and cook for 15–20 minutes or until the rice is tender and all the liquid has been absorbed.

Remove the pan from the heat, spoon the rice onto a serving dish and serve immediately.

# sabzi pollo

## herb rice

*Better a dish of herbs where love is than a fattened ox and hatred with it.*
Arab Wisdom
This classic pilav from Iran makes great use of fresh herbs.
Unfortunately some of these are not easily available in Europe, e.g. fresh leaf
fenugreek. Use it, if available, otherwise substitute dried.

9 oz (250g) long-grain rice, washed thoroughly under cold water and drained
1 tablespoon salt
2 tablespoons butter
3 tablespoons chopped fresh dillweed
2 tablespoons chopped fresh fenugreek or 1/2 teaspoon dried
3 tablespoons finely chopped parsley
3 tablespoons finely chopped Chinese parsley
3 tablespoons finely chopped tarragon leaves
2 spring onions, finely chopped (discard the white bulbs)

Bring 3 pints (1.8 litres) of water to the boil in a large saucepan. Add the rice and salt and stir. Boil for 10 minutes, then strain through a colander. Rinse the rice with cold water and leave to drain.

Melt the butter in a medium-sized saucepan and add one third of the rice. Sprinkle half the chopped herbs and all of the spring onions over the rice. Add another third of the rice and top with the remaining herbs. Layer the remaining rice over the top.

Cover the pan tightly first with a teatowel and then with the lid, lifting the edges of the towel well away from the heat, and steam over a low heat for about 30 minutes.

# roz ou hamoud

## rice with sauce

This is a favourite Egyptian recipe. It consists of a plain rice pilav with
a separately served sauce. Traditionally, the sauce is made with chicken bones,
giblets and so on, but it is still very tasty and satisfactory without.

Sauce
1 turnip, peeled and cut into small pieces
2 potatoes, peeled and cubed
2 leeks, washed thoroughly and thinly sliced
2 sticks celery, coarsely chopped
2 tablespoons finely chopped parsley
2 cloves garlic
juice of 1 lemon
1 teaspoon salt
1/2 teaspoon black pepper
1 oz (25g) butter

**plain rice (Roz) recipe from page 108**

Put all the ingredients, except the rice, in a large saucepan and add about 1¹/₂ pints
(900ml) water. Bring to the boil, lower the heat and simmer for about an hour, or until
the vegetables are very tender and about to disintegrate.

Meanwhile, prepare the rice, following the basic recipe.

Serve sauce and rice separately, then pour some of the sauce over each serving of rice.

# banirov pilav

## cheese pilav

This is an Armenian speciality which is not only delicious with its crunchy topping, but also extremely attractive to present.

Although Feta or Haloumi are traditionally used, Cheshire or Cheddar cheeses are equally successful and tasty. The garnish adds an extra touch to the look of the dish, although it is perfectly acceptable without it.

2 oz (50g) butter
9 oz (250g) long-grain rice,
washed thoroughly under cold running water and drained
1 pint (600ml) water, boiling
1 teaspoon salt
6 oz (175g) brown or white breadcrumbs
6 oz (175g) grated cheese – Feta, Haloumi, Cheddar or Cheshire

Garnish
1/2 oz (15g) butter
1 oz (25g) blanched almonds
1 oz (25g) pine kernels
1/2 teaspoon sumak powder

Prepare the rice, following the recipe for Roz on page 108. Leave it to 'rest'.

Lightly grease a shallow ovenproof casserole dish, about 8–9in (20–22.5cm) in diameter. Add half the rice, spreading it evenly over the base. Spread half the breadcrumbs over the rice, then half the cheese over the breadcrumbs.

Spread the remaining rice evenly over the layer of cheese, and top with the remaining cheese. Finally, sprinkle over the remaining breadcrumbs and press down firmly.

Place in the centre of an oven preheated to 350F (180C) gas 4, and bake for about 30 minutes, or until the breadcrumbs are toasted and golden.

When ready to serve, make the garnish by melting the butter in a small pan. Add the almonds and pine kernels and fry until golden. Remove with a slotted spoon and sprinkle over the pilav.

Sprinkle with the sumak and serve.

# plov shashandaz

## rice and omelette pilav

This recipe is from Azerbaijan.

2 oz (50g) butter
1/2 teaspoon saffron
9 oz (250g) long-grain rice, washed under cold running water and drained
1 pint (600ml) water, boiling
1 teaspoon salt
1 oz (25g) butter
1 small onion, finely chopped
1 tablespoon lemon juice
1 teaspoon sugar
4 eggs
1/2 teaspoon salt
2 oz (50g) melted butter
good pinch of cinnamon

Prepare the pilav following the Roz recipe on page 108, adding the saffron to the melted butter before adding the rice. While the rice is 'resting', make the omelette.

Melt the 1 oz (25g) of butter in a large frying pan; add the onion and fry, stirring occasionally, until it is golden. Stir in the lemon juice and sugar.

Beat the eggs in a mixing bowl with the salt until they are frothy. Pour the egg mixture over the onion and let it spread out evenly. Reduce the heat to very low and leave the omelette to cook without disturbing it.

When the centre is beginning to firm, invert a plate over the pan and turn the omelette over on to the plate. Slide the omelette back into the pan to cook on the other side until golden.

Remove the omelette from the pan and roll it up as you would a pancake.

Shred it across the roll into 1/2in (1cm) strips.

Pile the rice on to a serving platter and garnish it with the omelette strips. Dribble the butter over it and sprinkle with cinnamon.

# kasmag pilav

## rice and dough pilav

A pilav from Azerbaijan, where the rice is cooked on a kasmag –
a thin round layer of dough. It is a colourful dish, being garnished with fresh
pomegranate seeds.

1 egg
salt
3 oz (75g) plain flour
4 pints (2.4 litres) water
8 oz (250g) long-grain rice, washed thoroughly in cold water and drained
1/4 teaspoon powdered saffron (optional)
1/4 teaspoon vegetable oil
4 oz (110g) butter, melted

Garnish
1 fresh pomegranate

Beat the egg in a medium-sized mixing bowl until it is frothy. Add a pinch of salt. Add 2 oz (50g) of the flour and mix well. Add the remaining flour a little at a time, until the dough is smooth and does not stick to the fingers. Flour a work surface and roll out the dough.

Place a flameproof casserole on the dough and cut round it so that you have a piece of dough which will fit into the base of the casserole. Set the dough aside.

In a large saucepan, bring the water to the boil with the saffron and 1 tablespoon salt. Slowly add the rice so as not to disturb the boiling. Boil briskly for 10 minutes, then drain the rice in a colander.

Brush the base of the casserole with the oil and place the kasmag in the bottom. Brush this liberally with some of the melted butter. Add the rice to the casserole and sprinkle with the remaining butter. Cover the casserole with a teatowel to absorb the steam, and a lid, and cook on a low heat for 35–40 minutes.

To serve, pile the rice on to a large plate and garnish with wedges of the golden-brown kasmag crust. Peel the pomegranate and sprinkle the seeds over the rice.

# soongov pilav

## pilav with mushrooms

A delightful pilav from Armenia using mushrooms, which are not generally well known in Middle Eastern cuisine.

This pilav has a delicate golden colour and the addition of sumak gives it a sharp lemony flavour. You should find sumak powder at Middle Eastern stores.

2 oz (50g) butter
1 small onion, finely chopped
1 small green pepper, thinly sliced
4 oz (110g) mushrooms, wiped clean and thickly sliced
1 large tomato, blanched, peeled and chopped
1 clove garlic, crushed
9 oz (250g) long-grain rice, washed thoroughly under cold water and drained
1 pint (600ml) water, boiling
1 teaspoon salt
1/2 teaspoon saffron

Garnish
1 tablespoon sumak powder

Melt the butter in a saucepan. Add the onion, green pepper and mushrooms and fry until soft. Add the tomato and garlic and fry for 2–3 minutes. Stir in the saffron and rice and proceed as for Roz (plain rice pilav) on page 108.

Just before serving, sprinkle the pilav with the sumak.

# kabak pilavi

## rice and courgette pilav

'Kabak kafasi!' People do not have 'thick' heads in Turkey. Theirs are made of courgette, marrow or pumpkin – depending on the shape of the person one is insulting. However, this charming, simple pilav is eaten by both 'thick' and 'thin', the bright and the dumb. It is often served with yoghurt spooned over the top and accompanied by fresh herbs or pickles.

1 lb (450g) small courgettes
4 oz (110g) long-grained rice, washed thoroughly under cold water and drained
1¹/2 teaspoons salt
2 oz (50g) butter
1 onion, coarsely chopped
1 oz (25g) currants
1/2 teaspoon black pepper

Garnish
2 spring onions, finely chopped

Top and tail the courgettes and rinse them well. Cut the courgettes into ¹/4in (6mm) rounds. If the courgettes are quite plump, cut them in half lengthways before slicing crossways.

Bring about 1 pint (600ml) water to the boil in a saucepan and add 1/2 teaspoon of the salt and the rice. Boil for 8–10 minutes, then drain and set aside.

Melt the butter in a large saucepan, add the onion and fry, stirring frequently, until soft and turning golden. Add the courgette slices and fry for 2–3 minutes, occasionally turning carefully.

Add the rice, currants, the rest of the salt and the pepper and stir carefully. Cover and cook over a low heat for about 10 minutes, or until the rice and courgettes are tender. Set aside to 'rest' for 10–15 minutes.

Spoon into a shallow dish, sprinkle with the spring onions and serve.

*One day Nasretin Hoça quarrelled with his wife. She wept and wept and finally ran out of the house and sought refuge in a neighbour's house. Angrily he followed her.*

*It came to pass that a wedding feast was in progress and the host and guests did all they could to calm him down, and vied with each other to reconcile the couple. Plates of pilav followed each other accompanied by bowls of salads and pickles. Then came the desserts and sherbets. Hoça forced himself to eat 'a little of this, a little of that'.*

*Satisfied with himself, he lay against the wall and said to his wife, 'Woman, remind me*

# rice and leek pilav

A lovely pilav from Jordan, similar to many Turkish and Syrian rice dishes.
The west bank of the Jordan and the Jordan valley are famed for their delicious
leeks – this is not really surprising as it is one of the 'original' homes
of this vegetable.

Although delicious hot, this pilav is often cooled to room temperature
before serving.

1 lb (450g) leeks, trimmed of roots and coarse outer leaves
2 fl oz (60ml) oil
1 onion, coarsely chopped
2 medium-sized carrots, peeled and cut into 1/4in (1/2cm) rounds
1 teaspoon salt
1/2 teaspoon black pepper
1/2 pint (300ml) water
4 oz (110g) long-grain rice, washed thoroughly under cold water and drained

Cut the leeks into 1in (2.5cm) pieces, place them in a colander and rinse very
thoroughly under cold running water to remove all sand and grit. Set aside to drain.

Heat the oil in a large saucepan, add the onion and carrots and fry for about 10
minutes, or until the onion is soft. Add the leeks, salt, pepper and water and bring to
the boil.

Stir in the rice, lower the heat and simmer for about 20 minutes, or until the rice is
tender and all the liquid absorbed. Cover and set aside to 'rest'.

Serve hot, or at room temperature.

# baklali ve tereotu pilavi

## rice and broad bean pilav with dill

From Turkey – with love, and spoonfuls of dill!

6 oz (175g) long-grain rice, washed thoroughly under cold water and drained
8 oz (225g) shelled broad beans with their transparent skins removed
6 tablespoons melted butter
4 tablespoons coarsely chopped fresh dill, or 2 tablespoons dried dillweed
8 fl oz (250ml) stock or water

Garnish
1/2 teaspoon black pepper

Half-fill a large saucepan with lightly salted water and bring to the boil. Add the rice and beans and cook for 8 minutes. Turn into a mesh strainer and leave to drain.

Put 2 tablespoons of the melted butter into a medium-size saucepan and swirl to coat the base. Add a third of the rice-bean mixture and half the dill.

Repeat this with a second third of the rice-bean mixture and the rest of the dill. Top with the remaining rice-bean mixture.

Pour in the stock, seasoned with a little salt if necessary; drizzle the remaining butter evenly over the surface. Cover the pan and cook over a low heat for 20–30 minutes, or until the rice is tender and the liquid absorbed. Turn off the heat.

Remove the lid, cover the pan with a teatowel, replace the lid and leave to 'rest' for 10–15 minutes.

Fluff up the pilav carefully with a long-pronged fork, pile into a shallow serving dish and sprinkle with the black pepper for serving.

# dampokht

## rice with broad beans

This popular Iranian pilav is eaten on its own with yoghurt, or as an accompaniment to meat dishes.

1 oz (25g) butter
1 large onion, thinly sliced
1 teaspoon turmeric
1 teaspoon salt
6 oz (175g) dried broad beans or 8 oz (225g) fresh broad beans
1 pint (600ml) water
9 oz (250g) long-grain rice, washed under cold running water and drained
1 oz (25g) melted butter

Melt the butter in a saucepan, add the onion and fry until golden.

If using dried broad beans, add the turmeric, salt, beans and a third of the water; stir and simmer for 10 minutes before adding the rice and remaining water.

If using fresh beans, add the turmeric, salt, beans and rice and fry for 2–3 minutes before adding the water.

Bring the water to the boil, lower the heat and simmer for about 20 minutes, or until all the water has been absorbed. Remove from the heat, cover with a clean teatowel and then with the saucepan lid and place over a very low heat for a further 10–15 minutes until the rice is fairly dry.

Just before serving, pour the melted butter over the rice.

# chelo sabzamini

## rice and potato pilav

This variation of Chelo contains beautiful golden potatoes.

Serve, as with the plain Chelo, with butter, raw egg yolks and sumak.
This is definitely a meal in itself.

12 oz (350g) long-grain rice,
washed thoroughly under cold running water and drained
2¹/2 pints (1.5 litres) water
2 tablespoons salt
¹/2 teaspoon saffron
1 teaspoon sugar
1 teaspoon warm water
3 oz (75g) melted butter
2 large potatoes, peeled and cut into slices about ¹/4in (6mm) thick
1 oz (25g) butter cut into small pieces

Begin preparing this dish by following the instructions for Chelo on page 109, draining the rice into a sieve.

Mash the saffron and sugar together in a small bowl and add the teaspoon of warm water and the melted butter. Pour the mixture into the saucepan, add the potato slices and turn them until they are well coated in the mixture.

Spread the potato slices out flat over the bottom of the pan. Spoon the rice over them and dot the pieces of butter over the top. Cover the pan, place it over a moderate heat and cook for 5 minutes.

Remove the lid, cover the pan with a teatowel and replace the lid, making sure the ends of the teatowel are kept away from the heat. Reduce the heat to very low and leave to steam for 35–40 minutes.

To serve, first spoon the rice on to a serving dish and then, using a palette knife, remove the potato slices and arrange them around the rice.

# harem pilav

## an avocado, wine and mushroom pilav

This recipe uses tomatoes, mushrooms, avocado and wine. It is an interesting concoction and very appetising.

4 oz (110g) butter
1 clove garlic, finely chopped
1 onion, finely chopped
12 oz (350g) long-grain rice, washed thoroughly under cold water and drained
1 pint (600ml) water
7 fl oz (210ml) white wine
2 teaspoons salt
1 teaspoon black pepper
6 oz (175g) button mushrooms, wiped clean and halved
6 tomatoes, blanched, peeled and chopped – use canned ones if you prefer
1/4 teaspoon dried oregano
1 ripe avocado, peeled and diced
a few fresh parsley or tarragon leaves, finely chopped

Preheat oven to 350F (180C) gas 4.

Melt 2 oz (50g) of the butter in an ovenproof casserole. Add the garlic and onion and fry until the onion is golden brown. Add the rice and cook for 2 minutes, stirring constantly.

Pour in the water and wine, stir in 1 teaspoon of the salt and 1/2 teaspoon of the black pepper and bring to the boil. Cover the casserole, place in the oven and leave for 15–20 minutes until the liquid is absorbed.

Meanwhile, in a frying pan, melt the remaining butter and sauté the mushrooms for 2–3 minutes. Stir in the tomatoes, oregano and the remaining salt and pepper and allow to simmer for a further 2 minutes. Scatter the mixture with the diced avocado; remove the pan from the heat and keep warm.

On a large serving plate, arrange the rice in a ring and fill the centre with the vegetable mixture. Sprinkle with the chopped parsley or tarragon and serve at once.

# tutum pilav

## pumpkin with rice

The simple pumpkin is very widely used in the Turkish and Armenian cuisines. This is a pilav of pumpkin slices with sultanas and rice, slightly sweet and extremely unusual; it is often eaten as a main meal with pickles, salads or plain yoghurt.

6 oz (175g) long-grain rice, washed thoroughly under cold water and drained
8 fl oz (250ml) water
1 teaspoon salt
1 teaspoon dillweed
2 oz (50g) sultanas
3–4 dried apricots, thinly sliced (optional)
1 lb (450g) pumpkin, peeled and sliced lengthwise into 1/2in (1cm) slices
2 oz (50g) sugar
3 oz (75g) melted butter

Place the rice in a saucepan with the water, bring to the boil and then simmer for 10 minutes. Stir in the salt, dill, sultanas and apricots and simmer for a further 5 minutes. Strain into a sieve and run cold water through the rice.

Lightly butter a baking or casserole dish. Arrange half the pumpkin slices over the bottom and sprinkle with a third of the sugar and a third of the melted butter.

Put the rice in a bowl, add half of the remaining sugar and butter and mix thoroughly. Spread the rice over the pumpkin slices.

Pour the remaining butter into a frying pan and sauté the remaining pumpkin slices for a few minutes, turning once. Arrange the pumpkin slices decoratively over the rice and sprinkle with the remaining sugar and any butter left in the frying pan. Cover and place in the centre of an oven preheated to 350F (180C) gas 4, and bake for 40–45 minutes.

Remove from the oven and serve.

# miveh pollo-ba-sabz

## vegetable and fruit pollo

A rich Iranian dish which can be eaten as a meal in its own right! Brilliantly colourful with an appetising aroma that lingers well after the last morsel has been consumed.

It can be cooked on top of the stove or in the oven.

~✻~

9 oz (250g) long-grain rice, washed thoroughly under cold water and drained
1 tablespoon salt
2 oz (50g) butter or ghee
1 onion, thinly sliced
1 green pepper, sliced
2 carrots, peeled and cut into thin rounds
3 oz (75g) peas
black pepper
2 oz (50g) dried apricots, soaked overnight and chopped
1 oz (25g) raisins
1 oz (25g) blanched almonds
$1/2$ teaspoon cinnamon
$1/4$ teaspoon ground nutmeg
2 tablespoons orange juice
about 6 tablespoons water, boiling

Place the rice in a bowl, add half the salt and enough water to cover by about 1in (2.5cm). Leave to soak for about 2 hours.

Half-fill a large saucepan with a well-fitting lid with water and bring to the boil. Add the remaining salt. Drain the rice thoroughly, then pour it slowly into the boiling water so that the water does not go off the boil. Stir a few times and then boil, uncovered, for 5 minutes. Drain the rice into a sieve.

Melt 1 oz (25g) of the butter in a frying pan, add the onion, green pepper and carrots and fry for 5–10 minutes, or until the vegetables have softened. Add the peas and cook for a further 5 minutes, stirring frequently. Season to taste with salt and black pepper and set aside.

Melt half the remaining butter in a small pan, add the apricots, raisins, almonds, cinnamon and nutmeg and fry for a few minutes, stirring frequently, until the raisins are plumped up and the almonds are golden. Stir in the orange juice and set aside.

If cooking on top of the stove, melt the remaining butter in a large saucepan. If baking in the oven use the butter to coat the base and sides of an ovenproof casserole. Spread half the rice over the base and cover evenly with the vegetable mixture. Spread with half the remaining rice, top with the fruit and nut mixture and cover with the remaining rice.

Pour the boiling water over the top and then cover with a teatowel and close-fitting lid. Bring the ends of the towel up over the lid to prevent it burning. Simmer over a low heat or bake in an oven at 350F (180C) gas 4, for 25–30 minutes.

To serve, tip on to a large dish and use the golden crust in the base to garnish.

noushov pilav

## pilav with almonds

A regional speciality from Armenia and Turkey, this is the national pilav of the Anatolians, in whose region grow the finest almonds in the world.

**2 oz (50g) butter or ghee**
**9 oz (250g) long-grain rice, washed thoroughly under cold water and drained**
**1 pint (600ml) water, boiling**
**1 teaspoon salt**
**1/2 oz (15g) butter**
**1 oz (25g) blanched almonds**
**1/4 teaspoon salt**

Cook the plain pilav following the recipe for Roz on page 108. Leave to 'rest'.

While the pilav is resting, melt the 1/2 oz (15g) butter in a small pan. Add the almonds and sauté until golden brown. Remove the almonds with a slotted spoon and drain on kitchen paper. Sprinkle with salt.

Serve the rice pilav topped with the almonds.

# roz-bil-tamar

## pilav with almonds and dates

*A Bedouin dish mixing the commonplace with the highly prized - i.e. dates, which are abundant in the desert, with almonds which have to be imported at great expense from Turkey and Iran.*

2 oz (50g) butter
9 oz (250g) long-grain rice,
washed thoroughly under cold running water and drained
1 teaspoon salt
1 pint (600ml) water, boiling

Garnish
2 oz (50g) butter
2 oz (50g) blanched almonds
3 oz (75g) stoned dates, chopped
2 oz (50g) seedless raisins or sultanas
1 teaspoon rose water

Cook the rice, following the recipe for Roz – plain rice pilav – on page 108. Leave the rice to 'rest'.

While the rice is resting, prepare the garnish. Melt 1 oz (25g) of the butter in a large frying pan, add the almonds and fry, stirring frequently, until they begin to turn a light golden colour.

Add the remaining butter, the dates and the raisins or sultanas. Fry for a few more minutes, stirring frequently. Remove from the heat and stir in the rose water.

To serve, spoon the rice on to a serving dish and arrange the fruit and nut mixture over the top.

# adas pollo

## rice, lentils and raisins

This light and simple rice dish comes from Iran.

✿

12 oz (350g) long-grain rice, washed thoroughly in cold water and drained
4 tablespoons salt
6 oz (175g) red lentils
2 oz (50g) butter
1 oz (25g) toasted slivered almonds (optional)
1 oz (25g) raisins, optional

Three-quarters fill a large saucepan with water and bring it to the boil. Add the rice and salt and boil for just 10 minutes. Drain the rice into a sieve, rinse under cold, running water and set aside to drain well.

Meanwhile, wash the lentils, place them in a saucepan, add enough water to cover by about 1in (2.5cm). Bring to the boil, add a pinch of salt and boil for just 10 minutes. Drain in a sieve and set aside.

Melt the butter in a large saucepan. Spread a third of the rice over the bottom and spread half of the lentils over the top. Add another third of the rice and then the remaining lentils. Finish with the remaining rice. If you are using the almonds and raisins, sprinkle them over the top layer of rice.

Spread a clean teatowel over the pan and firmly replace the lid. Lift the corners of the cloth over the lid to prevent them burning. Place over a very low heat and steam for 20–30 minutes.

# kitry

## rice and lentil pilav

This recipe from Iraq is also popular in the Gulf States and Kuwait.
It is often eaten on its own as a full meal, but it is at its best when accompanying
cooked vegetable dishes.

3 oz (75g) whole brown lentils
2 tablespoons oil
2 cloves garlic, finely chopped
1 tablespoon tomato purée
1/2 teaspoon turmeric
1 teaspoon salt
6 oz (175g) long-grain rice washed thoroughly under cold running water and
drained
3/4 pint (450ml) water

Place the lentils in a saucepan with enough water to cover by about 2in (5cm), and simmer until the lentils are just tender. Strain the lentils into a colander and set aside.

Heat the oil in a large saucepan and sauté the garlic, stirring occasionally, for 2 minutes. Add the tomato purée, turmeric and salt and fry, stirring frequently, for 2 more minutes. Add the rice and lentils and toss in the mixture until well coated. Pour in the water and bring to the boil.

Reduce the heat, cover and simmer until the moisture has been absorbed and the rice and lentils are tender.

Leave to 'rest' for 10 minutes and then serve.

# mujaddarah

## lentils and rice

This is an Arab favourite, sometimes called 'Esau's favourite'. It is often eaten as a main meal accompanied by fresh salad, pickles and a bowl of yoghurt.

Although this recipe uses rice, you can use burghul – cracked wheat – as the Armenians and Kurds do.

6 oz (175g) brown lentils washed and drained
1¹/2 pints (900ml) cold water
¹/3 pint (200ml) olive or cooking oil
2 large onions, thinly sliced
2 teaspoons salt
¹/2 teaspoon black pepper
¹/2 pint (300ml) boiling water
6 oz (175g) long-grain rice, washed thoroughly under cold water and drained

Put the lentils into a large saucepan, cover with the 1¹/2 pints (900ml) water and bring to the boil. Lower the heat, cover and cook for 25–30 minutes, or until the lentils are almost cooked and the water mostly absorbed.

Meanwhile, heat the oil in a frying pan, add the sliced onions and fry, stirring frequently, until they are a dark golden, but take care not to burn them. Reserve half of the onions and the oil; stir the other half into the lentils.

Add the salt, pepper and ¹/2 pint (300ml) boiling water and bring back to the boil. Stir in the rice and bring to the boil again. Lower the heat, cover and simmer for a further 15–20 minutes, or until the lentils and rice are tender and the water absorbed. Remove from the heat and leave to stand for 10–15 minutes.

Pile the Mujaddarah on to a plate and garnish with the remaining onions and oil.

# burghul pilav

## cracked wheat pilav

This is a standard recipe for burghul pilav.

Burghul is available from many Middle Eastern and Continental stores; for 'pilav' always use the large-grained variety.

❧

9 oz (250g) large-grain burghul
2 oz (50g) butter or ghee
1 small onion, finely chopped
3/4 pint (450ml) water, boiling
1 teaspoon salt
1/2 teaspoon black pepper

Put the burghul into a bowl or fine sieve and wash several times until the water runs clear. Leave to drain.

Melt the butter or ghee in a saucepan. Add the onion and fry gently until soft and golden. Add the burghul and fry over a moderate heat for 2–3 minutes, stirring constantly.

Add the boiling water, salt and pepper and stir well. Bring to the boil and boil vigorously for 5 minutes, then lower the heat and simmer gently for about 8–10 minutes, or until the water has been absorbed.

Turn off the heat, cover the pan with a clean teatowel, clamp on the lid and leave to 'rest' for 15 minutes. Serve with fresh yoghurt.

## burghul pilav with basil

The Armenian cuisine has done with *tzavar* (burghul) what the Iranians have done with rice – exploited it to its full potential. Here is a typical recipe using cracked wheat, vermicelli and basil.

Serve with a fresh salad and pickles.

❧

2 oz (50g) butter
2 oz (50g) vermicelli, broken into 1in (2.5cm) pieces
6 oz (175g) large burghul, washed in a bowl until the water poured away is clear
1/2 pint (300ml) stock or water
salt to taste
4 tablespoons chopped fresh basil, or 2 tablespoons crushed dried basil
1/2 teaspoon black pepper

Melt the butter in a saucepan, add the vermicelli and fry, stirring frequently, until evenly golden. Add the burghul and fry for 1–2 minutes, stirring constantly to coat it with the butter.

Add the stock or water and salt to taste and bring to the boil. After 2–3 minutes, lower the heat and simmer for 10 minutes. Add the basil, stir carefully and cook for a further 5–10 minutes or until the burghul is tender and the liquid absorbed.

Turn off the heat, cover the pan with a teatowel and set aside to 'rest' for 10–15 minutes. Stir gently with a long-pronged fork, spoon onto a serving dish and sprinkle with the black pepper.

# burghul-bi-spanikh

## cracked wheat with spinach pilav

This is an Arab speciality from the Lebanon, but it is popular throughout
the Middle East, especially with the Kurds and Assyrians of Syria.
It can be served by placing a plate over the saucepan, inverting it and
thus serving the burghul topped by the spinach.

9 oz (250g) large-grain burghul
8 tablespoons vegetable oil
1 medium-sized onion, finely chopped
1 clove garlic, finely chopped
1/2 lb (225g) fresh spinach, washed thoroughly and coarsely chopped
1 teaspoon salt
1/2 teaspoon black pepper
3/4 pint (450ml) water, boiling

Put the burghul in a bowl or fine sieve and wash several times until the water runs clear.
Leave to drain.

Heat the oil in a saucepan, add the onion and fry for a few minutes until soft. Add the
garlic and fry for a few more minutes. Add the spinach, stir; cover and cook until the
spinach is slightly limp. Now add the burghul, salt, pepper and water and cook for 15
minutes over a moderate heat.

Lower the heat and simmer for a few more minutes until all the water has been
absorbed. Remove from the heat, cover and leave to 'rest' for 10–15 minutes.

Serve with salads and yoghurt.

# chirov burghul pilav

## cracked wheat with fruit and nuts

A rich and decorative way of preparing the humble cracked wheat pilav.

9 oz (250g) large burghul
2 oz (50g) butter or ghee
1 teaspoon salt
1 oz (25g) raisins or sultanas
2 oz (50g) dried apricots, soaked overnight, then thinly sliced
2 oz (50g) dried prunes, soaked overnight, stoned and then thinly sliced
3/4 pint (450ml) water, boiling

Garnish
2 oz (50g) butter
1 oz (25g) blanched almonds
1 oz (25g) hazelnuts, coarsely chopped
1 oz (25g) pine kernels

Put the burghul in a bowl or fine sieve and wash several times until the water runs clear. Leave to drain.

Melt the butter or ghee in a saucepan. Add the burghul and fry for a few minutes, stirring constantly.

Add the salt, raisins or sultanas, apricots, prunes and boiling water and stir well. Boil vigorously for 5 minutes, then reduce the heat and simmer gently for 8–10 minutes or until all the water has been absorbed.

Turn off the heat, cover with a clean teatowel, clamp on the lid and leave to 'rest' for 10–15 minutes.

Meanwhile, melt the remaining 2 oz (50g) butter in a frying pan, add the almonds, chopped hazelnuts and pine kernels and fry, stirring frequently, until they begin to turn a light golden colour. Remove the nuts from the pan with a slotted spoon.

Spoon the burghul pilav into a serving dish, sprinkle the fried nuts over the top and serve.

# burghul pilav with a tahina sauce

A rich and colourful Armenian pilav which is a meal in its own right.

Serve with fresh salad and pickles.

1 oz (25g) chickpeas, soaked overnight in cold water
1¼ pints (750ml) water
1½ teaspoons salt
2 medium-sized carrots, peeled and diced
½ red pepper, diced
½ green pepper, diced
6 oz (175g) large-grain burghul, rinsed
3 tablespoons oil, preferably sesame oil
½ teaspoon chilli pepper

Sauce
2 cloves garlic, crushed
4 fl oz (120ml) water
4 fl oz (120ml) tahina paste

Garnish
1 tablespoon chopped parsley or dill

Drain the chickpeas and remove the skins by squeezing each pea between thumb and forefinger. Place the chickpeas in a medium saucepan with the water and bring to the boil. Simmer for 20–30 minutes or until tender.

Add the remaining ingredients and cook for a further 20–25 minutes, or until the burghul is tender and the liquid absorbed.

Remove from the heat, cover with a teatowel, add the lid and set aside while you prepare the sauce.

Mix the garlic and water together in a small bowl. Slowly pour the tahina into the bowl, stirring all the time. The mixture should have the consistency of thick cream. If it seems too thick, stir in a little more water.

Stir the pilav carefully, spoon into a shallow dish and either spoon the sauce over the top or serve it in a sauce boat.

Sprinkle the pilav with the parsley or dill and serve.

# cracked wheat with chickpeas

*I merely said 'lap', but he understood 'laplabou' (chickpeas).*
*(To make a mountain out of a molehill.)*
Armenian Saying

A popular Lenten dish which is also served in the *meyhanes* and *kinedouns*
(cafe-cum-pubs) of Turkey and Armenia.

4 oz (110g) chickpeas, soaked overnight in cold water
2 tablespoons oil
1 onion, finely chopped
6 oz (175g) large-grain burghul
2 heaped tablespoons tomato purée
1 teaspoon salt
1/2 teaspoon black pepper
1/2 pint (300ml) reserved cooking liquid

Place the chickpeas in a saucepan with plenty of water and bring to the boil. Lower the heat and simmer until tender. Add more boiling water if necessary. Drain the chickpeas and reserve the liquid.

Heat the oil in a saucepan, add the onion and fry until soft and golden. Add the chickpeas and burghul and fry for 1 minute. Stir in the tomato purée, salt, pepper and 1/2 pint (300ml) of the reserved liquid. Bring to the boil, lower the heat and simmer for 15–20 minutes or until all the liquid has evaporated.

Remove from the heat. Cover the pan with a clean teatowel and leave to 'rest' for 10–15 minutes. Stir carefully with a long-pronged fork and turn into a serving dish.

**Note:** This dish is sometimes chilled and served as a salad, garnished with parsley.

# dzedzadzi pilav

## wheat pilav

Dzedzadz is the Armenian name for uncooked wheat. This is not all that easy to obtain outside the Middle East, but if you can find it then it is worth trying. It gives a new dimension to a pilav dish. The grains are large and slightly chewy with a nutty flavour.

If you cannot find dzedzadz, pearl barley makes a fine substitute.

2 pints (1.2 litres) water
9 oz (250g) dzedzadz or pearl barley
1 teaspoon salt
1 oz (25g) butter
1 small onion, finely chopped
3 tablespoons finely chopped parsley
1 teaspoon dried basil

Bring the water to the boil in a saucepan. Wash the dzedzadz, add it to the saucepan with the salt, cover and simmer until the water is absorbed and the grains are tender. This will probably take 40–45 minutes.

Melt the butter in a small pan, add the onion and fry until soft and turning golden. Stir the parsley and basil into the onion and then add this mixture to the pilav.

Stir the pilav, cover and leave to 'rest' for 10–15 minutes before serving.

**Note:** If using pearl barley, you will only need 1¹/2 pints (900ml) water and the cooking time will be about 30 minutes.

# hadig pilav

## wheat and pomegranate pilav

This is an exciting pilav from Armenia; hadig is the whole wheat boiled (like burghul) and then dried. It can usually be bought in Greek and Middle Eastern stores.

4 oz (110g) butter
12 oz (350g) hadig, washed in a colander or sieve until the water runs clear, then drained
1¹/2 pints (900ml) water
1 teaspoon salt
1 large red pomegranate
1 teaspoon cinnamon

Melt the butter in a saucepan, add the hadig and fry over a moderate heat, stirring frequently, for 2–3 minutes. Stir in the water and salt and boil vigorously, uncovered, for 5–6 minutes. Reduce the heat and simmer gently for a further 7–8 minutes, or until the liquid has been absorbed.

Turn off the heat, cover the pan with a teatowel and leave to 'rest' for 15–20 minutes. Cut the pomegranate in half and remove the seeds. Pile the hadig onto a platter and sprinkle the pomegranate seeds over the top. Sprinkle with cinnamon to give extra flavour.

# kasha

## buckwheat pilav

Kasha is an essential ingredient in the Russian and Polish cuisines, and it has now made its appearance in the Middle Eastern cuisine.

It is very simple to cook and there are countless variations.

## plain kasha

8 oz (225g) kasha (buckwheat)
1 egg, lightly beaten
2 tablespoons butter
1/2 tablespoon salt
3/4 pint (450ml) water, boiling

Put the kasha into a bowl, add the lightly beaten egg and mix until all the grains are coated with the egg. Put into an ungreased frying pan and cook, stirring constantly, until the grains are lightly toasted and dry. Do not let them burn.

Lightly grease an ovenproof casserole dish with 1 tablespoon of the butter and transfer the kasha to it. Add the remaining butter, the salt and the water. Cover the casserole and place in an oven preheated to 350F (180C) gas 4, and cook for 20 minutes.

Remove the casserole from the oven, fluff up the kasha with a fork and serve.

## kasha with mushrooms and onions

1 oz (25g) butter
1 large onion, finely chopped
8 oz (225g) mushrooms, wiped clean and sliced
1 teaspoon salt
1/2 teaspoon black pepper
1 tablespoon finely chopped parsley
8 oz (225g) kasha, cooked as in the previous recipe
2 tablespoons smetana (soured cream), double cream or yoghurt

Melt the butter in a large frying pan; add the onion and fry, stirring occasionally, for a few minutes until soft but not brown.

Add the mushrooms and fry for 5 minutes. Add the salt, pepper and parsley and stir well.

Stir in the cooked kasha. Reduce heat to low and cook for 10 minutes, stirring occasionally until the kasha is heated through. Transfer to a serving dish, spoon the smetana, cream or yoghurt over the top and serve.

# cold and warm dishes

Under this heading I have grouped together:

### Stuffed vegetables

Dolmas (*dolmades* in Greek, *litsk* in Armenian and *mahshi* in Arabic) are an integral part of the Middle Eastern cuisine. The ancient Akadians, Babylonians and Sassanians were in the habit of wrapping minced meat or wheat and spices in vine, cabbage, fig and apricot leaves and then cooking them in water flavoured with spices and herbs. The masters of this method of cooking are undoubtedly the Armenians and Turks.

### Olive oil-based

Olive oil-based dishes are found in the lands along the Mediterranean coast, i.e. Greece, Turkey, Syria, Lebanon and Egypt where olives grow in abundance. These dishes are of Greek–Byzantine origin and pre-date the Muslim era by millennia. They play an important role in the calendar of the Christian churches as they are usually (but not exclusively) prepared during the forty days of Lent when meats, animal fats and suchlike are not permitted.

The rest of the Middle East prefers to use fats – butter and ghee – particularly the Iranians and the Arabs of the Gulf States.

### Pastas and cereals

Pastas and cereals are very popular and people still prepare their own rishta – home-made pasta.

### Vegetables

The finest aspect of the Middle Eastern kitchen is its versatile use of vegetables. No other people have created such diverse and rich dishes as the Middle Easterners. They are, of course, fortunate in having this great variety of high-quality vegetables locally available, but this fact should not detract from the immense wealth, imagination and brilliance of the tastes created over the centuries by the people.

### Savouries – pies and pastries

These are various fillings encased in pastry and boiled, baked or fried. The masters are the Turks, who no doubt brought many of them from their original homeland in Central Asia.

# enginar dolmasi

## stuffed artichokes

An attractive recipe from Istanbul, which is delicious either hot or cold and equally satisfactory served either as a side vegetable or as an appetiser.

6 globe artichokes
1 lemon, halved
1 carrot, peeled and cut into 1/2in (1cm) rounds
3 small onions, halved
6 fl oz (180ml) water
3 tablespoons lemon juice
1/4 teaspoon sugar

### Filling
2 fl oz (60ml) olive oil
8 oz (225g) spring onions, chopped
4 tablespoons chopped fresh dill or 2 tablespoons dried dillweed
2 tablespoons pine nuts
1 teaspoon salt

To prepare the artichokes, first fill a large bowl with cold water and squeeze in the juice of half the lemon.

Wash the artichokes well under cold running water. Taking one artichoke at a time, cut off the stem close to the base and rub the cut surface with the remaining half lemon. Turn it on to its side and trim the top of the leaves by cutting down with a sharp knife. Rub each cut edge with the lemon.

Using kitchen scissors, snip off the tops of the lower leaves, then pull away any loose leaves from the base with your fingers. Continue to rub each cut edge with the lemon. Scoop out the hairy choke with a spoon or a sharp knife, then drop the artichoke into the bowl of acidulated water.

Prepare the remaining artichokes in the same way and leave them in the water while you prepare the filling.

Heat the oil in a small saucepan, add the onions and dill and cook over a low heat for about 5 minutes, stirring occasionally. Remove with a slotted spoon, place in a small bowl and stir in the nuts and salt. Reserve the oil in the pan.

Remove the artichokes one at a time from the water, shaking off any excess water. Poke your finger into the centre, enlarging the opening without breaking any leaves; spoon some filling into the centre of each artichoke, pressing it down firmly to the bottom.

Arrange the stuffed artichokes upright in a saucepan just large enough to hold them; scatter the onions and carrots over the top, add the water and bring to the boil. Add the lemon juice, sugar and oil remaining in the pan; cover, lower the heat and simmer for 15–20 minutes or until the artichokes are tender. Remove the pan from the heat and set aside for 15 minutes.

Lift the artichokes out carefully and arrange in a serving dish. Spoon out the onions and carrots with a slotted spoon and arrange around the dish.

Serve warm or cold.

# kabakli imam bayildi

## courgettes stuffed with onion, garlic and tomatoes

This is the courgette version of the classic Imam Bayildi – aubergines stuffed
with onions and tomatoes (see page 161).
This dish is particularly favoured by Turks and Armenians.

Serve cold as an appetiser.

**4 medium courgettes**

Filling
**1 small bunch spring onions, chopped – including most of the green parts**
**2 cloves garlic, crushed**
**2 tablespoons finely chopped parsley**
**1 tablespoon mint, finely chopped**
**1/2 teaspoon salt**

Sauce
**2 tomatoes, blanched, peeled and chopped**
**2 1/2 fl oz (75ml) olive oil**
**2 tablespoons lemon juice**
**water**

Garnish
**lettuce leaves**
**lemon wedges**

Slit the courgettes lengthways and half-way through, leaving about 1in (2.5cm) at each
end uncut. Remove a little flesh from each courgette with a sharp knife and a
teaspoon.

Mix the filling ingredients together in a small bowl; fill each courgette with some of this
mixture and lay them, side by side, in a saucepan.

Mix the tomatoes, oil and lemon juice together and pour over the courgettes. Add
enough water to half-cover the courgettes, then bring to the boil and cover the pan.
Lower the heat and simmer for about 45 minutes–1 hour, or until the courgettes are
tender. Test with a fork and add a little more water during cooking if necessary.
Remove from the heat and leave to cool.

When cold, arrange on a bed of lettuce leaves and garnish with lemon wedges.

# kishuyim memulaim

## courgettes stuffed with chickpeas

A recipe from Israel to serve with a fresh salad of your choice.

This dish can be eaten hot or cold, but I prefer the former.

3 oz (75g) chickpeas, soaked overnight
8 courgettes
4 tablespoons vegetable oil
1 onion, finely chopped
2 tomatoes, finely chopped
3 oz (75g) rice, washed thoroughly under cold running water
1 tablespoon parsley, finely chopped
1/2 teaspoon oregano
2 teaspoons salt
1/2 teaspoon black pepper
1/2 teaspoon chilli pepper

Place the chickpeas in a large saucepan three-quarters filled with water; bring to the boil, lower the heat and simmer until tender. Drain, rinse and set aside.

Slice the stalk end off each courgette and then, using an apple corer, remove as much as possible of the pulp leaving a shell about 1/4in (1/2cm) thick. Take care not to split or to make a hole in the skin.

Heat the oil in a saucepan, add the onion and sauté until golden brown. Add the cooked chickpeas, tomatoes, rice, parsley, oregano, salt and peppers and mix thoroughly.

Three-quarters fill each courgette with this mixture. Do not pack it down too tightly as the rice will expand during cooking. Place the courgettes side by side in a casserole dish and completely cover with lightly salted water. Bring to the boil and then cook over a very low heat for about 1 1/2 hours, or until the courgettes are cooked. Keep the water level topped up so that the courgettes are cooked through.

# kizi-inzi

## vegetables stuffed with rice and nuts

In olden days when families were large, the peasants of Anatolia prepared enormous quantities of this dish at one go. The vegetables included tomatoes, green peppers, aubergines, courgettes, and vine leaves were also stuffed.

Kizi-Inzi means 'one for you and one for me', which beautifully illustrates the concept of a large family dinner with each person taking a stuffed tomato, then an aubergine, then a green pepper – and so on.

The following quantities make a fine lunch for 2. Increase the proportions accordingly if you wish to make more.

2 medium-sized green peppers,
with 1/2 in (1cm) sliced off each stem end and reserved, seeds removed
2 large tomatoes, 1/4in (1/2cm) cut off stem ends and reserved;
pulp scooped out and reserved

### Filling
4 fl oz (120ml) olive oil
2 onions, finely chopped
3 oz (75g) long-grain rice,
washed thoroughly under cold running water and drained
1/2 teaspoon allspice
1/2 teaspoon cayenne pepper
1 teaspoon salt
1/2 teaspoon black pepper
4 fl oz (120ml) water
2 tablespoons finely chopped parsley
1 tablespoon lemon juice

### Sauce
2 tablespoons tomato purée
3/4 pint (450ml) water

### Garnish
lemon wedges
1 tablespoon finely chopped parsley

Make the filling: heat the oil in a saucepan, add the onions and fry, stirring frequently, until soft and lightly browned. Add the rice and cook for 2–3 minutes, stirring frequently. Stir in the reserved tomato pulp, allspice, cayenne pepper, salt, black pepper and water and bring to the boil.

Reduce the heat, cover the saucepan and simmer until all the liquid has been absorbed. Remove from the heat, stir in the parsley and lemon juice and set aside to cool for 10 minutes.

Spoon the mixture into the tomatoes and peppers and cover with the reserved tops. Place the vegetables side by side in a casserole dish, tops uppermost.

Dilute the tomato purée in the water and pour into the casserole dish. Cover and cook over a moderate heat for 45–50 minutes or until tender. Remove from the heat and allow to cool, then transfer to a serving dish and garnish with the lemon wedges and parsley.

# letzonadz dakdegh

## green peppers stuffed with carrots

An Armenian classic from Aparan, high up in the hills, famed for her 'thick' populace – both physically and mentally . . .

One day Vartanig, a cousin of the famed wit Boloz Mugoush, decided to try his luck in Town since work was scarce in Aparan. After a few weeks of bad luck, he landed a good job – as a policeman. He was given a new uniform, all spick and span, and a donkey to ride on.

The first thing he did was to be photographed by one of those street photographers who abounded in the city square.

Three days later he collected the snaps and sent one to his cousin. He wrote: 'Dear cousin, I am now an honourable policeman in the big city. Everyone respects me and is afraid of me. Here is a photo of me seated on my donkey "Aboush". I am very pleased with it. I hope you like it.

My deepest regards to everyone and especially to you.

Your loving cousin Vartanig, the policeman.

PS I am the one seated above; the donkey is the one below!'

Serve the dish warm with salads and a pilav of your choice. It also makes an excellent appetiser.

4 medium-sized peppers, tops sliced off, but reserved;
seeds and pith removed and discarded

### Filling
3 tablespoons oil
1 small onion, finely chopped
2 large carrots, peeled and grated
1 large tomato, blanched, peeled and chopped
1/2 teaspoon salt
1 teaspoon sugar
1/4 teaspoon cinnamon
2 tablespoons finely chopped tarragon leaves or 2 teaspoons dried tarragon

### Sauce
water
1 tablespoon oil
1 teaspoon salt

### Garnish
1 tablespoon finely chopped parsley

Make the filling: heat the oil in a saucepan, add the onion and fry until soft. Add the grated carrots and fry for a few more minutes until the onion is golden. Add the tomato, salt, sugar, cinnamon and tarragon, stir well and cook for a few more minutes, then remove from the heat and reserve.

Meanwhile, bring a saucepan half-filled with lightly salted water to the boil, add the peppers and simmer for 2–3 minutes. Remove from the water and drain.

Fill the peppers with the stuffing and arrange them snugly in a saucepan. Half-fill with water, add the oil and salt, cover and bring to the boil. Simmer for about 40 minutes or until tender.

Remove the pan from the heat and transfer the peppers to a serving dish. Sprinkle with the parsley and serve warm.

# lahana dolmasi

## stuffed cabbage leaves

Stuffed cabbage leaves are as popular as stuffed vine leaves throughout the Middle East, especialy with Turks and Armenians.

Here is a Turkish recipe using nuts and raisins. There are simpler recipes – in Anatolia, for example, the peasants use only rice and spices.

Serve cold or warm with lemon wedges and a bowl of yoghurt.

2–3 lb (1–1.35kg) head of white cabbage
3 tablespoons olive oil
2 onions, finely chopped
4 oz (110g) long-grain rice,
washed thoroughly under cold running water and drained
1 tablespoon pine kernels
1 tablespoon blanched almonds, coarsely chopped
1 tablespoon raisins
1/2 teaspoon allspice
pinch of paprika
11/2 teaspoons salt
1/2 teaspoon black pepper
8 fl oz (250ml) water
juice of 1 lemon

Garnish
2 tablespoons chopped parsley
lemon wedges

Bring a large saucepan two-thirds filled with lightly salted water to the boil. Remove as much of the thick core of the cabbage as possible; place the cabbage in the water and boil for 7–8 minutes. Drain and remove the cabbage to a large plate and, when cool enough to handle, carefully peel away the outer leaves taking care not to tear them. Place the leaves in a colander to cool.

When it becomes difficult to remove the leaves, return the cabbage to the water and boil for a few more minutes. Continue removing leaves until you have all that you need. Reserve the small inner leaves.

Meanwhile, heat the oil in a saucepan, add the onions and fry until soft. Add the rice, pine kernels and almonds and fry, stirring frequently, until the nuts begin to turn golden. Add the raisins, spices and water and bring to the boil. Reduce the heat, cover and simmer until the liquid is absorbed.

Remove the pan from the heat, stir in half the lemon juice and set aside.

To stuff a leaf, place one on a board, veins uppermost, and cut out the hard stem. With the cut end towards you, place about 1 tablespoon – the exact amount depends on the size of the leaf – near the cut end. Fold the cut end over the filling and then fold the two sides in over the filling towards the centre. Roll the leaf away from you towards the tip and the result will be a long cigar-shaped parcel.

Continue in this way until you have used up all the leaves and filling. Use any remaining leaves to cover the base of a medium-sized saucepan. Pack the stuffed leaves carefully and closely into the saucepan in layers and sprinkle with the remaining lemon juice.

Place a plate over the leaves to cover as many as possible and hold it down with a small weight – this prevents the leaves from moving and unwrapping while cooking. Pour in enough water to cover and bring to the boil. Lower the heat and simmer for about 1 hour or until the leaves are tender. Add a little more water if necessary.

Remove the pan from the heat and take off the weight and plate. Allow to cool and then arrange on a serving plate.

Serve with the lemon wedges and garnished with the parsley.

# derevi blor

## vine leaves stuffed with onions and rice

Vine leaves have been used as an outer covering for rice and nut mixtures, burghul and fruit, lentil, small fish and meat fillings from time immemorial. Ancient Greeks and Sassanian Persians were fond of such dishes.

There are many variations. Most meatless versions are eaten cold; a traditional way is to spoon natural yoghurt or Sughtorov Madzoun (garlic-yoghurt sauce – see page 245) over the blor – also called sarma or dolma.

Serve with bread and pickles. This recipe makes enough for 6–8 people.

3/4 lb (350g) vine leaves – fresh ones are perfect, but if they are not available, you can buy packets of dried leaves from Greek or Arab delicatessens

### Filling
1/4 pint (150ml) olive oil
2 onions, thinly sliced
1 green pepper, seeded and thinly sliced
6 oz (175g) long-grain rice, thoroughly washed in cold water and drained
1 1/2 tablespoons tomato purée
1 teaspoon salt
1/2 teaspoon chilli pepper
1 teaspoon allspice
1 oz (25g) chopped almonds
1 tablespoon chopped parsley

### Sauce
1 tablespoon tomato purée
2–3 pints (1.2–1.8 litres) water
4 cloves garlic, crushed
1 teaspoon salt
1/2 teaspoon chilli pepper
3 tablespoons lemon juice

Wash the vine leaves in cold water, place in a saucepan and fill the pan with water until the leaves are covered. Bring to the boil and simmer for 15–20 minutes, then drain into a colander.

Heat the olive oil in a large saucepan over a moderate heat. Add the sliced onions and green pepper and cook for 5–10 minutes, stirring occasionally, until the onions are soft but not brown.

Stir in the washed rice, tomato purée, salt, chilli pepper and allspice and cook gently for a further 10 minutes, stirring occasionally to prevent the rice sticking to the pan. Remove the pan from the heat, stir in the chopped almonds and parsley, turn into a large bowl and leave to cool.

To make each blor, spread a leaf out flat, smooth side down and veins uppermost. You will be left with small cigar-shaped parcels.

When you have used up all the filling and leaves, use any remaining broken leaves to cover the bottom of a medium-sized saucepan – this helps to prevent burning.

Pack the blor carefully and closely into the saucepan in layers, then place a plate on top to cover as many of the blor as possible. Hold it down with a small weight – this will prevent the blor from moving around while cooking and so coming undone.

Mix the ingredients for the sauce together in a bowl and pour into the saucepan. The sauce should cover the blor completely. If it doesn't, then add a little more water. Bring the sauce to the boil, lower the heat and simmer for 1½–2 hours.

Remove the pan from the heat, take off the weight and plate and remove the blor to test if the leaf is tender. If so, allow to cool, remove from the saucepan and arrange on a plate.

## how to fold your vine leaves

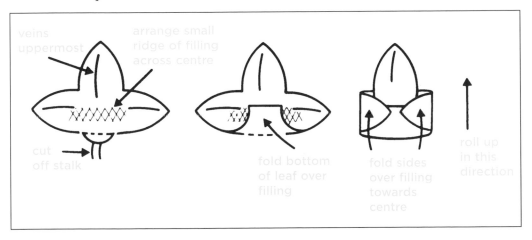

veins uppermost

arrange small ridge of filling across centre

cut off stalk

fold bottom of leaf over filling

fold sides over filling towards centre

roll up in this direction

# yarma dolmasi

## vine leaves stuffed with cracked wheat

In Central Anatolia where rice was not easily available and where sometimes even the peasant's staple diet – burghul – was difficult to come by, the villagers made use of yarma – a coarse-ground wheat flour. Since yarma is virtually unknown outside Anatolia, I suggest you use pearl barley and grind it coarsely or, better still, use a medium or large-grained burghul for this simple, wholesome peasant dish.

In Anatolia apricot, cherry or vine leaves are used; the most easily available here are vine leaves, but if you can find apricot leaves then do try them as they have a delightful flavour.

12 oz (350g) vine leaves
8 oz (225g) yarma (use coarsely ground pearl barley or coarse-grained burghul)
1 teaspoon salt
water
1 oz (25g) coarsely ground walnuts

Sauce
2 oz (50g) butter
2 large onions, finely chopped
1 pint (600ml) yoghurt
juice of 1 lemon

Wash the leaves in cold water, place in a saucepan, cover with water and bring to the boil. Simmer for 15 minutes, then strain into a colander and leave to cool.

Put the yarma, cracked pearl barley or burghul, into a bowl and sprinkle with the salt. Make a well in the centre and slowly add water, stirring all the time. Knead until the mixture binds together. Add the walnuts and knead a little more.

To make each dolma, follow the instructions for Derevi Blor in the previous recipe.

Line the bottom of a saucepan with any remaining leaves. Pack the dolmas carefully and closely together in layers in the saucepan. Place an inverted plate over the top to cover as many dolmas as possible and hold in place with a small weight. Add sufficient water to cover and simmer for about 1 hour. Take out 1 dolma and test to see if the leaf is tender. If not, simmer a little longer.

Meanwhile, make the sauce by melting the butter in a small pan. Add the onions and fry until soft and lightly browned. Stir in the yoghurt, lemon juice and a few tablespoons of the dolma juice and remove from the heat.

Arrange the dolmas on a plate, pour the yoghurt sauce over the top and serve.

**Serves6-8**

# vospov litsk

## vine leaves stuffed with lentils, burghul and prunes

A stuffed vine leaf recipe from the Caucasus, this dish is traditionally served during the forty days of Lent. The unusual combination of flavours works extremely well.

In the Caucasus they use fresh plums and plum syrup; I suggest you use prunes and either pomegranate syrup or lemon juice.

1/2 lb (225g) vine leaves
3 oz (75g) whole brown lentils
2 oz (50g) coarse burghul
4 tablespoons vegetable oil
1 small onion, finely chopped
6 stoned prunes, soaked overnight and then sliced
1 tablespoon raisins
1 teaspoon salt
1/2 teaspoon black pepper
1/2 teaspoon dried mint
1/2 teaspoon nutmeg
1 tablespoon pomegranate juice or 2 tablespoons lemon juice
8 fl oz (250ml) water
1 tablespoon oil
1 teaspoon salt

Wash the vine leaves in cold water, place in a saucepan half-filled with water and bring to the boil. Simmer for 15 minutes, then drain in a colander. Meanwhile, boil the lentils in lightly salted water for 15 minutes; strain and set aside. Wash the burghul in a bowl until the water you pour off is clear.

Heat the oil in a saucepan, add the onion and fry for a few minutes until soft. Add the lentils, burghul, prunes, raisins, salt, pepper, mint and nutmeg and stir. Add the pomegranate or lemon juice and the 8 fl oz (250ml) water and simmer over a low heat until all the water is absorbed. Remove from the heat and leave to cool.

To stuff a leaf, spread it out, veins uppermost. Cut off the stem and follow as for Derevi Blor (see page 151). Continue until you have used up all the filling and leaves.

Use any remaining leaves and/or broken ones to line the base of a saucepan. Pack the stuffed vine leaves carefully into the pan in layers. Place an inverted plate over the top, covering as many of them as possible and place a weight on top. This will prevent the vine leaves moving about and unrolling during cooking.

Add the oil, salt and sufficient water to cover the vine leaves. Bring to the boil, then lower the heat and simmer for about 1 1/2 hours. Remove from the heat and take off the weight and plate. Leave until cool, then arrange on a serving plate.

## iraqi stuffed potato balls

From the outset, I was warned by my aunts and cousins who live in Baghdad that if a book about Middle Eastern food does not include their famed and much loved Batatat Charp then it has no right to its claims. 'After all,' wrote my cousin, who apparently lives on these fried potato balls, 'it's like Shehrazade reciting the 1000 nights and missing out the 1. It's just not done!'

These stuffed balls are the 'fish and chips' or 'hot dogs' of Iraq. They are sold at street corner shops and are the nearest thing to a 'take-away', apart from the Mayyi – turnips cooked with beets – that Baghdadis have.

There are several fillings. The one I have chosen is – naturally – a vegetable one and the recipe is my aunt's.

1 lb (450g) potatoes, peeled, boiled and drained
1 egg, beaten
1 tablespoon plain flour
3/4 teaspoon salt
1/2 teaspoon black pepper

Filling
2 tablespoons oil
1 onion, finely chopped
1/2 teaspoon turmeric
1 large ripe tomato, blanched, peeled, seeded and chopped
3 tablespoons finely chopped parsley
1 tablespoon chopped hazelnuts or walnuts
1 teaspoon salt
1/2 teaspoon black pepper
1/4 teaspoon cinnamon
flour
oil for frying

Mash the potatoes until smooth and set aside to cool.

Meanwhile, prepare the filling by heating the oil in a frying pan and sautéing the onion until soft. Add the turmeric and fry for another 2 minutes. Add the remaining ingredients for the filling, mix well and set aside to cool.

Add the egg, flour, salt and pepper to the potato and mix until smooth.

Keep your hands damp while you make these balls. Take a tablespoon of the potato mixture and flatten it in the palm of your hand. Put a teaspoon of the filling in the centre and carefully close the potato around it. Shape into a ball by rolling it gently in your palms. Keeping your hands damp, shape the remaining ingredients into stuffed balls. Roll each one in flour.

Add enough oil to a frying pan to cover the base by 1in (2.5cm) and fry the balls, a few at a time, until golden all over.

Remove with a slotted spoon, drain on kitchen paper and keep warm while you fry the remaining balls in the same way.

Serve garnished with fresh vegetables and pickles.

## potatoes stuffed with spinach

An Israeli recipe, but there are several similar dishes throughout the region.
Stuffed potatoes are particularly popular in Saudi Arabia and Iraq.
This can be served as a starter, or a main dish accompanied by pickles and
a fresh salad of your choice.

4 large potatoes
1 oz (25g) butter or margarine
1 onion, finely chopped
1/2 lb (225g) spinach, thawed if frozen and thoroughly washed if fresh
4 tablespoons stock
1/4 teaspoon allspice
1 hard-boiled egg, shelled and chopped
1 teaspoon salt
1/2 teaspoon black pepper
2 tablespoons matzo meal (optional)
oil for frying
1/2 pint (300ml) garlic-yoghurt sauce (see page 245)

Garnish
finely chopped lettuce
pinch of paprika

Wash and peel the potatoes and place in a saucepan of water. Bring to the boil and simmer for about 10 minutes. Drain and set aside until cool enough to handle.

Meanwhile, heat the butter in a saucepan and sauté the onion until it is soft. Squeeze excess water from the spinach, chop it and add it to the onion, together with the stock. Cook for 5–7 minutes, or until the spinach is limp. Stir in the allspice and drain off any liquid which has not evaporated. Put this mixture into a bowl and add the chopped egg, salt, pepper and matzo meal and mix well.

Cut the potatoes in half lengthways and carefully scoop out the centre, leaving a shell about 1/2in (1cm) thick. Fill the centres with the spinach mixture.

Heat some oil in a large frying pan, add the halved potatoes and cook until the potatoes are golden and crusty. This is easiest if you add enough oil to come just to the rim of each halved potato.

Garnish a serving dish with the chopped lettuce leaves, arrange the potatoes on top and spoon a little of the garlic-yoghurt sauce over each. Sprinkle with paprika and serve.

# bamyi-bil-zayt

## okra in olive oil

An Arab recipe. Okra (ladies' fingers) is a very popular vegetable in the Middle East. There are many recipes for it and I think that it is at its very best in stews.

This is a Lenten dish (i.e. cooked in olive oil) and although it is traditionally served cold, there is no reason why it cannot be eaten warm with a pilav of your choice.

1 lb (450g) small, whole okra
1/4 pint (150ml) olive oil
1 onion, finely chopped
3 cloves garlic, finely chopped
2 teaspoons coriander seeds, or 1/2 teaspoon ground coriander
1 teaspoon salt
1/2 teaspoon black pepper
2 tablespoons tomato purée diluted in 1/4 pint (150ml) water
juice of 1 lemon

Wash the okra with a slightly damp cloth and cut off the stems.

Heat the oil in a saucepan, add the okra and sauté for a few minutes until lightly browned. Remove the okra with a slotted spoon and set aside.

Add the onion to the oil in the pan and fry for a few minutes until soft. Add the garlic, coriander, salt and pepper. Add the okra and stir well.

Stir in the diluted tomato purée and just enough water to cover the vegetables. Bring to the boil and simmer, stirring occasionally and carefully in order not to break up the okra, for about 15 minutes or until tender. Do not overcook, or the okra will break up and become stringy.

Remove from the heat and stir in the lemon juice. Transfer to a serving dish and serve warm or cold.

# fasulya piyazi

## haricot beans in olive oil

One of the most popular dishes from Turkey, beloved by the millions of peasants who often virtually live on this – and similar vegetable dishes.

This dish is best served cold, but is often eaten warm for breakfast – in which case use butter instead to the oil. Eat with bread.

1/2 lb (225g) haricot beans, soaked overnight in cold water
3 tablespoons oil (or butter if this is to be eaten warm)
1 large onion, thinly sliced
5 tomatoes, blanched, peeled and chopped
2 cloves garlic, crushed
1/2 teaspoon dried basil
3 tablespoons finely chopped parsley
1 teaspoon salt
1/4 teaspoon black pepper
1/4 teaspoon allspice

Garnish
lemon wedges

Bring a large saucepan half-filled with lightly salted water to the boil, add the drained beans and simmer until soft. The time will depend on the quality and age of the beans, so add a little more water if necessary.

Heat the oil or butter in a large saucepan, add the onion and fry until soft and golden. Add the tomatoes, garlic, basil, parsley, salt, black pepper and allspice and mix thoroughly. Cook over a low heat for 5–10 minutes, stirring frequently.

Strain the beans and place them in a serving dish. Retain a little of the cooking liquid. Pour the tomato mixture over the beans and mix well. If you think the mixture is too dry, then stir in a little of the bean water.

If this dish is to be eaten cold, then refrigerate for 2–3 hours. Serve with lemon wedges and bread.

# yoghov shogham

## turnips in olive oil

A simple recipe that enhances the rather bland flavour of the turnips.
It is an Armenian recipe and can be served hot or cold.

✦

1 lb (450g) turnips, peeled, washed and cut into 1–1¹/₂in (2.5–3.5cm) pieces
10–12 small onions, peeled
¹/₄ pint (150ml) olive oil
1 teaspoon sugar
³/₄ pint (450ml) water
salt and black pepper to taste

Garnish
2 tablespoons finely chopped parsley
2 tablespoons finely chopped dill or 2 teaspoons dried dillweed
2 tablespoons finely chopped mint or 2 teaspoons dried mint
lemon slices

Place all the ingredients (except for the garnish) in a large saucepan and bring to the boil. Cover, lower the heat and simmer for about 30 minutes, or until the turnips are tender. Transfer to a serving dish and sprinkle with the parsley, dill and mint. Serve with the lemon slices.

# bras yahni

## leeks with olive oil

This popular Lenten dish from Armenia can be eaten hot or cold.

1¹/₂ lb (675g) leeks
¹/₄ pint (150ml) olive oil
1 onion, thinly sliced
¹/₄ pint (150ml) water
2 tomatoes, blanched, skinned, seeds removed and flesh coarsely chopped
8–10 whole peppercorns
salt to taste
3 oz (75g) rice, washed thoroughly and drained
2 tablespoons lemon juice

Garnish
1 tablespoon sumak powder

Slice roots off leeks and discard any discoloured leaves. Cut leeks into 1in (2.5cm) pieces and place in a colander. Wash very thoroughly under cold running water to remove all the sand and grit. Drain and dry on kitchen towels.

Heat the oil in a large saucepan, add the onion and fry until soft. Add the leeks and sauté for a few more minutes, stirring frequently. Stir in the water, tomatoes, peppercorns, salt and rice and bring to the boil.

Lower the heat and simmer, with the lid of the pan slightly ajar, for 20–30 minutes or until tender. Add the lemon juice, stir well and cook for a further 5 minutes.

Serve hot or cold, sprinkled with the sumak powder.

# imam bayildi

## aubergines in olive oil

A classic of the Turkish cuisine, this is probably – and deservedly – the most famous dish in the Middle Eastern repertoire. It is no wonder that the Imam (priest) fainted when he tasted this dish for the first time!

It makes an excellent hors d'oeuvre and is usually served cold with pita or lavash bread. It will keep in the refrigerator for several days.

4 medium-sized aubergines
6 tablespoons olive oil
2 onions, thinly sliced
2 green peppers, thinly sliced
2 cloves garlic, coarsely chopped
2 ripe tomatoes, thinly sliced
3 tablespoons tomato purée
2 teaspoons salt
1/2 teaspoon paprika
1 teaspoon allspice
3 tablespoons finely chopped parsley
8 fl oz (250ml) cooking oil
1 pint (600ml) boiling water

Wash and dry the aubergines, leaving on the stalks. Make a slit about 1–2in (2.5–5cm) long down each aubergine. Sprinkle salt inside the slits and set aside for 15 minutes.

Meanwhile, heat the olive oil in a saucepan, add the onions, green peppers and garlic and fry gently for about 10 minutes.

Add the tomatoes, tomato purée, salt, paprika and allspice; stir well and cook for a further 5 minutes. Stir in half the parsley and remove from the heat.

Rinse out the aubergines and pat dry with kitchen paper.

Heat the cooking oil in a frying pan and fry the aubergines, turning a few times, until the flesh begins to soften. Remove from the heat and place the aubergines in an ovenproof dish, slit sides uppermost. Carefully prise open the slits and spoon the onion mixture into each slit.

If there is any onion mixture left, add this to the dish and then pour in the boiling water. Place in the centre of an oven preheated to 400F (200C) gas 6 and cook for 1 hour.

Remove from the oven, let cool and then refrigerate. Before serving, garnish with the remaining parsley.

# soong yahni

## braised mushrooms

Mushrooms in general are not much used in Middle Eastern cuisine.
However, there are certain exceptions – and certain regional specialities such as the
recipe below, which is from Turkish Armenia.

This delicious vegetable dish can be served hot or cold; I prefer it hot.

2 fl oz (60ml) olive oil
2 onions, thinly sliced
2 cloves garlic, finely chopped
1 lb (450g) mushrooms, wiped clean and quartered
4 tablespoons chopped parsley
1$^1$/2 teaspoons salt
$^1$/2 teaspoon black pepper
8 fl oz (250ml) water
1 tablespoon finely chopped fresh dill or 1 teaspoon dried dillweed
1 tablespoon finely chopped fresh mint or 1 teaspoon dried mint

Garnish
lemon wedges

Heat the olive oil in a saucepan. Add the onions and garlic and fry for a few minutes
until the onion is soft and transparent. Add the mushrooms and fry for a few minutes,
stirring frequently.

Stir in the parsley, salt, pepper and water and bring to the boil. Simmer for about 20
minutes, or until the mushrooms are just tender.

Transfer to a serving dish, sprinkle with the dill and mint and garnish with the lemon
wedges.

patates plakisi

# potato plaki

This is a Turkish speciality that originated, most probably, in the Balkans. There are several plaki recipes, some using vegetables, others fish, chicken, oysters or mussels . . .

It makes an ideal salad eaten with pita bread or fried vegetables such as aubergines, courgettes and so on.

4 potatoes, peeled and sliced
1 large carrot, peeled and diced
1 stick celery, diced
1 large tomato, blanched, peeled and chopped
2 cloves garlic, finely chopped
2 tablespoons finely chopped parsley
1 tablespoon finely chopped fresh dill or 1/2 tablespoon dried dillweed
1 teaspoon salt
1/2 teaspoon black pepper
12 fl oz (360ml) water
2-3 tablespoons olive oil

Garnish
lettuce leaves
lemon wedges

Place the potatoes, carrot, celery, tomato, garlic, parsley and dill in a large saucepan and mix carefully. Add the salt, pepper and water. Cover the pan and simmer over a low heat for 40-45 minutes or until the vegetables are nearly tender. Add a little more water if necessary.

Uncover the pan, pour in the olive oil and cook for a further 15-20 minutes or until the vegetables are well cooked. Remove from the heat and leave to cool.

Arrange the lettuce leaves around a serving plate and pile the plaki into the centre. Serve with the lemon wedges.

# barbunya fasulya yagli

## red beans in oil

A popular cold vegetable dish from Turkey: serve with bread.

1/2 lb (225g) red kidney beans, soaked overnight
2 tablespoons olive oil
1 onion, thinly sliced
2 cloves garlic, finely chopped
3 tomatoes, blanched, peeled and chopped
2 tablespoons finely chopped parsley
1/2 teaspoon dried dillweed
1/4 teaspoon chervil
1 teaspoon salt
1/2 teaspoon black pepper
1/2 pint (300ml) bean stock
juice of 1/2 lemon
1/2 teaspoon paprika
2 teaspoons finely chopped parsley or tarragon leaves

Drain the soaked beans, reserving 1/2 pint (300ml) of the soaking water to use as stock. Half-fill a large saucepan with lightly salted water, add the beans and cook until tender. Drain and set aside.

Meanwhile, heat the oil in a saucepan, add the onion and fry until soft and turning brown. Add the garlic, tomatoes, parsley, dill, chervil, salt and pepper and mix thoroughly.

Add the beans and the 1/2 pint (300ml) of bean stock. Simmer for 10–15 minutes.

Transfer to a serving dish and refrigerate for at least 2 hours. Before serving, stir in the lemon juice and sprinkle with the paprika and parsley or tarragon.

# rishta

## home-made pasta

Before the commercial pastas penetrated the kitchens of Middle Eastern housewives, women prepared their own – known as rishta in Arabic, arsha in Armenian, reshda in Iranian and sehriye in Turkish. The word in old Persian means 'thread'.

Today in most villages throughout the region, people still make their own pastas which come in many shapes and sizes. The recipe below is a typical one used throughout the Middle East. It is for long thin 'threads' of dough similar to flat pastas such as tagliatelli or plain noodles. Try using rishta instead of the macaroni or spaghetti suggested in some of the recipes in this book.

Vary the quantity as required.

1 lb (450g) plain flour
1 teaspoon salt
2 eggs, beaten
5–6 tablespoons water

Sift the flour and salt into a large bowl. Make a well in the centre and add the beaten eggs and 4 tablespoons of the water. Mix well and knead until the dough is firm. Add a little more water if necessary. Knead for about 10 minutes.

Lightly flour a working top and divide the dough into 3–4 portions. Roll each portion out as thinly as possible, working from the centre. When all the sheets are rolled, leave the pastry to rest for about 45 minutes.

Carefully roll up each sheet tightly – like a Swiss roll – and then cut them into 1/4in (6mm) – or narrower – slices. Unroll the threads and spread them out on the floured surface for at least 10 minutes.

To serve, boil some lightly salted water in a saucepan, add the rishta and simmer for about 5 minutes. Drain and serve as required.

# banirov arsha

## macaroni with cheese

An Armenian favourite which makes a fine lunch with fresh salad and pickles.

1 egg
5 tablespoons finely chopped parsley
1/2 teaspoon salt
1/2 teaspoon black pepper
1 clove garlic, crushed
6 tablespoons melted butter
3/4 lb (350g) grated cheese, e.g. Haloumi, Kashkaval or Cheddar
8 oz (225g) macaroni

Mix the egg, parsley, salt, pepper, garlic and 2 tablespoons of the melted butter together in a bowl. Add the grated cheese, mix well and set aside.

Bring a large saucepan half-filled with lightly salted water to the boil. Add the macaroni and cook for 10–12 minutes. Strain into a colander and rinse under hot water. Mix 2 tablespoons of the butter into the macaroni.

Lightly grease an ovenproof dish about 9in (22.5cm) in diameter and spread half the macaroni over the bottom. Spread two-thirds of the cheese mixture over the macaroni and top with the remaining macaroni. Spread the remaining cheese over the top and sprinkle with the remaining butter. Place in the centre of an oven preheated to 400F (200C) gas 6 and bake for 20–30 minutes.

Cut into squares and serve hot.

# makaruni

## macaroni in olive oil

This recipe from Syria will make a change for those used to the 'Italian' way of cooking macaroni. It is simple, cheap and very filling.

❧

8 oz (225g) macaroni or noodles of your choice, broken into 2in (5cm) pieces
4 tablespoons olive oil
1 onion, finely chopped
2 cloves garlic, finely chopped
1 teaspoon sweet basil
1 teaspoon salt
1/2 teaspoon black pepper
pinch of ground cinnamon
8 fl oz (250ml) water

Half-fill a large saucepan with lightly salted water and bring to the boil. Add the macaroni or noodles, stir and simmer until just cooked. Drain into a colander and rinse under cold water.

Heat the oil in a saucepan, add the onion and garlic and fry until golden brown. Stir in the basil, salt, pepper and cinnamon and fry for a minute or two.

Add the water, bring to the boil and stir in the macaroni or noodles. Simmer for 5 minutes, transfer to a serving dish and serve.

# makaruni-bil-beid

## spaghetti with boiled eggs

A popular Arab dish traditionally made with rishta – home-made pasta
(see page 165) but spaghetti or macaroni both make good substitutes.
This is a very tasty and substantial dish, and needs only a salad and/or yoghurt as
an accompaniment.

2 large aubergines, sliced
2 tablespoons oil
1 onion, finely chopped
1 lb (450g) ripe tomatoes, blanched and peeled or a 14 oz (400g) can tomatoes
1 teaspoon dried oregano
1/2 teaspoon allspice
1 teaspoon salt
1/2 teaspoon black pepper
1/4 pint (150ml) water
vegetable oil for frying
12 oz (350g) spaghetti
1 1/2 oz (75g) butter
3–4 hard-boiled eggs, thinly sliced
2 oz (50g) grated cheese, e.g. Cheddar or Parmesan

Arrange the aubergine slices over a large plate, sprinkle with salt and set aside for 30 minutes.

Meanwhile, heat the oil in a large saucepan, add the onion and fry until soft and turning brown. Add the tomatoes, oregano, allspice, salt, pepper and water and mix thoroughly. Cover and simmer for 25–30 minutes.

Meanwhile, rinse the aubergine slices under cold running water and drain on kitchen paper. Heat some vegetable oil in a frying pan, add a few of the aubergine slices and fry gently, turning once, until soft. Remove the slices and drain on kitchen paper. Fry the remaining slices, adding more oil if necessary, and drain.

Bring a large saucepan half-filled with lightly salted water to the boil; add the spaghetti, stir once and simmer until just tender. Drain the spaghetti and rinse under cold water. Transfer the spaghetti to the vegetable saucepan and mix thoroughly. Add the butter and mix so that it is spread evenly.

Butter a large baking dish. Spread a third of the pasta mixture over the bottom. Cover with half the aubergine slices, then half the egg slices.

Spread another third of the pasta over the top and then cover with the remaining aubergine and egg slices. Top with the remaining spaghetti and sprinkle the cheese over the top.

Place in the centre of an oven preheated to 375F (190C) gas 5, and bake for about 40–45 minutes, or until the top is golden.

Remove from the oven, cut into squares and serve. **Serves 6–8.**

## makaruni-bil-tarator

### macaroni with tahiniyeh sauce

Another macaroni recipe from Syria; it is simple and filling, but rather rich and I suggest you serve it with a fairly plain vegetable dish or salad.

**8 oz (225g) macaroni or spaghetti, broken into 2in (5cm) pieces**
**1/2 quantity of tahiniyeh sauce – see page 246**

Bring a large saucepan half-filled with lightly salted water to the boil. Add the macaroni or spaghetti, stir and cook until just tender. Strain into a colander and rinse under cold water.

Return the macaroni or spaghetti to the saucepan, pour in the tahiniyeh and mix thoroughly.

This dish can be eaten hot or cold.

# rishta-bil-adas

## pasta with lentils

Here is a really delicious Lebanese recipe making use of home-made pasta or rishta (see page 165). It's as old as the mountains and certainly much older than Marco Polo and his 'spaget'! When preparing it, cut the 'threads' into lengths of about 2¹/2–3in (6–7.5cm). However, this dish works equally well with bought spaghetti.

8 oz (225g) whole lentils, rinsed
8 oz (225g) rishta, cut into 2¹/2 –3in (6–7.5cm) lengths or 8 oz (225g) spaghetti, broken into 2¹/2 –3in (6–7.5cm) lengths
6 tablespoons oil or melted butter
1 onion, finely chopped
1 teaspoon salt
1 clove garlic, finely chopped
1 tablespoon finely chopped fresh coriander or ¹/2 tablespoon ground coriander

Place the lentils in a saucepan half-filled with water; bring to the boil, then simmer for about 45 minutes or until the lentils are tender. Drain and set aside.

Meanwhile, bring another pan half-filled with lightly salted water to the boil. If using rishta, add it to the pan and simmer for 5 minutes before draining. If using spaghetti, add it to the pan and simmer until tender before draining.

While the rishta or spaghetti is cooking, heat the oil or butter in a saucepan. Add the onion, salt, garlic and coriander and fry until the onions are soft and turning golden brown. Add the drained lentils and rishta or spaghetti and mix thoroughly.

Gently heat through, stirring frequently to prevent it sticking. Transfer it to a serving dish and serve with yoghurt and a salad.

# kilisi kufta

## sumak-flavoured kufta

A traditional recipe from Kilis, Southern Turkey, this is another of those countless burghul-vegetable dishes loved by the Armenians, Kurds and Syrians.
Sumak powder (available from Middle Eastern stores) gives not only a strong lemony flavour, but it darkens the colour a little.

You can shape the kufta into small patties and serve, or pile it into a serving dish as suggested here.

4 tablespoons vegetable or olive oil
1 small onion, finely chopped
3 large tomatoes, fincly chopped
2 tablespoons tomato purée
1 teaspoon cayenne pepper
1 teaspoon salt
3 tablespoons sumak powder
5 tablespoons water
8 oz (225g) fine or medium-grained burghul
3 tablespoons finely chopped parsley
2 spring onions, finely chopped
1 small green pepper, chopped

Heat the oil in a large frying pan, add the onion and fry until soft and turning golden. Add the tomatoes, tomato purée, cayenne pepper and salt and mix well.

Meanwhile, place the sumak and water in a small saucepan and bring to the boil. Strain through a fine sieve and reserve the juice. Add the sumak juice to the tomato mixture and remove from the heat.

Wash the burghul in a bowl until the water you pour away is clear, then stir the burghul into the mixture. Cover and leave to stand for about 20 minutes, so that the burghul is softened by the juices.

Mix the parsley, spring onions and green pepper in a small bowl.

Knead the kufta for about 5 minutes until it is well blended. Mix in the chopped vegetables from the bowl and knead a little longer. Arrange the kufta in a dish and serve with a spoon.

Serve with pickles and salads of your choice.

# baki sini kufte

## burghul and nuts in the tray

This is an Armenian version of the famed Arab Kibbeh-Bi'sinya. Eaten during the forty days of Lent, this recipe substitutes potatoes, walnuts and pomegranate juice for the meat. Serve with a bowl of fresh salad and some yoghurt.

Filling
1 tablespoon butter
1 small onion, finely chopped
4 oz (110g) chopped walnuts
1 teaspoon allspice
1 teaspoon salt
1/2 teaspoon black pepper
2 oz (50g) pine kernels
1 tablespoon pomegranate juice or 11/2 tablespoons
lemon juice

Kufte
6 oz (175g) fine burghul
2 potatoes, peeled, boiled, strained and mashed
2 tablespoons very finely chopped onion
1 teaspoon basil
1 teaspoon salt
1 teaspoon black pepper
11/2 oz (40g) butter
pinch of allspice
2 tablespoons cooking oil
4 tablespoons water

Prepare the filling by melting the butter in a saucepan. Add the onion and fry until soft. Stir in the walnuts, allspice, salt, pepper, pine kernels and pomegranate juice or lemon juice. Stir thoroughly and cook for a few more minutes.

Remove from the heat, stir in the parsley and set aside to cool.

Meanwhile prepare the kufte by placing the burghul in a bowl or fine sieve and wash until the water runs away clear. Squeeze out excess water and spread the burghul out on a baking sheet; leave for 10 minutes.

Add the mashed potato, onion, basil, salt and pepper. Keeping the palms of your hands damp, knead the mixture for at least 10 minutes until it is very smooth. Divide into two.

Using some of the butter, grease a shallow ovenproof casserole or pie dish about 8in (20cm) in diameter. Sprinkle a little allspice over the base. Spread half the kufte mixture over the bottom of the dish and press down firmly. Cover evenly with the walnut mixture. Now spread the remaining kufte over the top, pressing it firmly into place. Cut down through with diagonal lines to form lozenge shapes and put a dab of butter on each lozenge.

Mix the oil and water together and pour over the top. Place in an oven preheated to 375F (190C) gas 5, and cook for about 30 minutes, or until it is golden and crisp on top. Serve immediately.

# vospov kufta

## lentil and burghul balls

This is a regional speciality from Turkey, popular with Armenians, Kurds and Turks. It is often eaten as a main dish with an accompanying fresh salad, home-made pickles and a yoghurt and cucumber mixture called Jajig (see page 73).

6 oz (175g) red lentils, washed and drained
1 pint (600ml) water
1 small onion, finely chopped
4 oz (110g) fine burghul
2 tablespoons melted butter
1 teaspoon paprika
1/4 teaspoon cayenne pepper
1 teaspoon salt
2 spring onions, finely chopped
2 tablespoons finely chopped parsley
2 tablespoons fresh mint, finely chopped
1 small green pepper, finely chopped

Place the lentils, water and chopped onion in a saucepan and bring to the boil. Lower the heat, cover and simmer for 10–15 minutes, or until the lentils are tender. Make sure that all the water is NOT absorbed; the mixture should have a 'soupy' consistency. Remove from the heat and stir in the burghul, butter, paprika, pepper and salt. Cover and leave to rest for 10 minutes.

When cool enough, knead well, keeping your hands damp with cold water. Mix in half the spring onion, parsley, mint and green pepper. Taste and add more salt if necessary.

Pile into a serving dish and sprinkle with the remaining spring onion, parsley, mint and green pepper and serve warm.

# topig

## lenten kufte stuffed with nuts and spices

Another traditional Lenten dish which is served chilled with olive oil, lemon, pickles and a salad of your choice.

Follow the instructions carefully and if you cannot find whole-grain wheat, use mashed potato.

Filling
3 tablespoons olive oil
1 large onion, finely chopped
2 tablespoons flour
3 tablespoons pine kernels
3 tablespoons raisins or sultanas
2 tablespoons finely chopped parsley
1/4 teaspoon allspice
1 1/2 teaspoons salt
1/2 teaspoon black pepper
pinch of ground cinnamon
3 tablespoons tahina paste

Kufte Shells
4 oz (110g) whole-grain wheat (skinless). If this is not available,
peel 1/4 lb (110g) potatoes, boil until tender and mash
6 oz (175g) chickpeas, soaked overnight in cold water
4 oz (110g) fine burghul
3 tablespoons finely chopped onion
1 egg
1/2 teaspoon paprika
1 teaspoon salt
1/4 teaspoon cayenne pepper

boiling water
2 teaspoons salt
cumin
paprika
olive oil
lemon wedges

Prepare the filling first – preferably the day before – by heating the oil in a large saucepan. Add the onion and fry until soft. Add the flour and fry for 2–3 more minutes, stirring frequently. Remove from the heat and stir in the remaining filling ingredients. Mix thoroughly, transfer to a bowl and chill in the refrigerator – preferably overnight.

To prepare the kufte, first half-fill a saucepan with water, bring to the boil, add the wheat, turn off the heat and leave the wheat to soak for 2 hours.

Drain and rinse the chickpeas and place in a large saucepan half-filled with water. Bring to the boil, then lower the heat and simmer until the chickpeas are tender. If necessary, add more water. Drain the chickpeas and when they are cool enough to handle, remove and discard the skins by pressing each chickpea gently between thumb and forefinger.

Pass the chickpeas and wheat (if you are using it) through a mincer or chop very finely.

Place the burghul in a bowl and wash with cold water until the water you pour off is clean.

Place the burghul, chickpeas and wheat or mashed potato in a large bowl. Add the onion, egg, paprika, salt and cayenne pepper and knead for about 5 minutes, or until the mixture is smooth. Add a little water if necessary, but do not make it too damp or it will be difficult to shape.

To make the stuffed kufte, break off a piece of the kufte and roll it into a ball about 1½in (3.5cm) in diameter. Keeping your palms damp, hold the ball of kufte in one hand and make a hole in it with the index finger of the other hand. Press the index finger down into the palm of the other hand, squeezing out the kufte and making the shell a little thinner. Slowly rotate the ball of kufte so that the finger is pressing down on a new part of the kufte shell and making it thinner.

Fill the opening with 1–1½ teaspoons of the filling and then close the opening by drawing the edges together and sealing. Roll the kufte between your palms to make a smooth round shape.

Continue until all the kufte and filling have been used.

Two-thirds fill a large deep saucepan with water, add the salt and bring to the boil. Drop in a few kuftes at a time and simmer for 10 minutes. Remove with a slotted spoon to a large plate. Repeat until all the kuftes are cooked.

Sprinkle the kuftes generously with the cumin and paprika and refrigerate for a few hours. Sprinkle with olive oil and serve with lemon wedges. **Serves 6–8.**

# baki kufta

## lenten stuffed wheat balls

This is a Lenten version of one of the classic Middle Eastern specialities, kibbeh. These are stuffed wheat and meat balls popular throughout Syria, Armenia and Kurdistan.

Matzo meal mixes well with burghul and, indeed, Israelis have a similar dish entirely made of matzo meal plus a filling. It can be served hot or cold. (I prefer it hot!)

Accompany with a salad of your choice.

### Filling
2 tablespoons oil
4 oz (110g) chopped walnuts
2 oz (50g) pine kernels
1 large onion, finely chopped
1 teaspoon salt
1 teaspoon black pepper
1 teaspoon allspice
2 teaspoons finely chopped parsley

### Kufta
8 oz (225g) fine burghul
2 potatoes, peeled, boiled and mashed or 8 oz (225g) medium matzo meal
2 tablespoons very finely chopped onion
2 teaspoons salt
1 teaspoon black pepper
oil for deep-frying

### Garnish
lemon wedges

First prepare the filling by heating the oil in a small saucepan. Add the nuts, fry gently until they turn golden and then remove them and drain. Add the onion to the oil and fry until soft. Stir in the fried nuts, salt, black pepper, allspice and parsley and then set aside.

Wash the burghul in a bowl until the water you pour away is clear. Pour out excess water. Spread the burghul out on a baking sheet and knead for a few minutes.

Add the mashed potatoes or matzo meal, the chopped onion, salt and pepper and knead for about 15 minutes, keeping your hands damp with cold water.

To make the stuffed kufta, wet your hands and break off a piece of kufta about the size of an egg. Hold the ball of kufta in the palm of one hand and with the index finger of the other hand make a hole in the kufta. Press the index finger down into the palm of the other hand, squeezing out the kufta and making the shell a little thinner. Slowly rotate the ball of kufta so that the finger is pressing down on a new part of the kufta shell and making it thinner. Continue turning the shell round and round and pressing it up your finger until you have a long oval shape with a slightly wider mouth.

Place a tablespoon of the filling into the shell and then close the opening by drawing the edges together and sealing. Dampen your hands again and roll the kufta between your palms to smooth it off and ensure it is a real oval shape.

Continue in this way until you have used up all the kufta mixture and the filling.

To cook, add sufficient oil to a pan to deep fry and heat until hot. Add a few kufta at a time and fry in batches until golden brown all over. Remove and drain.

Serve with the lemon wedges. To eat, cut the kufta in half and squeeze the lemon juice into the filling. **Serves 6–8.**

# kibbeh hali

## burghul ball in tomato sauce

This is a Syrian speciality popular with the Alouites in the north of the country.
It is not a soup as such, but is often regarded as one.

8 oz (225g) fine burghul
4 oz (110g) plain flour or oatmeal
1 egg

### Sauce
4 tablespoons oil
1 onion, finely chopped
2 cloves garlic, finely chopped
1 tablespoon ground coriander
3 tablespoons tomato purée diluted in 1/2 pint (300ml) water
11/2 teaspoons salt
2 bay leaves
1/2 teaspoon allspice
1 teaspoon cayenne pepper
1/2 teaspoon black pepper
11/2 pints (900ml) water
juice of 1 lemon

### Garnish
2 tablespoons finely chopped parsley

Wash the burghul in a bowl until the water runs clear; pour away excess water. Spread the burghul out on a baking tray and knead for a few minutes.

Add the flour or oatmeal. Add the egg, mix it in and then knead until you have a paste thick enough to mould. If you find the mixture a little too sticky, leave it for 15–30 minutes by which time the burghul will have absorbed much of the excess moisture.

Keeping your palms damp, shape teaspoonfuls of the mixture into small balls about the size of marbles. Set these aside while you prepare the sauce.

Heat the oil in a saucepan, add the onion and fry until soft and lightly browned. Add the garlic and coriander and fry over a low heat for a further 2 minutes. Add the diluted tomato purée, salt, bay leaves, allspice, cayenne and black pepper and the water and stir well. Bring to the boil, add the balls of kibbeh and simmer for about 30 minutes until the sauce thickens.

Stir in the lemon juice. Transfer to a serving dish and sprinkle with the parsley.

**Serves 6–8.**

# torsh-e tareh

## iranian vegetable stew

This exotic, thick casserole is an Iranian favourite. It makes use of all kinds of greens and is served with rice pilavs. It is also often eaten as a soup with bread by the peasants.

Use fresh herbs and vegetables.

✳

4 tablespoons samna or ghee
1 large onion, thinly sliced
4 oz (110g) pinto or borlotti beans (dappled pink in colour) or pea beans (black-eyed beans) soaked in cold water for 3–4 hours
4 oz (110g) brown lentils, rinsed
3 pints (1.8 litres) water
2 tablespoons salt
1/2 teaspoon black pepper
3 cloves garlic, crushed
2 oz (50g) dillweed, finely chopped
1 bunch parsley, finely chopped
8–10 sprigs mint, finely chopped
4 tablespoons finely chopped coriander
11/2 lb (675g) spinach, washed thoroughly, drained, stemmed and coarsely chopped
2 oz (50g) rice flour
3 tablespoons water
4 eggs, beaten
juice of 1 lime or lemon
5 tablespoons pure orange juice

Melt 2 tablespoons of the fat in a large saucepan, add the onion and sauté until soft. Add the beans, lentils, water, salt and pepper; cover and simmer for 1–11/2 hours or until the beans are cooked.

In a frying pan, melt the remaining fat and sauté the garlic for 2 minutes. Add the dill, parsley, mint and coriander and fry for a further 2 minutes, stirring frequently. Add this mixture to the saucepan together with the spinach and cook for a further 20 minutes.

In a small bowl, mix the rice flour and water to a smooth paste. Add a few tablespoons of the hot stock, then add to the saucepan and cook, stirring constantly, until the sauce thickens.

Place the beaten eggs in a bowl and stir in the lime or lemon juice and a few tablespoons of the hot stock. Stir this into the saucepan together with the orange juice; cook for a few more minutes and then remove from the heat and serve.

**Serves 6–8.**

# gananchi porani

## aubergine stew

A classic recipe from the Armenian cuisine similar to those of Iran and Turkey, but in its overall treatment less 'overdone' as a great number of Iranian dishes tend to be. It is traditionally eaten with a garlic-yoghurt sauce (see page 245).

2 medium-sized aubergines, tops and stems removed
2 medium-sized courgettes, tops and stems removed
salt, for sprinkling
1/2 lb (225g) French beans
3 oz (75g) butter
1 green or red pepper, seeded and thinly sliced
1 clove garlic, crushed
1 1/2 teaspoons salt
3/4 teaspoon black pepper
2 eggs

Cut the aubergines and courgettes crossways into 1/4in (6mm) slices. Arrange the slices on a large plate, sprinkle with the salt and leave for 30 minutes.

Meanwhile wash, top and tail the French beans and cut into 2in (5cm) pieces. Put them into a pan of boiling, lightly salted water and cook for 5–10 minutes. Drain and dry with kitchen paper.

Rinse and dry the aubergine and courgette slices.

Melt the butter in a large saucepan or casserole, add the aubergine and courgette slices and fry, stirring occasionally, for 10 minutes. Add the beans, pepper, garlic, salt and black pepper and mix carefully. Cover and simmer, stirring occasionally and carefully, for about 20–30 minutes or until all the vegetables are just cooked.

Break the eggs into a bowl, beat with a fork and stir into the vegetables. As soon as the egg is cooked, remove from the heat and serve immediately with a rice pilav and a garlic-yoghurt sauce.

*One day, Nasretin Hoça climbed into a neighbour's garden and started filling a sack with onions, aubergines, courgettes, radishes – in short, every vegetable he could lay his hands on. The neighbour's son saw him and called his father, who came running – followed by wife, children, dog, cat, cockerel, hen and chicks.*

*'What are you doing, Hoça?'*
*'I was blown over by a mighty wind.'*
*'And who uprooted the vegetables?'*
*'I caught hold of them to stop myself being swept along.'*

*'What is the explanation for all these vegetables in your sack?'*
*'Funny you should ask that, neighbour! That is just what I was wondering about*
*when you interrupted me.'*

# loligov bamia

## okra with tomatoes

A traditional Armenian dish that goes well with pilavs, especially a burghul or cracked wheat pilav. You can use French beans or cabbage instead of okra.

2 tablespoons butter
1 onion, finely chopped
2 tomatoes, blanched, peeled, seeded and chopped
1 lb (450g) okra, washed and trimmed of stem ends
1 teaspoon salt
1/2 teaspoon black pepper
1/2 teaspoon dillweed
1/2 pint (300ml) water
juice of 1 lemon

Melt the butter in a large saucepan. Add the onion and fry, stirring frequently, until soft and lightly browned. Add the tomatoes and fry for 2 minutes, stirring frequently. Now add the okra, salt, pepper, dill and water and bring to the boil.

Lower the heat and simmer for 30 minutes, stirring carefully from time to time, or until the okra is tender. Do not overcook or the okra will disintegrate.

Five minutes before serving, stir in the lemon juice. Serve hot.

# etsis turlu

## rich vegetable stew

This recipe – one of literally hundreds – for a rich stew comes from Turkey. In the cold climate of Eastern Turkey, the Caucasus and Russia, rich stews are not the fashion, but a necessity of life. Chunks of meat are often added to enrich the stew still further.

The vegetables vary with the seasons and also with your own preferences. In this stew – anything goes! But it makes a filling meal for a cold winter's day when served with a pilav of your choice.

2 large aubergines
4 oz (110g) butter
1 green pepper, seeded and cut into 8 pieces
2 courgettes, sliced into 1<sup>1</sup>/2in (3.5cm) pieces crosswise
2 large potatoes, peeled and each cut into 8 pieces
2 large tomatoes, blanched, peeled and quartered
2 large onions, quartered
4 oz (110g) okra, stems trimmed
4 oz (110g) French beans, trimmed and halved
3 cloves garlic, finely chopped
2 tablespoons coarsely chopped parsley
2 turnips, peeled and quartered
2 sticks celery, cut into 1in (2.5cm) pieces
2 bay leaves
1/4 teaspoon dried basil
1/4 teaspoon dillweed
1/2 teaspoon sumak (optional)
1/4  teaspoon ground cumin
1/2 teaspoon cayenne pepper
1<sup>1</sup>/2 teaspoons salt
1/2 teaspoon or more black pepper
2 tablespoons butter

Slice the aubergines crosswise, arrange on a large plate, sprinkle generously with salt and leave for 30 minutes. Meanwhile, prepare all the other vegetables as suggested.

Melt the butter in a very large saucepan or casserole, add all the vegetables apart from the aubergines, and stir well for a minute or two until coated with the butter. Add about 1<sup>1</sup>/2 pints (900ml) water, the bay leaves and the remaining herbs and spices and stir thoroughly.

Rinse the aubergines under cold running water and dry on kitchen paper.

Melt the 2 tablespoons of butter in a frying pan, add the aubergine slices and fry for a few minutes, turning occasionally. Add them to the other vegetables, bring to the boil, cover the pan tightly and simmer for about an hour – carefully turning the vegetables a few times – or until the vegetables are tender. **Serves 6–8.**

# ghalieh esfanaj

## spinach in pomegranate juice

*'Polished delicates are we
Ruby mines in silver earth,
Maiden's blood of light degree
Curdled into drops of worth,
Breasts of women when they see
Man is near, and stand them forth.'*
1001 Nights

This simple dish from the Caspian coastline of Northern Iran is tangy and delicious. Serve it with a rice pilav and yoghurt.

6 oz (175g) whole lentils, washed
1½ lb (675g) fresh spinach or 1 lb (450g) frozen leaf spinach
2 tablespoons butter
1 onion, thinly sliced
1 teaspoon salt
3 tablespoons pomegranate juice

Bring a large saucepan half-filled with lightly salted water to the boil, add the lentils and simmer until tender – about 30–40 minutes. Drain the lentils and set aside.

If using fresh spinach, wash it thoroughly; if using frozen, let it thaw. Squeeze excess moisture out of the spinach and chop it coarsely.

Melt the butter in a saucepan, add the onion and fry, stirring frequently, until golden brown. Add the chopped spinach, stir well and cover the pan. Lower the heat and simmer for 10 minutes.

Stir in the lentils, salt and pomegranate juice, then cover the pan and simmer for a further 20 minutes.

Transfer to a serving dish and serve immediately.

# spanaki me ladi eyas key domates

## spinach with olive oil and tomatoes

This recipe is from Cyprus – though I hasten to add that it is typical of the entire region, barring Iran and the Gulf States where olive oil is hardly ever seen.

Serve with a pilav of your choice.

1 lb (450g) fresh spinach
3 tablespoons olive oil
2 cloves garlic, crushed
3 large ripe tomatoes, blanched, peeled and coarsely chopped
1 teaspoon salt
1/2 teaspoon black pepper

Discard coarse stems and damaged leaves and rinse the spinach thoroughly to remove soil and sand. Place the spinach in a large saucepan and cook until limp just in the water that clings to the leaves. Drain in a colander and, when cool enough to handle, squeeze out the excess water and chop coarsely.

Heat the oil in a large frying pan, add the garlic and fry for 2–3 minutes. Add the spinach and stir to coat with the oil. Scatter the tomatoes over the spinach and sprinkle the salt and pepper over the top. Cover the pan and cook for 5–10 minutes, stirring occasionally.

Serve hot.

# khorak-e kadoo ba ja'fari

## courgettes with parsley

This is a simple, tasty and easily prepared dish from Iran.
Serve with a rice pilav of your choice.

4 medium-sized courgettes, washed
1 onion, finely chopped
2 cloves garlic, finely chopped
4 tablespoons finely chopped parsley
4 tablespoons vegetable oil
1/2 pint (300ml) water
2 teaspoons salt
1/2 teaspoon black pepper
1/2 teaspoon paprika

Garnish
1 teaspoon ground cumin

Slice the top and tail off each courgette and then cut each one lengthwise into quarters. Arrange the courgettes in the bottom of a flameproof casserole dish.

Mix the chopped onion, garlic and parsley together and sprinkle over the courgettes. Add the vegetable oil and water and sprinkle with the salt, pepper and paprika. Cover the casserole and cook over a low heat for 20–25 minutes or until the courgettes are tender. Add a little more water if necessary, but take care not to make the sauce too watery.

Just before serving, sprinkle with the cumin.

# kapuska

## cabbage and tomatoes

This is a Caucasian way of preparing cabbage and it is absolutely delicious.
The cabbage is steamed in its own juices and the toasted almonds
give a contrasting flavour and texture.

This is also a popular dish in Eastern Turkey.

1 medium-sized cabbage
1¹/2 oz (40g) butter
1 large onion, thinly sliced
3 tomatoes, blanched, skinned and chopped
1¹/2 teaspoons salt
¹/2 teaspoon paprika
¹/2 teaspoon black pepper
¹/2 teaspoon dillweed
1 tablespoon lemon juice
3–4 tablespoons water
2 tablespoons blanched almonds, toasted under the grill until golden

Discard any coarse outer cabbage leaves, then quarter the cabbage. Slice the quarters into thin strips, discarding any thick stalk.

Melt the butter in a large saucepan, add the onion, tomatoes, salt and paprika and mix thoroughly. Add the cabbage slices, black pepper, dill and lemon juice and stir well.

Add the water, cover the pan and simmer over a low heat, stirring occasionally, for about 20–30 minutes, by which time the cabbage should be tender.

Just before serving, stir in the toasted almonds.

# baklali havuçi

## broad beans with carrots

*'One has no appetite for eating – the other has no eating for his appetite.'*
Jewish Wisdom

A typical Anatolian (Turkish–Armenian) dish which is part of the staple diet of the peasantry. It's a healthy dish, often topped with yoghurt or Sughtorov Madzoun – garlic-yoghurt sauce (see page 245) and served with bread, or a pilav and salads.

1 lb (450g) broad beans, either shelled or, if the pods are young,
simply string them and cut the pods into 1in (2.5cm) pieces
1 onion, chopped
8 fl oz (250ml) water
2 cloves garlic, coarsely chopped
2 carrots, peeled and cut into 1in (2.5cm) sticks
2 tablespoons chopped dill or mint or 1 tablespoon dried dillweed or mint
1 teaspoon salt
1/4 teaspoon black pepper
1/2 teaspoon sugar
2 fl oz (60ml) olive oil

Rinse the beans and place in a large saucepan with the onion and water. Bring to the boil, cover the pan and simmer for 30 minutes.

Stir in all the remaining ingredients, cover and cook for a further 20–30 minutes, or until the vegetables are tender.

Serve hot or at room temperature.

# kharperti gakhos

## carrots and celery

A tasty dish from Karpert, a once prosperous city now in ruins in Western Armenia.
You can increase the amount of chilli pepper if you wish.

Although usually served hot, this dish is also delicious cold
and can be served as a salad.

1 lb (450g) carrots, peeled
1 head celery, trimmed
2 oz (50g) butter
4 tablespoons olive oil
1 small onion, thinly sliced
2–3 cloves garlic, coarsely chopped
1 red pepper, cut into small chunks
1¹/2 teaspoons salt
¹/2 teaspoon chilli pepper

Cut the carrots into 1in (2.5cm) strips. Cut the leaves off the celery, chop them coarsely and set aside. Cut the celery sticks into 1in (2.5cm) pieces. Place the carrot and celery pieces in a colander and rinse thoroughly.

Melt the butter in a large saucepan, add the oil, carrots and celery (not the leaves); cover the pan and cook for 10 minutes.

Stir in the celery leaves, onion, garlic, red pepper, salt and pepper. Cover and cook for a further 30 minutes or until the vegetables are tender, shaking the pan occasionally to prevent sticking.

Serve hot or cold.

# gakhosi drtzak

## celery bundles

A very decorative dish from the Caucasus, which will provide a talking-point for a dinner party.

1 large head celery
4 carrots, peeled and cut into 1in (2.5cm) rounds
2 large onions, each cut lengthways into 8 pieces
4 tablespoons oil
8 fl oz (250ml) water
1 teaspoon salt
1/2 teaspoon chilli pepper
1 tablespoon lemon juice

Sauce
2 tablespoons olive oil
2 tablespoons flour
1/4 pint (150ml) stock, retained from cooking the above vegetables
1/4 teaspoon salt
1 tablespoon chopped fresh dill or 1 teaspoon dried dillweed

Garnish
1 teaspoon paprika

Separate the sticks of celery and wash them thoroughly. Cut them into pieces 6in (15cm) long and 1/4in (1/2cm) wide, cutting the leafy ends into similar lengths. Tie the sticks up in bundles – 6 to 8 pieces in each – using thin household string.

Place the bundles in a large saucepan and arrange the carrots and onions over the top. Add the remaining ingredients and bring to the boil. Lower the heat, cover the pan and simmer for about 20 minutes, or until the celery is just tender. Do not overcook. Remove from the heat and set aside for 15 minutes.

Lift the bundles carefully out of the pan and arrange them on an oval serving dish. Stack them in a pyramid arrangement with about 5 bundles on the bottom row, 4 on the next, and so on. Put the leafy bundles on the top. Drain and arrange the carrots and onions around the edge.

Reserve the liquid left in the pan. There should be about 1/4 pint (150ml) – if not, make up the quantity with water.

Heat the olive oil in a small saucepan, add the flour and stir until smooth. Cook, stirring constantly, until the flour is golden, then slowly stir in the reserved stock and the salt. Remove from the heat and stir in the dill. Drizzle the sauce over the celery to give a ribbon effect. Sprinkle with the paprika and serve immediately.

## mashed potatoes with tahina

*'He is so mean that he charges for the fat on a fly.'*
Armenian Wisdom

A simply delicious Lebanese dish. The mashed potatoes are mixed with fried onions and tahina and baked in the oven until the top is crisp.

Serve with bowls of fresh salads and pickles.

1¹/₂ lb (675g) potatoes, peeled
1¹/₂ teaspoons salt
pinch of baking powder
3 tablespoons milk
4 tablespoons olive oil
1 onion, finely chopped
6 tablespoons tahina paste
¹/₂ teaspoon chilli pepper

Garnish
a sprinkling of paprika

Place the potatoes in a large saucepan, cover with water and bring to the boil. Add 1 teaspoon of the salt and simmer for 20–30 minutes or until the potatoes are cooked. Drain and mash, adding the remaining salt, the baking powder and the milk.

While the potatoes are cooking, heat 1 tablespoon of the oil in a small pan. Add the onion and fry, stirring frequently, until soft. Add half the onion and 5 tablespoons of the tahina to the potatoes and mix thoroughly.

Brush a shallow ovenproof dish with a little of the oil and spoon in the potato mixture, leaving small peaks on the surface.

Add the remaining oil, tahina and the pepper to the onion in the pan and stir to blend. Spoon this sauce over the potatoes and sprinkle paprika over the surface.

Place in an oven preheated to 400F (200C) gas 6 and bake for 10 minutes. Put under a preheated hot grill for about 1 minute to brown the top lightly, then serve immediately.

# tutum printzov

## pumpkin with apricots and rice

This is a Caucasian dish using two diverse ingredients – pumpkin and apricots.
It makes an excellent meal – with a fresh salad of your choice.

2 oz (50g) butter
1 onion, finely chopped
2 lb (900g) pumpkin, peeled and cut into 1–1¹/₂in (2.5–3.5cm) cubes
4 oz (110g) dried apricots, chopped
2 oz (50g) long-grain rice, washed thoroughly under cold water and drained
2 oz (50g) sugar
salt and pepper to taste
¹/₂ pint (300ml) water

Melt the butter in a large saucepan, add the onion and fry until soft and golden, stirring frequently. Add all the remaining ingredients and stir well. Bring to the boil, lower the heat, cover and simmer for 20–25 minutes until the pumpkin and rice are tender and the water has been absorbed.

Leave to 'rest' for 10–15 minutes, then pile into a serving dish.

# tziranov bami

## okra with apricots

*'Who doubts you sweet*
*with savoury almond-stores*
*Apricots?*
*When you were young*
*You had star flowers.*
*Now you are little suns*
*Ripe in the leaves.'*
1001 Nights

A vegetable and a fruit come together to create one of the greats of Armenian cuisine. Caucasians, and to some extent the Iranians, have a great penchant for vegetable dishes with fruit and nuts. This tradition can be traced back to Urartian–Sassanian cultures and to the religious concept of Good and Evil, Sweet and Sour, Light and Dark – Zoroastrianism.

1 lb (450g) small fresh okra
1 lemon, halved
2 fl oz (60ml) olive oil
1 onion, thinly sliced
2 tablespoons tomato purée diluted in 8 fl oz (250ml) warm water
12 dried apricot halves, each cut into 2 or 3 strips
1 teaspoon salt
1/4 teaspoon black pepper
1/2 teaspoon dried basil

Trim the stems of the okra into cone-shapes. Do not cut into the pods. Rinse and dry the okra. Place in a bowl, squeeze one lemon half over them and then shake well.

Cut the remaining half lemon into thin, half-moon slices.

Heat the oil in a large saucepan, add the onion and fry until soft and just turning golden. Add the okra, the diluted tomato purée and the lemon slices; cover the pan and simmer gently for 20 minutes.

Stir in the apricots, salt, pepper and basil and cook, uncovered for a further 15–20 minutes, or until the apricots are tender and the sauce has thickened.

Remove from the heat, set aside for 10 minutes, then serve with a pilav of your choice.

# glazed pumpkin

This is an attractive pumpkin dish which goes well with pilavs and other vegetable dishes.

8 fl oz (250ml) water
6 oz (175g) sugar
1in (2.5cm) piece root ginger, peeled and halved
3 lb (1.35kg) pumpkin, peeled and cut into 1in (2.5cm) cubes
pinch of salt
Juice of 1 lemon
2 tablespoons blanched almonds
1 tablespoon slivered pistachios

Bring the water to the boil in a large saucepan. Stir in the sugar and root ginger. Add the pumpkin and salt and cook until tender, occasionally stirring carefully.

Remove and discard the ginger. Stir in the lemon juice and transfer the pumpkin to a serving dish.

Toast the almonds and pistachios under a hot grill for a few minutes, turning frequently to prevent burning. Sprinkle the nuts over the pumpkin and serve.  **Serves 6–8.**

# vospov tutum

## lentils with pumpkin

*An Anatolian recipe making use of two 'humble' ingredients – lentils and – once again – the much-neglected pumpkin.*

*Serve with fresh yoghurt on the side.*

3 oz (75g) whole brown lentils
1¹/2 lb (675g) peeled pumpkin, cut into slices 2in (5cm) long and ¹/2in (1cm) thick
2 oz (50g) butter
1 onion, finely chopped
1 oz (25g) sugar
¹/2 teaspoon salt
3 tablespoons finely chopped parsley

Rinse the lentils and place them in a saucepan with enough water to cover them to a depth of about 2in (5cm). Bring to the boil, then simmer for about 30 minutes or until the lentils are tender. Add more water if necessary. Drain the lentils and set aside.

Put the pumpkin pieces in a saucepan and add enough water to cover by about 1in (2.5cm). Bring to the boil and simmer until the pumpkin is just tender. Do not overcook. Drain the pumpkin and set aside.

Melt the butter in a large, deep pan, add the onion and sauté until golden-brown. Add the lentils and pumpkin and sprinkle the sugar and salt over the top. Mix gently and heat through for about 5 minutes.

Transfer to a serving dish, sprinkle with the parsley and serve.

# ghalieh-ye kadoo

## lentils with courgettes

This is an extremely tasty and nourishing Iranian recipe from the Shiraz region.

Eat it with a pilav of your choice and with the finest of all Middle Eastern ingredients – yoghurt.

1 oz (25g) butter
2 onions, thinly sliced
3/4 lb (350g) brown lentils, washed
water (see method)
3–4 courgettes, cut crosswise into 1/2in (1cm) slices
1 tablespoon lemon juice
11/2 teaspoons salt
1/2 teaspoon black pepper
1 teaspoon ground cumin
1 tablespoon butter
1 small onion, finely chopped
2 tablespoons finely chopped parsley

Melt the butter in a large saucepan, add the sliced onions and fry until golden brown. Add the lentils and enough water to cover by 1in (2.5cm) and bring to the boil. Lower the heat and simmer for 15 minutes.

Stir the courgette slices into the lentils, cover and simmer for a further 20 minutes, or until the courgettes and lentils are tender. Add the lemon juice, salt, pepper and cumin and stir thoroughly.

Melt the tablespoon of butter in a small pan, add the chopped onion and fry until lightly browned.

To serve, transfer the lentil–courgette mixture to a serving dish and sprinkle with the fried onion and parsley.

# shesh havij

## carrots and nuts

A very attractive, tasty dish from Iran, which goes beautifully
with a saffron rice pilav (see page 110).

3 tablespoons butter
3/4 lb (350g) carrots, peeled and thinly sliced crossways
1 large onion, finely chopped
5 stoned dates, thinly sliced
1 tablespoon raisins or sultanas
1 tablespoon white wine vinegar
1 tablespoon pomegranate juice or 2 tablespoons lemon juice
4 eggs
1 teaspoon salt
1/2 teaspoon black pepper
1 tablespoon blanched, slivered almonds
1 tablespoon slivered pistachio nuts

Melt the butter in a saucepan. Add the carrots and fry for a few minutes, stirring
frequently to coat them with the butter. Add the onion and fry until soft and turning
golden.

Add the dates, raisins or sultanas, vinegar and pomegranate or lemon juice and mix
well. Cover the pan, lower the heat and simmer for 30 minutes. Transfer this mixture
to a large frying pan or shallow casserole dish.

Break the eggs into a bowl, add the salt and pepper and beat well. Pour the eggs over
the carrot mixture and cook over a low heat until set.

Sprinkle with the nuts and serve immediately.

## pastry for borek

Below is one of many recipes used for making pastry for boreks. Two others
are described in Yogurtlu Kabak Boregi and Spanakh Boregi (pages 206-11).
All these can be interchanged with the various fillings suggested.

This dough, which makes enough for 30-36 boreks, takes a little time to make, but
it is deliciously soft and flaky.
However, bought puff pastry makes a satisfactory substitute.

1 lb (450g) plain flour
1 teaspoon salt
8 fl oz (250ml) cold water
1 teaspoon lemon juice
2 oz (50g) clarified butter or ghee, melted
8 oz (225g) block margarine or butter, chilled
1 egg, beaten

Sift the flour and salt into a large bowl. Make a well in the centre, add the water and
lemon juice and mix thoroughly, using a wooden spoon. Add the melted clarified
butter and knead for 10 minutes until smooth. Shape the dough into 1 large ball, cover
with a damp cloth and leave for 30 minutes.

Lightly flour a worktop and roll out the dough until 1/4in ( 1/2cm) thick.

Put the block of margarine or butter in the middle of the dough and fold the pastry
over the fat so that it is completely enclosed. With a well-floured rolling pin, flatten the
dough to a 1/2in (1cm) thickness. Fold the dough in half and refrigerate for 10 minutes.

Return the dough to the floured worktop and roll out in 1/4in ( 1/2cm) thickness. Fold
in half and refrigerate for a further 10 minutes.

Keeping the worktop well floured, roll out the dough once more as thinly as possible.
Now cut into the desired sizes and shapes for the boreks (see pages 207-8). The most
usual ones are 3–4in (7.5–10cm) circles or squares.

Put 1–2 teaspoonfuls of your chosen filling in one half of each shape. Dampen the
edges with cold water and fold over to make half-moons or rectangle shapes; seal the
edges with your finger tips or a fork.

Arrange the boreks on greased baking trays and brush each with a little beaten egg.
Bake in an oven preheated to 350F (180C) gas 4, for 20–30 minutes, or until puffed
and golden.

Other suggested savoury fillings follow on the next two pages.

## aubergine

1 lb (450g) aubergines, unpeeled and cut into $1/2$in (1cm) cubes
2 teaspoons salt
3 tablespoons oil
2 onions, finely chopped
2 large tomatoes, blanched, peeled and chopped
$1/2$ teaspoon allspice
$1/2$ teaspoon salt
$1/2$ teaspoon black pepper
$1/2$ teaspoon chilli pepper
2 tablespoons finely chopped parsley or fresh mint

Place the aubergine cubes in a colander, sprinkle with the salt and set aside for 30 minutes.

Rinse under cold running water, drain and pat dry with kitchen paper.

Heat the oil in a saucepan, add the onions and fry until soft. Add the aubergines and fry until soft, stirring frequently. Add a little more oil if necessary.

Add all the remaining ingredients, mix well and simmer until the vegetables are very soft. Mash with a fork and set aside to cool, When cold, pour off any excess oil.

## pumpkin

1 lb (450g) pumpkin flesh, cut into 1in (2.5cm) cubes
2 tablespoons samna or ghee
1 large onion, finely chopped
2 tablespoons fresh pomegranate juice or 1 tablespoon lemon juice
$1/2$ teaspoon cinnamon
1 teaspoon salt
$1/2$ teaspoon black pepper

Cook the pumpkin flesh in lightly salted boiling water until tender. Drain and either mash with a fork or purée in a blender.

Heat the samna or ghee, add the onion and fry until soft and turning golden. Place the mashed pumpkin, fried onion and remaining ingredients in a bowl and mix well. Set aside to cool.

## ganachi borek

### fresh vegetables and herbs

2 leeks, trimmed, cut in half lengthways, washed thoroughly and drained
1/2 lb (225g) fresh spinach, stems trimmed, washed thoroughly and drained
2 tablespoons samna or oil
3 spring onions, finely chopped
1/4 lb (110g) sorrel (optional), trimmed, wilted leaves removed, washed thoroughly and finely chopped
4 tablespoons finely chopped parsley
3 tablespoons fresh dill, chopped
3 tablespoons fresh pomegranate juice or 2 tablespoons lemon juice
1/2 teaspoon cinnamon
1 teaspoon salt
1/2 teaspoon black pepper

Chop leeks into 1/4in (6mm) pieces and chop the spinach.

Heat the samna or oil, add the leeks and onions and fry until soft. Add the spinach, sorrel, parsley and dill; cover the pan and cook for 5–6 minutes or until the greens are tender.

Stir in the pomegranate juice, cinnamon, salt and pepper; mix well and set aside to cool.

## lent pizza

This is a pizza with a difference, for this indeed is the source of all pizzas – that is, vegetables on bread.

Pizzas, of course, are of Neapolitan origin; but the Neapolitans were of Greek origin, the Greeks received their culture from Asia Minor and it was in Asia Minor that miss hatz – meat or vegetables on bread – was born.

The name 'pizza' comes from the Greek pita, meaning bread. This comes from the Armenian *petag* meaning 'hive' – a hole or pocket which can be filled with meats and vegetables.

This is an Armenian recipe which makes about 15–20 pizzas – allow 2-3 per person.

### Dough
1/2 oz (15g) fresh yeast or 1/4 oz (8g) dried yeast
1 teaspoon sugar
7 fl oz (220ml) tepid water
12 oz (350g) plain flour
1 teaspoon salt
1/2 teaspoon allspice

### Topping
1 large onion, finely chopped
8 oz (225g) finely chopped walnuts
4 oz (110g) blanched almonds, finely chopped
1 large green pepper, finely chopped
4 tablespoons finely chopped parsley
8 black olives, stoned and chopped
2 cloves garlic, crushed
1 lb (450g) ripe tomatoes, blanched, peeled and chopped
1 tablespoon pomegranate syrup or 2 tablespoons lemon juice
11/2 teaspoons salt
1/2 teaspoon cayenne pepper
1/2 teaspoon black pepper
1 tablespoon tomato purée

### Garnish
lemon wedges

Dissolve the yeast and sugar in a cup with a little of the water and leave in a warm place until the mixture begins to froth.

Sift the flour, salt and allspice into a large bowl. Make a well in the flour and add the yeast mixture. Adding a little of the water at a time, knead until you have a soft dough. Transfer to a worktop and knead for at least 10 minutes until the dough is smooth and elastic.

Cover the bowl with a damp cloth and leave in a warm place for about 2 hours, or until the dough has doubled in bulk.

Meanwhile, prepare the topping by putting all the ingredients into a large bowl and mixing until well blended.

When the dough is ready, punch it down and knead it for a minute or two, then divide it into golf ball-sized balls. Cover them with a cloth and leave for 10 minutes.

Heat the oven to 450F (230C) gas 8, and grease some baking sheets.

Lightly flour a work top and roll each ball of dough out into a circle about 6in (15cm) in diameter. As you roll them out, place them on the greased baking sheets, leaving an inch or two (2.5–5cm) between each one. Spread a generous layer of topping over the entire surface of each circle.

Bake for 12–15 minutes until the dough is cooked through and lightly golden, but still soft enough to fold.

Serve hot with the lemon wedges. To eat, squeeze some lemon juice over the surface and roll up like a pancake. A salad makes an ideal accompaniment.

**Note:** These will keep for several days in the refrigerator. To reheat, place some foil over the grill rack and place the Baki Miss Hatz, face downwards, on the foil under a hot grill for a few minutes.

# tzavarov-shomini borek

## small patties of spinach, burghul and dough fried in oil

These are ideal as an appetiser, as part of a buffet, or as a main course with salad. Any not required can be frozen before or after frying – in the latter cases, warm through before serving.

The quantities below will make about 36 patties.

### Dough
1/2 oz (15g) fresh yeast or 1/4 oz (8g) dried yeast
1/2 teaspoon sugar
8 fl oz (250ml) tepid water
8 oz (225g) plain flour
1/2 teaspoon salt
2 teaspoons cooking oil

### Filling
3 oz (75g) fine-grain burghul
11/2 lb (675g) fresh spinach
1 tablespoon plus 1 teaspoon salt
1 oz (25g) coarsely chopped parsley
1/2 oz (15g) coarsely chopped fresh mint or 1/4 oz (8g) dried mint
4 cloves garlic, crushed
3 oz (75g) finely chopped onion
1 oz (25g) chopped spring onions
11/2 oz (40g) chickpeas, soaked overnight in cold water, then cooked until tender
2 tablespoons ground coriander
1 teaspoon chilli pepper
1 teaspoon black pepper
1 teaspoon bicarbonate of soda
1/2–3/4 pint (300–450ml) oil

Place the yeast and sugar in a small bowl, add 3 tablespoons of the water, stir and set aside in a warm place for about 10 minutes, or until the mixture begins to froth.

Sift the flour into a large bowl, make a well in the centre and add the yeast mixture, salt and oil. Stir to mix and add just enough of the remaining water to make a soft dough.

Knead for 5–10 minutes until smooth and elastic, place in the cleaned bowl, cover with a teatowel and set aside in a warm place for about 1 hour, or until the dough has doubled in bulk.

Meanwhile, prepare the filling: place the burghul in a small bowl and rinse with cold water until the water poured off is clean

Discard coarse stems and bruised leaves from the spinach, rinse very thoroughly under cold running water, then shake off any excess water. Shred the spinach finely, sprinkle 1 tablespoon of salt over it, mix and pile into a colander. After 30 minutes, squeeze the spinach dry and place in a large bowl.

Add the burgul, the remaining salt and all the other ingredients except the oil. Mix.

Place a little of the dough and the filling in another large bowl and mix together with your fingers. Continue to mix the two in this way until all the dough and filling are well blended.

Keeping your hands damp, take small lumps of the mixture, roll into balls and shape into very thin patties about 3in (7.5cm) in diameter.

Heat half the oil in a large frying pan, add a few of the patties and cook until golden, allowing about 3 minutes for each side.

Remove with a slotted spoon, arrange on a large plate and keep warm while you fry the remaining patties in the same way. After some time you may find that the oil has darkened, in which case discard it, wipe the pan clean, heat the remaining oil and continue frying.

Serve warm.

# sou boreki

## water pastry

The word *beoreg* comes from the Turkish word *bobreg* meaning kidney, since the traditional borek is kidney-shaped. The pastry is dipped in boiling water, then almost immediately into cold water to give that crisp effect.

An excellent buffet dish or a first course, accompanied by a salad. The quantities given make enough for 6–8 people.

Pastry
**6 eggs**
**1 teaspoon salt**
**2 teaspoons cooking oil**
**1 lb (450g) plain flour**

Filling
**1 lb (450g) cooking cheese, grated**
**3 tablespoons chopped parsley**
**salt and pepper to taste**

**6 oz (175g) butter, melted**

Grease a baking try. Beat the eggs together in a large mixing bowl. Stir in the salt and cooking oil. Add the flour and mix until you have a soft dough. Knead for several minutes until the dough is smooth, then divide it into about 12 portions and roll each into a ball.

Place the balls on a tray, setting them well apart; cover with a teatowel and leave to rest overnight in a cool place.

Roll each ball out very thinly to cover the whole of the baking tray. Set each one aside.

In a very large saucepan, boil up about 12 pints (7.5 litres) of water with 1 tablespoon of salt.

Fill another large pan with cold water.

Dip each sheet of dough into the boiling water and hold for about 30 seconds. Remove, and dip immediately into the cold water. Dry carefully on a clean teatowel and set aside.

Make the filling by mixing together the cheese and parsley in a bowl with salt and pepper to taste.

Place 2 sheets of dough on the baking tray. Brush 1–2 tablespoons of the melted butter over the second sheet. Continue buttering every second sheet until you have used up half the sheets. Spread the filling over this sixth sheet.

Continue adding the sheets of pastry and buttering every second one until they are all used up. Pour any remaining butter over the last sheet.

Cook in an oven preheated to 400F (200C) gas 6, for about 30 minutes.

Remove from the oven and leave to rest for 5 minutes. If you like it soft, cover this for 5 minutes; if you prefer it crunchy then do not cover.

Cut into 3in (7.5cm) squares and serve warm.

# banirov borek

## savoury pastry with cheese

This makes an excellent hors d'oeuvre; it can be served hot or cold as part of a buffet, or with salad as a main course. This recipe comes from Armenia; the quantities given make 16–20 boreks.

8 oz (225g) cheese (Traditionally Feta or Haloumi-type cheeses are used, but Cheddar or Edam are both delicious)
2 eggs, beaten
1 heaped tablespoon chopped parsley
1/4 teaspoon nutmeg
1/2 teaspoon black pepper
12 oz (350g) flaky pastry (You can make this yourself, or use the frozen variety, which I find most acceptable)

Glaze
1 beaten egg or milk

Grate the cheese and add the egg, parsley, nutmeg and pepper. Mix well.

Preheat the oven to 350F (180C) gas 4.

Roll out the pastry very thin and cut into 3in (7.5cm) squares. Put a heaped teaspoon of the cheese mixture in the middle of each square. Wet the edges with a little water, fold over and seal the edges with a fork to create a decorative effect. Place on a greased baking tray and brush each borek with some beaten egg or milk.

Bake for 15-20 minutes until golden brown, and serve warm with a fresh salad – or cold for a buffet.

# yogurtlu kabak boregi

## yoghurt pastry stuffed with courgettes

An extremely tasty Turkish savoury, which should be served warm with a salad of
your choice. The quantities given below make 30–35 boreks.

### Dough
8 oz (225g) unsalted butter or margarine
2 tablespoons vegetable oil
1 large egg
1/2 pint (300ml) yoghurt
11/4 lb (560g) plain flour
1/4 teaspoon salt
1/4 teaspoon bicarbonate of soda

### Filling
1 lb (450g) courgettes, peeled
6 oz (175g) grated Feta, Lancashire, Cheddar or Gruyère cheese
1 teaspoon salt
1/4 teaspoon black pepper
1 teaspoon dried mint
1 egg, beaten

Before preparing the dough, grate the courgettes and place them in a sieve to drain.

Mix the melted butter, oil, egg and yoghurt together in a large bowl. Sift in the flour,
salt and bicarbonate of soda. First stir in the flour, then knead until it forms a dough.

Lightly flour a worktop, place the dough on it and knead for a few minutes until the
dough is smooth and no longer sticks to your fingers. If the dough is still a little sticky,
knead in a little more flour.

Divide the dough into 2 portions and roll each out as thinly as possible. Cut the dough
into 4in (10cm) circles.

Prepare the filling by first squeezing as much moisture as possible out of the
courgettes and then placing them in a mixing bowl. Add the grated cheese, salt,
pepper, mint and half of the beaten egg. Mix until the ingredients are well blended,
then place 11/2–2 teaspoons of the filling in one of the pastry circles. Fold it over to
form a semi-circle and seal the edges by pressing with a fork.

Continue until you have used up all the pastry and filling; place the boreks on greased
baking sheets and brush with the remaining beaten egg.

Cook in an oven preheated to 350F (180C) gas 4, for about 25–30 minutes or until
golden. Serve warm.

# filo pastry boreks

Filo pastry is often used for making boreks. Ready-made filo can be bought from most Middle Eastern shops and many continental delicatessen stores. These boreks can be stored for up to a fortnight in the refrigerator, or up to 3 months in the freezer – in the latter case, defrost slowly overnight in a refrigerator. You can use any filling you like; as well as the three (Betingan, Ganachi Borek and Tetumi Lidsk) I have included on pages 198-9. I suggest you try the spinach filling from the Spanakh Boregi recipe and the cheese filling in Banirov Borek.

Below, I have described the three most popular ways of preparing filo pastry boreks.

**1 packet (1 lb/450g) filo pastry**
**1/4 lb (110g) butter, melted**
**filling of your choice**

When preparing the boreks, use one sheet of pastry at a time and keep the others covered or they will dry out and go crumbly.

Pastry Triangles

1  The pastry sheets are usually about 20 x 12in (50 x 30cm).
2  Remove 1 sheet and cut it into 4 pieces each about 6 x 10in (15 x 25cm).
3  Brush each with melted butter and fold lengthways to form 3 x 10in (7.5 x 25cm) strips.
4  Place 1 teaspoon of the filling about 1in (2.5cm) in from the bottom of the strip nearest you and then fold up as illustrated below.

## pastry triangles

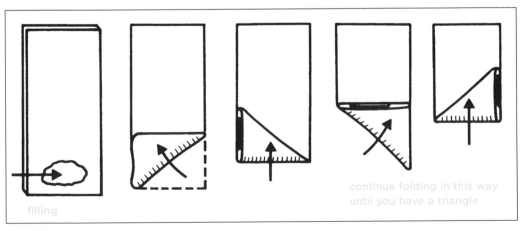

filling

continue folding in this way until you have a triangle

## Pastry Fingers

1  Remove 1 sheet and brush with melted butter.

2  Cut into 4 pieces 5 x 12in (12.5 x 30cm) and put two of the pieces on top of the other two to give 2 strips each of 2 layers.

3  Place 1 teaspoon of the filling about 1in (2.5cm) in from the edge nearest you and spread it out in a thin ridge.

4  Fold over and roll up as illustrated below.

## pastry fingers

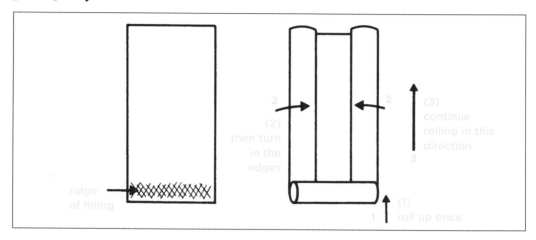

## Pastry Squares

1  Prepare pastry strips as described for pastry triangles 1–3.

2  Place 1 teaspoon of the filling about 1in (2.5cm) in from the edge nearest you and fold as illustrated below.

## pastry squares

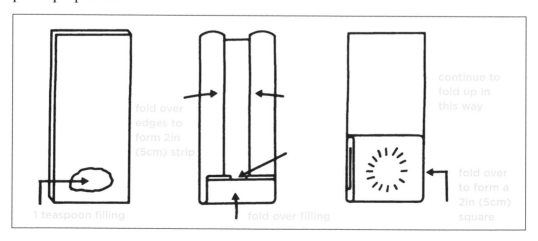

**Baked Boreks**

Arrange on greased baking trays and brush the top of each pastry with any remaining melted butter.

Place in an oven preheated to 375F (190C) gas 5, and bake for 30 minutes or until golden.

**Deep-Fried Boreks**

This method is particularly popular in North Africa where this type of pastry is known as brisk.

Deep-fry in moderately hot oil – it should not be smoking – until golden. Drain.

**Note:** Finger pastries are not usually cooked in this way as they may unroll.

# spanakh boregi

## pastry stuffed with spinach

Boreks are the glory of Turkish cuisine – there are many versions and versions of versions . . .

Spinach goes very well with pastry and onions and this dish is excellent  as an appetiser, for lunch or dinner (makes 16–20).

Serve with a fresh salad and/or a yoghurt and cucumber salad.

### Dough
1 oz (25g) fresh yeast or 1/2 oz (15g) dried yeast
about 1/4 pint (150ml) tepid water
8 oz (225g) plain flour
1 teaspoon salt
2 fl oz (60ml) cooking oil

### Filling
11/2 lb (675g) fresh spinach or 1 lb (450g) frozen leaf spinach
5 tablespoons olive oil
1 onion, finely chopped
11/2 teaspoons salt
1/2 teaspoon black pepper
juice of 1 lemon
3 tablespoons grated cheese (optional)

In a small bowl, dissolve the yeast in 4 tablespoons of the water and leave in a warm place until it begins to froth.

Sift the flour and salt into a large, warmed, mixing bowl. Make a well in the centre and pour in the yeast mixture. Add the oil to the yeast mixture and work it into the flour.

Adding a little of the tepid water at a time, work until you have a dough that is firm but not hard.

Cover with a damp cloth and leave in a warm place for about 2 hours, when it should have almost doubled in bulk.

Meanwhile, wash the spinach very thoroughly; place in a saucepan with a small quantity of water and cook until tender. Strain into a colander and leave to cool, then squeeze out any excess water and chop the spinach into small pieces. (Follow the directions on the package if using frozen spinach; cook and chop.)

Heat the oil in a saucepan, add the onion and fry for a few minutes until soft. Add the salt, pepper and chopped spinach, the lemon juice and grated cheese and stir well. Remove the pan from the heat and leave the mixture to cool.

When the dough is ready, divide it into small walnut-sized balls.

Lightly flour a worktop and roll the pastry out until thin. Cut into 3–4in (7.5–10cm) squares; place a tablespoon of the filling in each square; wet the edges with a little water, fold over into a triangle and seal the edges with a fork to create a decorative effect.

Arrange on a greased baking sheet and brush each borek with a little beaten egg. Place in an oven preheated to 350F (180C) gas 4, and bake for 20–30 minutes or until golden-brown. Serve hot or cold.

❧

# spanakopita

## spinach pie

A Greek classic which is also popular throughout the Middle East. It makes a fine main dish or, when cut into squares, a tasty appetiser or savoury. Packets of ready-made filo pastry can be found in Middle Eastern stores or on delicatessen counters.

❧

2 lb (900g) fresh spinach, washed thoroughly, coarse stems removed
4 fl oz (120ml) oil
1 onion, finely chopped
2 oz (50g) parsley, finely chopped
2 teaspoons fresh dill, chopped or 1 teaspoon dried dillweed
2 teaspoons fennel, chopped (optional)
1/4 teaspoon nutmeg
6 oz (175g) grated cheese – Cheddar, Feta or Gruyère
2 oz (50g) grated Parmesan
2 eggs, beaten
1 teaspoon salt
1/4 teaspoon black pepper
8–10 sheets filo pastry
3–4 tablespoons melted butter

Chop the spinach coarsely, put it into a large saucepan, cover and place over a low heat for about 10 minutes, mixing occasionally with a fork.

When the spinach has 'wilted', pour it into a colander to drain and, with the back of a large spoon, press tightly to remove as much juice as possible.

Heat the oil in a small pan, add the onion and fry for several minutes until soft and turning golden. Place the onion and spinach in a large bowl, add the parsley, dill, fennel, nutmeg, grated cheese, eggs, salt and pepper and mix thoroughly.

Lightly grease a baking dish or ovenproof casserole about 10 x 12in (25 x 30cm). Lay 4 or 5 sheets of the filo in the baking dish, brushing each one with the melted butter. Pour the spinach mixture into the dish and spread evenly with the back of a spoon. Lay the remaining sheets of filo over the top, again brushing each one with melted butter. Trim the edges of the pastry. Pour any remaining butter over the top and sprinkle with a little cold water – this should prevent the pastry curling at the edges.

Place in the centre of an oven preheated to 350F (180C) gas 4, and bake for about 45 minutes, or until golden.

Remove from the oven, let it rest for a few minutes, then serve.

**Note:** A variation is to use shortcrust pastry or to make borek pastry (see recipe for Sou Boreki). Divide the pastry into 2 equal parts. Roll out one half a little larger than the base of the dish to allow for shrinkage and place it in the bottom of the greased dish. Cover with the spinach mixture.

Roll out the other piece of pastry and arrange over the top, tucking in the edges. Prick the pie top in 2 or 3 places with a fork, then cook as above for at least 45 minutes until crisp and golden.

# breads

Middle Easterners still eat more bread than meat, vegetables or fruit and while in Britain the consumption of bread is decreasing, in the Middle East it is, if anything, on the increase. The choice is rich and the quality superb – despite the following humorous anecdote.

'Well, Ampagoum Aga, the price of wheat has fallen, but bread is still as expensive as ever.'

'So?'

'Well, the price of bread should fall as well.'

'On the contrary, it should rise even higher because the price of rope has risen.'

'What has rope got to do with bread?'

'You may well ask what . . . but it has something . . . every day from 1 kilo of bread I get 100 grams of rope!'

The most popular bread is pita which was well known to the bakers of Babylon and Assyria, although some would insist that lavash is older still. However, both of these and the others given in this chapter are as ancient as the walls of Jericho.

# lavash

## crispy thin bread

Lavash is the classic – and most probably the oldest – form of bread found in the Caucasus. It is thin and crispy, and normally prepared in a Tonir (the Caucasian version of Tandoor) but it can also be prepared, as indeed it is in Arab lands and Iran, on a 'domed' oven made of cast iron with the coal or wood burning underneath.

Below is a simplified version of lavash. This is ideal for dips, salads and as an accompaniment to all Middle Eastern foods.

1 oz (25g) fresh yeast or 1/2 oz (15g) dried yeast
tepid water
1 teaspoon sugar
3 lb (1.35kg) plain flour
2 teaspoons salt

Dissolve the yeast in 1 pint (600ml) tepid water. Stir in the sugar.

Sift the flour and salt into a large mixing bowl. Make a well in the centre of the flour and slowly work in the dissolved yeast and enough warm water to make a stiff dough. Knead well on a floured surface for about 10 minutes.

Place the ball of dough in a clean bowl, cover with a cloth and leave in a warm place for at least 3 hours.

Transfer the dough to a floured surface, punch it down and knead again for a few minutes. Leave it in the bowl, covered, for a further 30 minutes.

Flour the worktop again. Divide the dough into balls each about the size of an apple. This quantity of dough should make between 25–30 balls.

With a long rolling pin, roll out each ball into a thin sheet about 8–10in (20–25cm) in diameter. Sprinkle the worktop occasionally with more flour to prevent sticking.

Line the bottom of the oven with aluminium foil. Heat the oven to 400F (200C) gas 6.

Place each sheet of dough in turn on the foil and cook for about 3 minutes. Cover the cooked lavash with a cloth to keep it warm while the remaining ones are being cooked.

Serve immediately.

**Note:** If the lavash are not used immediately, they can be kept for many months wrapped in plastic or stored in a freezer. When you are ready to serve them, sprinkle lightly with water, wrap in a teatowel and leave for 10 minutes to absorb the water and soften.

# khubz arabi

## pita bread

This is the most popular and best-known of all Middle Eastern breads and today is widely available in supermarkets. Pita is a flat, hollow bread, and thus a perfect, edible food container, ideal with vegetable dishes, especially dips and salads. It is not difficult to prepare and the following recipe will make about 8 average breads.

1/2 oz (15g) fresh yeast or 1/4 oz (8g) dried yeast
about 1/2 pint (300ml) tepid water
a pinch of sugar
1 lb (450g) plain flour
1/2 teaspoon salt
oil

In a small bowl, dissolve the yeast in 3–4 tablespoons of the water. Stir in the pinch of sugar and leave in a warm place for 10–15 minutes or until it becomes frothy.

Sift the flour and salt into a warmed mixing bowl. Make a well in the centre and pour in the yeast mixture. Add enough tepid water to make a firm, but not hard, dough.

Lightly flour a work surface and knead the dough for about 15 minutes until it is smooth and elastic and no longer sticks to your hands. If you knead in a tablespoon of oil, it will make a softer bread.

Wash and dry the mixing bowl and oil it. Roll the dough round and round the bowl until it is covered all over with a film of oil – this will prevent the dough from going crusty and cracking while rising. Cover the bowl with a damp cloth and leave in a warm place for at least 2 hours, when it should have almost doubled in size.

Punch it down and knead it again for a few minutes. Divide the mixture into 6–8 pieces, depending on the size you want the pitas. Roll them around in the hands until they are round and smooth.

Lightly flour a board and flatten each one out on it with the palm of your hand or with a rolling pin, until it is about 1/4in (6mm) thick and as even and circular as possible. Dust with flour and cover with a floured cloth; leave to rise in a warm place for 20–30 minutes.

Preheat the oven to 450–475F (230–240C) gas 8–9, putting in 2 large oiled baking sheets halfway through the heating period. When the oven is ready, slide the rounds of dough on to the hot baking sheets, dampening the tops to prevent them browning, and bake for 10 minutes. Do not open the door during this time; after this it is safe to open it cautiously to see if the pitas have puffed up.

Put them on to wire racks to cool as soon as possible after you have removed them from the oven. They should be soft and white with a pouch inside.

# khubz basali

## onion bread

A truly magnificent bread of Capadocian origin, popular throughout Anatolia, Armenia and Northern Syria. Wonderful for breakfast, or with cheese, fish, vegetables, eggs, olives and salads.

This recipe will make a loaf 12in (30cm) long.

8 oz (225g) self raising flour
1/2 teaspoon salt
1/2 pint (300ml) water or slightly less
1 teaspoon baking powder
1/2 teaspoon ground cumin
1/2 teaspoon thyme
1/4 teaspoon chilli pepper
10 black olives, seeded and coarsely chopped
1 small onion, finely chopped
4–5 tablespoons olive or groundnut oil

Sift the flour and salt into a warmed mixing bowl. Make a well in the centre and add enough of the water to make a firm, but not hard, dough. Add the baking powder, cumin, thyme, chilli pepper, chopped olives and onion.

Lightly flour a work surface and knead the dough on it for about 15 minutes until it is smooth and elastic and no longer sticks to your hands. Knead in the oil. This will not only help to give the bread its particular flavour, but will also soften its texture.

Wash and dry the mixing bowl and lightly oil it. Roll the dough round and round the bowl until it is completely covered with a film of oil – this will prevent the dough from going crusty and cracking while rising. Place the dough in a greased bread tin, cover with a damp cloth and leave it to rise in a warm place for about 30 minutes.

Bake in an oven preheated to 350F (180C) gas 4, for 45–50 minutes, until the crust is golden brown.

Remove from the baking tin, cool and serve.

# nan-e barbari

## persian bread

The bread of Iran, oval-shaped and covered with sesame seeds, Nan-e Barbari should be eaten straight from the oven as it does not keep for long and when cold it loses much of that special flavour for which it is famed.

1/2 oz (15g) fresh yeast or 1/4 oz (8g) dried yeast
1 teaspoon sugar
1/2 pint (300ml) tepid water
2 tablespoons oil
1 lb (450g) plain flour
2 tablespoons melted butter
2 tablespoons sesame seeds

In a small bowl, dissolve the yeast and sugar in 4 tablespoons of the water and set aside until it begins to froth. Stir in the oil.

Sift the flour into a warmed mixing bowl. Make a well in the centre and pour in the yeast mixture. Add enough of the water to make a firm, but not hard, dough.

Lightly flour a work surface, turn the dough on to it and knead for about 10 minutes or until the dough is smooth and elastic. Cover with a cloth and leave in a warm place for about 2 hours or until it has doubled in bulk.

Punch the dough down and knead for a few more minutes. Divide the mixture into 3 portions. Roll them around between your palms until they are round and smooth.

Lightly flour a board and press each one out on it with the palms of your hands; shape it into an oval about 1/4in (1/2cm) thick.

With the forefingers of both hands press 4 ridges lengthwise over the surface of the dough. Brush each surface with the melted butter and sprinkle generously with the sesame seeds. Leave the loaves to rest for a further 30 minutes.

Preheat the oven to 450F (230C) gas 8, putting in greased baking sheets halfway through the heating period. When the oven is ready, slide the loaves onto the hot sheets and bake for 15 minutes or until golden brown in colour.

Serve while still warm.

## cilician thick bread

Several years ago, with great pleasure, I noted a medieval recipe described as the bread of 'Franks and Armenians' in what was perhaps the first serious work on Middle Eastern cuisine (*A Book of Middle Eastern Food* by Claudia Roden.) This recipe was so close to one I recall used by my grandmother and called by her Hasd Hats (thick or fat bread) which she only prepared on Ascension Day.

The recipe below however is not exactly that of my grandmother, but rather an adaptation based on memory and my Aunt's in Baghdad. The result is a fascinating, crunchy loaf, one that I am sure is still made in one form or other in the villages of Cilicia or, as it is better known today, the Hattay region of Southern Turkey.

Try this bread – it is nourishing and filling. Vary the topping to suit your own taste.

### Dough
1/4 pint (150ml) milk
1/4 pint (150ml) tepid water
3/4 tablespoon lard
3/4 tablespoon butter
1 tablespoon sugar
1/2 teaspoon salt
1/2 oz (15g) fresh yeast or 1/4 oz (8g) dried yeast
1 lb (450g) plain flour, sifted

### Topping
scant 1/4 teaspoon ground ginger
11/2 tablespoons sesame seeds, toasted
1 teaspoon cumin seeds, toasted
1 teaspoon aniseed
1 teaspoon poppy seeds
11/2 tablespoons grated cheese – preferably a dry crumbly one such as Parmesan, Cheddar or Lancashire
1 tablespoon chopped pistachio nuts
1 teaspoon salt
1/2 teaspoon black pepper
2 egg yolks

You can use all the seeds suggested above or else select the ones you prefer.

Scald the milk, then add half the water and the lard, butter, sugar and salt and allow to cool to tepid.

Meanwhile, dissolve the yeast in the rest of the warm water; set aside in a warm place for about 10 minutes, or until the mixture begins to froth.

Mix the yeast mixture into the milk and water mixture and pour into a large bowl. Add the flour gradually to the yeast mixture, mixing first with a wooden spoon and then by hand until you have a soft dough. Transfer to a floured work top and knead for 10–15 minutes until the dough is smooth and elastic.

Grease a bowl with a little oil, roll the dough around the bowl until it is covered with the oil. This prevents a crust forming. Cover the bowl with a damp cloth and set aside in a warm place for about 2 hours, or until the dough has doubled in bulk.

Punch the dough down and knead for a few more minutes. Pat into a round, flat shape about 1/2–1in (1–2.5cm) thick on an oiled baking sheet.

Put all the topping ingredients into a bowl and mix to a paste. Spread this paste over the top of the loaf and leave it in a warm place for another 30 minutes.

Preheat the oven to 450F (230C) gas 8, then bake the bread for 10 minutes at that temperature. Reduce heat to 350F (180C) gas 4, and bake for a further 30 minutes.

Test the loaf by tapping it on the bottom. If it sounds hollow, it is ready. Cool on a wire rack.

# mannaeesh

## thyme bread

A Lebanese favourite, Mannaeesh Zahtar, as it is sometimes called, comes in two shapes: one, as in the recipe below; the other a hollowed, round shape, Kaahk Mannaeesh, which one breaks, sprinkles the inside with Zahtar (page 37) and then eats with coffee.

The following recipe is for flat, round bread which is easy to prepare and is excellent for breakfast, or with tea and coffee.

1/2 oz (15g) fresh yeast or 1/4 oz (8g) dried yeast
1 teaspoon sugar
about 1/2 pint (300ml) tepid water
1 lb (450g) plain flour
1/2 teaspoon salt

Topping
5-6 tablespoons olive oil
1/2 oz (15g) dried thyme
1/4 oz (8g) dried marjoram
3 tablespoons sesame seeds

Prepare the dough as described in Khubz Arabi (pita bread) on page 215 . When ready, divide the dough into 10 pieces. Roll each portion between your palms until it is smooth and round.

Flour a board and flatten each ball with a rolling pin until it is circular and about 5in (12.5cm) in diameter and between 1/8-1/4in (3mm-1/2cm) thick. Leave in a warm place for a further 20 minutes.

Brush the tops with a little of the oil. Mix the thyme, marjoram, sesame seeds and oil together to form a paste. Spread this mixture evenly over the surface of each round.

Preheat the oven to 450F (230C) gas 8, and put 2 greased baking sheets into the oven halfway through the heating period. Slide the mannaeesh rounds on to the hot sheets and cook for about 8 minutes. The bread should be soft and white.

Remove and cool on wire racks.

# pakhtakata

## 'fortune bread'

A sweet bread which is usually served at a family dinner during Lent. This quantity makes 2 loaves and each has a coin hidden in it – hence the name.

1 lb (450g) self raising flour
2¹/2 teaspoons salt
2 teaspoons baking powder
4 fl oz (120ml) plus 2 teaspoons clear honey
4 fl oz (120ml) plus 2 tablespoons cooking oil
about 4 fl oz (120ml) water
2 clean coins

Sift the flour, salt and baking powder into a large bowl. Place 4 fl oz (120ml) each of honey, oil and water in a small saucepan and heat over a low heat until lukewarm. Stir this mixture into the flour, mix and then knead for at least 5 minutes until smooth. Add a little more water if needed and coat your hands with some of the remaining oil while kneading. The dough should be a little stiff. Roll the dough into a ball, place in a polythene bag, wrap in a towel and set aside for 30 minutes.

Divide the dough into 2 balls and bury a coin in each. Roll out each ball into a 6–8in (15–20cm) circle. Use the prongs of a fork to make a decorative pattern over the top of each loaf. Either run the prongs over the surface, pressing down lightly or press tiny 'dimples' into the surface.

Place on a large baking sheet greased with the remaining oil and leave for a further 30 minutes.

Brush the surface of each loaf with the remaining honey. Place on the middle shelf of an oven preheated to 350F (180C) gas 4, and bake for 20 minutes, then place on the top shelf and cook for a further 20 minutes. The bread will not rise much and it should be golden brown when done.

Cut the bread into as many pieces as there are people present. The lucky one is the person who finds the coin.

# nazug

## spiced bread

*'The mother is newly made bread, still warm.*
*Whoever eats, will be nourished*
*and filled.*
*The father is unwatered wine.*
*Whoever sips will be intoxicated.*
*The brother is the rising sun*
*that lights the valley*
*and the mountainside alike.'*
Armenian Folk Poem

An aromatic bread from Armenia which is ideal for breakfast and at tea-time.

1/2 oz (15g) fresh yeast or 1/4 oz (8g) dried yeast
2 fl oz (60ml) warm milk
2 eggs, lightly beaten
6 tablespoons melted butter
4 oz (110g) sugar
1/2 teaspoon salt
2 teaspoons cinnamon
1 teaspoon vanilla essence
12–14 oz (350–400g) plain flour

Garnish
beaten egg

Place the yeast in a large bowl, add the milk and stir until the yeast has dissolved. Add the eggs, cooled melted butter, sugar, salt, cinnamon and vanilla and stir well. Gradually sift in enough flour to make a soft dough.

Transfer the dough to a lightly floured surface and knead for about 10 minutes or until the dough is smooth and elastic.

Wash and dry the mixing bowl and oil it lightly. Add the dough and roll it round the bowl until the surface is lightly greased. Cover with a cloth and set aside in a warm place for at least 2 hours or until it has doubled in bulk.

Punch the dough down and knead for a few more minutes. Divide the mixture into 4 portions. Roll or press each one out into a round about 1/2in (1cm) thick. Place on greased baking sheets about 2in (5cm) apart and set aside in a warm place for a further 30 minutes.

Brush the surface of each with beaten egg and bake in an oven preheated to 375F (190C) gas 5, for 10–15 minutes or until golden and baked through.

# pickles

Pickling is an art form in its own right, and as well as all the fruits and vegetables that are usually pickled in this country the Middle Easterners pickle – among others – olives, okra, aubergines, apricots, oranges, dates, cherries and grapes.

When these vegetables and fruits are in season, try the following recipes and enrich your palate.

Serve them generously, as do the Iranians who eat pickles with practically everything – often substituting them for salads.

# zeytun msabbah

## spiced olives

This is an Arab speciality from Syria. It gives a hot, spicy flavour to the olives which are an ideal accompaniment to salads and other vegetable pickles.

Fresh olives are rather difficult to find in Britain, but can sometimes be ordered by specialist grocers.

**1 lb (450g) fresh green olives**
**3 tablespoons salt**
**2 tablespoons cayenne pepper**
**water**

Soak olives overnight in water. Drain, then drop the olives into sterilised jars, sprinkling the layers with salt and cayenne pepper. Add water to completely cover. Seal the jars tightly and then leave for about 5 months.

To serve, arrange some on a plate and sprinkle with the juice of 1 small lemon and 2–3 tablespoons of olive oil.

# enginar turşusi

## pickled artichokes

A recipe from Ismir famed for her figs, grapes, kufte and artichokes.
This pickle is equally popular with Greeks.

When serving these delicious pickles, garnish with olive oil
and a little chopped parsley.

8–10 lemons
3/4 pint (450ml) water
8–10 artichokes
3 tablespoons coarse salt
2 tablespoons wine vinegar
olive oil

Squeeze enough lemons to produce 8 fl oz (250ml) juice. Strain the juice into a large bowl. Place any pulp in the strainer and pour the water through it into the bowl.

To prepare the artichokes, follow the instructions given in the recipe for Enginar Dolmasi on page 140. Use one of the squeezed lemons to rub the cut edges. Now cut the artichokes in half lengthways and scoop out each hairy choke with a knife or spoon. As you finish preparing each artichoke, drop it into the bowl of lemon-water.

Wash and dry three 1-pint (600ml) wide-neck jars. Remove the halved artichokes from the bowl and pack tightly into the jars to within 1in (2.5cm) of the top.

Strain the lemon-water into a large jug, discarding any residue. Add the salt and vinegar and mix well. Pour the brine into each jar to cover the artichokes by 3/4in (2cm). Reserve any leftover brine. Add a film of olive oil to the top of each jar.

Seal the jars and leave in a cool place for at least 2 weeks. If some of the liquid is absorbed during this time, top up with the reserved brine. Any brine left in the jars can always be used as a salad dressing.

# pickled onions

This is an Iranian method of pickling onions.

1 lb (450g) pickling onions, peeled
4 cloves garlic, finely chopped
a few sprigs fresh mint or 3 tablespoons dried mint
3 tablespoons salt
2 pints (1.2 litres) white wine vinegar

Soak the onions in water for 2 hours.

If using fresh mint chop it finely. Mix the garlic, mint and salt together in a small bowl. Drain the onions and dry on kitchen paper.

Place a few of the onions in sterilised jars and sprinkle with a little of the garlic mixture. Add a few more onions, sprinkle with a little more of the mixture and continue like this until all the ingredients have been bottled.

Fill the jars completely with the vinegar, seal lightly and leave for at least 2 weeks.

This is an Anatolian version of pickled onions.

1 lb (450g) pickling onions, peeled
3 tablespoons salt
1 pint (600ml) white wine vinegar
1 tablespoon brown sugar

Place the onions in a bowl, sprinkle with the salt and leave to stand overnight.

Turn the onions into a colander and rinse under cold running water.

Place the vinegar and sugar in a saucepan, add the onions and bring to the boil. Simmer for 5 minutes, then remove from the heat and pack the onions into sterilised jars. Top up with the hot vinegar. Seal the jars tightly and leave for at least 2 weeks.

# hiyar turşusi

## cucumber pickles

Adana cucumbers are famed for their aroma and sweetish flavour. They are usually
3–4in (7.5–10cm) long and make excellent pickles. However, in my opinion,
the best way to eat them is to peel them, thinly slice them lengthways and sprinkle
with salt. Try this and the humble cucumber will taste more like a delicious fruit.
These cucumbers can be found in Indian and Middle Eastern grocery stores.

2<sup>1</sup>/2 lb (1.2kg) small pickling cucumbers
1<sup>1</sup>/4 pint (750ml) water
2 oz (50g) coarse salt
8 fl oz (250ml) white or cider vinegar
4 large cloves garlic, halved
8 sprigs fresh dill

Scrub and rinse the cucumbers thoroughly. Prick each one 3 or 4 times with the prongs of a fork.

Bring the water to the boil in a saucepan. Add the salt and vinegar and stir until the salt has dissolved.

Wash and dry two 2-pint (1.2-litre) wide-neck jars. Place 2 half-cloves of garlic and 2 sprigs of dill in the bottom of each jar. Pack the cucumbers in tightly and place the remaining garlic and dill on top. Pour the hot brine over the cucumbers to cover and place a small, flat, clean stone over the cucumbers to keep them submerged. Loosely cover the jars and set aside in a warm place for 3–4 days, then cover tightly and refrigerate.

**Note:** A variation is to add courgettes to the cucumbers. Use small, tender ones, top and tail them, scrub and cut into 1/2in (1cm) rounds.

# pancar turssi

## pickled beetroot

This recipe creates a slightly spicy beetroot pickle, which is excellent with salads, pilavs and cooked vegetable dishes. This recipe should produce enough for three 2-pint (1.2-litre) jars.

5 lb (2.25kg) beetroot
8 pints (5 litres) water
2 pints (1.2 litres) white wine vinegar
1 pint (600ml) beetroot juice (see method)
8 oz (225g) sugar
1 1/2 tablespoons salt
2in (5cm) stik cinnamon
1 teaspoon whole cloves

Wash the beetroot – do not cut off the root ends and leave 2in (5cm) of the top of the stem to prevent it bleeding while cooking. Place the beetroot in a large pan, add half the water and bring to the boil. Lower the heat and simmer for an hour, or until the beetroot is almost tender. Drain, reserving 1 pint (600ml) of the juice for later use.

Place the beetroot in cold water, cut off the roots and stems and peel off the skins. Cut the beetroot into quarters. Bring the rest of the water to the boil in a pan, add the vinegar, reserved beetroot juice, sugar, salt, cinnamon and whole cloves. Drop the quartered beetroot into the brine and cook for 1 minute, then lower the heat and simmer for 5 minutes.

Fill sterilised jars with the beetroot and brine. Seal tightly and keep for 2–3 weeks before using.

# karnabahar turşusi

## cauliflower pickles

The beetroot gives the cauliflower a beautiful red colour and adds a distinctive flavour.

This is one of the most popular pickles throughout the Middle East. Some people add shredded red cabbage, which also enhances both the flavour and the colour of the cauliflower.

3 lb (1.35kg) young white cauliflower
2 raw beetroot, peeled and sliced
2 chilli peppers, sliced so the pods are exposed
2 pints (1.2 litres) water
3/4 pint (450ml) white wine vinegar
6 tablespoons salt

Wash the cauliflower and separate into florets. Arrange the florets in layers in a jar. Add a few slices of beetroot in between the layers.

Add the slit chilli peppers, one in each jar – or cut into the appropriate number – depending on the number of jars.

Mix the water, vinegar and salt in a bowl.

Pour the mixture into sterilised jars. Top up with water, if necessary.

Seal tightly and store. They should be ready in 4 weeks.

# bami titvash

## pickled okra

An Armenian recipe.

Use small, firm okra and leave the pickle for at least 8 weeks before using.

2 lb (900g) fresh small okra
6 small hot pepper pods and
6 cloves garlic (the exact number depends on the number of jars)
4 fl oz (120ml) water
6 tablespoons salt (not iodised)
1 tablespoon mustard seed
2 pints (1.2 litres) white wine vinegar

Wash okra. Pack into large sterilised pickling jars. Put 1 hot pepper and 1 clove of garlic into each jar.

In a large saucepan, bring the water, salt, mustard seed and vinegar to the boil. Now pour over the okra.

Seal tightly and leave to stand for at least 8 weeks.

# sumpoogi titvash

## stuffed aubergine pickles

This is a masterpiece of Middle Eastern pickling: it is absolutely delicious.

Select very small aubergines.

✳

3 lb (1.35kg) small aubergines
1 small green pepper, coarsely chopped
1 medium-sized red pepper, coarsely chopped
1/4 teaspoon chilli pepper
4 tablespoons finely chopped parsley
2 cloves garlic, finely chopped
1/2 teaspoon salt

Brine
1¹/4 pints (750ml) white wine vinegar
3/4 pint (450ml) water
5 tablespoons sugar
5 tablespoons iodised salt

Remove the stems from the aubergines, wash and place in a large saucepan. Cover with water and bring to the boil. Lower the heat and simmer for 10–15 minutes, then drain into a colander and leave to cool.

In a bowl, mix together the chopped peppers, chilli pepper, parsley, garlic and salt.

When the aubergines are cold, make a slit on one side of each about 1in (2.5cm) long. Press 1–2 teaspoons of the stuffing, depending on size of aubergines, into each opening. When all the aubergines are stuffed, set them aside for 10 minutes.

Meanwhile, in a large saucepan, bring the vinegar, water, sugar and salt to the boil. Carefully place the aubergines in the boiling brine, lower the heat and simmer for 3 minutes.

Remove the aubergines with a slotted spoon and pack them into two 2-pint (1.2-litre) sterilised jars. Fill the jars with the brine to completely cover the aubergines.

Seal tightly and keep for at least 2 weeks.

# titvash

## mixed pickles

This is probably the most popular form of pickling throughout the Middle East.
There are naturally regional variations, especially in the choice of vegetables,
but basically the following ones are those most commonly used.
However, I suggest that you use those which are most easily obtainable and
which are to your own taste.

It is advisable to make a fairly large quantity of this pickle.
The recipe below is for 1 gallon (4.5 litres). However, you can increase or decrease
the quantities accordingly.

2 small cauliflowers, separated into florets
8 carrots, peeled, quartered lengthwise and cut into 3in (7.5cm) pieces
8 small cucumbers
1/2 lb (225g) green beans, trimmed
6 sweet yellow peppers, quartered, seeded and deribbed
6 small hot red peppers
6 cloves garlic, peeled and halved
6 fresh dill sprigs
3 pints (1.8 litres) water
1 pint (600ml) white wine vinegar
4 oz (110g) salt

Wash the vegetables thoroughly. Pack them into 3 large sterilised jars. Add 2 cloves of garlic and 2 sprigs of dill to each jar.

Put the water, vinegar and salt in a large saucepan and bring to the boil. Pour the vinegar mixture over the vegetables until they are completely covered.

Seal tightly and store for at least 4–5 weeks.

# lemoun makbouss

## lemons in oil

*'Snow that takes on saffron*
*Silver turning gold*
*And lemons.*
*Moons which waver into suns,*
*Chrysolite bells and manifold*
*Are lemons, lemons.*
*Camphor ripening to corn light,*
*Breasts that else could not be told*
*Are lemons, lemons, lemons.'*
1001 Nights

**20 lemons, scraped and sliced**
**6 teaspoons salt**
**2 teaspoons paprika**
**oil (corn or olive oil)**

Sprinkle the sliced lemons with the salt in a large colander and leave overnight.

Arrange lemon slices in layers in sterilised jars, sprinkling a little of the paprika between each layer. Cover lemon slices with oil.

Seal the jars and let them rest for 3–4 weeks; by this time the lemons will be soft and orangy in colour.

# torshi-ye barg-e holoo

## pickled peaches

*'We think we fell in proud virgin's blood,*
*Therefore we fend our velvet with a mesh*
*Against the airs;*
*Eat through our scarlet skin to soft wet flesh,*
*To sweet gold flesh, best guard lest in full flood*
*You meet the heart of poison unawares.'*
1001 Nights

An Iranian recipe using dried peaches.

2 lb (900g) dried peaches
1<sup>1</sup>/2 pints (900ml) white wine vinegar
6 oz (175g) sugar
1 teaspoon ginger
1 teaspoon ground coriander
2 cloves garlic, finely chopped
1 tablespoon tamarind
1 teaspoon dry mustard
1 teaspoon paprika
1/2 teaspoon cinnamon

Place the dried peaches in a large bowl, add the vinegar and leave to soak for 2 days.

Transfer to a saucepan, add the remaining ingredients and bring to the boil. Lower the heat and simmer for 1 hour. Pour the mixture into sterilised jars, making sure you distribute the peaches evenly.

Seal the jars tightly and leave for at least 10 days.

# pickled cherries

Pickled cherries taste delicious, and this Iranian recipe shows how easy they are to prepare – marvellous to eat!

3/4 pint (450ml) white wine vinegar
4 tablespoons salt (not iodized)
2 lb (900g) cherries, stemmed, over-ripe ones discarded, washed
4 sprigs tarragon
10 peppercorns

In a saucepan, bring the vinegar and salt to the boil and simmer for 3 minutes. Remove from the heat and leave to cool.

Meanwhile, put the cherries into sterilised jars. Pour the vinegar mixture over the cherries. Add the tarragon leaves and peppercorns to the jars and seal them tightly.

Three to four days later, pour out the vinegar mixture, make up a new mixture and, when it is cool, pour it into the jars.

Seal the jars tightly and leave for a fortnight.

# khaghoghi titvash

## pickled grapes

A delicious and exotic appetiser, especially with drinks.

4 lb (1.8kg) mixed black, red and green grapes
1³/4 pints (1.05 litres) cider vinegar
1³/4 pints (1.05 litres) water
8 oz (225g) sugar
8 teaspoons salt
2 teaspoons whole cloves
4 3in (7.5cm) sticks cinnamon, roughly broken up
3 whole nutmegs, crushed

Wash the grapes thoroughly, discarding any damaged or over-ripe ones. Leave them in small bunches. Pack the bunches into four wide-mouthed 2-pint (1.2-litre) jars.

Put all the remaining ingredients into a large saucepan, bring to the boil, lower the heat, cover and simmer for 10 minutes. Set aside, uncover and leave to cool.

When the brine is lukewarm, pour it into the jars, distributing the seasonings evenly and filling the jars to the top.

Seal the jars and set aside for at least 2 weeks, then store in a cool place.

# torshi-ye-khorma

## pickled dates

*'We grow to the sound of the wind*
*Playing his flutes in our hair,*
*Palm tree daughters.*
*Brown flesh Badawi*
*Fed with light*
*By our gold father.*
*We are loved of the tree-tented,*
*The sons of space, the half-forgotten*
*The wide-handed, the bright-sworded*
*Masters of horses.*
*Who has rested in the shades of our palms*
*Shall hear a murmur ever above his sleep.'*
1001 Nights

This is an Iranian speciality but is also very popular with the Kurds and
the Iraqis, who produce the best dates in the world, both in quantity and quality.

Both sumak and tamarind can be purchased from Continental
and Middle Eastern shops. Tamarind is also easily found in most Indian shops.
It comes in 1 lb (450g) blocks.

3 oz (75g) sumak
8 oz (225g) dried tamarind
1¹/2 pints (900ml)  water
juice of 1 lemon
1 lb (450g) dates, stoned
2 cloves garlic, pressed through a garlic press
1/2 teaspoon salt
1/4 teaspoon black pepper
1/4 teaspoon cinnamon
1/4 teaspoon nutmeg

Soak the sumak in a bowl in 3/4 pint (450ml) of the water overnight. Do the same with
the tamarind in another bowl. Strain both the sumak and the tamarind through a
cheesecloth and reserve the liquid.

In a pan, mix the liquids, add the lemon juice and boil for 3 minutes. If a blender is
available, blend the dates, or use a mincer, or chop them finely. Add to the boiling
sumak mixture. Add the garlic, salt, pepper, cinnamon and nutmeg. Pour the mixture
into a 2-pint (1.2-litre) sterilised jar. Seal tightly. Use after a week.

# torshi-ye-gheysi

## dried apricot pickle

*'Feed the mouth and the eye will be bashful.'*
1001 Nights

A spicy Iranian pickle.

1 lb (450g) dried apricots
1 in (2.5cm) piece root ginger, peeled and finely chopped
1¹/₂ pints (900ml) vinegar – malt or white wine
2 tablespoons coriander seeds
4 oz (110g) sugar
¹/₄ teaspoon chilli pepper
10 cloves garlic, peeled
1 teaspoon salt
¹/₂ teaspoon black pepper

Place the apricots and ginger in a bowl, cover with the vinegar and set aside for about 8 hours.

Pour the contents of the bowl into a large saucepan, add the remaining ingredients and bring to the boil. Lower the heat and simmer until the mixture thickens. Set aside for 15–20 minutes.

Spoon into a hot, sterilised 2-pint (1.2-litre) jar, filling to the top with the syrup.

When cold, seal tightly and store in a cool place for at least 1 week. This pickle should be eaten within 2 months.

# mixed fruit pickles

This is an Iranian recipe also popular in the Caucasus. It is a fascinating pickle which really has the appearance of a thick pulp – more akin to a chutney than a pickle.

Use fresh fruits whenever available and use whatever are most easily available and to your taste. As well as those mentioned in the recipe, you could use pineapple, guavas, mangoes etc.

An excellent accompaniment to salads.

**1 lb (450g) each of the following fruits:**
grapes
pears
apples
quinces
figs
apricots
peaches
plums
watermelon – optional
white wine vinegar
2 teaspoons nutmeg
2 teaspoons cinnamon
1 teaspoon coarse salt

Stem the fruit and remove cores, pips and stones. Cut the fruit into small pieces and place in a large saucepan with a little water. Bring to the boil, then simmer until the fruit is soft and mushy.

Pass the mixture through a sieve, rubbing through as much of the pulp as possible. Bring to the boil and stir in enough vinegar to make a thin mixture. Stir in the nutmeg, cinnamon and salt and pour the fruit into several 2-pint (1.2-litre) sterilised jars.

Seal tightly and leave for at least 2 weeks.

# torshi-ye poost-e porteghal

## pickled orange rinds

Why waste your orange rinds or, for that matter, lemon or lime rinds when you can make an exquisite pickle that goes well with cooked vegetables and pilavs, and especially salads?

Follow the instructions for this Iranian recipe and you will make yourself a really tasty and original pickle.

You can use the same method to pickle lemon or lime rinds.

**2 cups (500ml) fresh orange rind**
**2¹/₂ pints (1.5 litres) white wine vinegar**
**¹/₂ teaspoon salt**
**¹/₂ teaspoon white pepper**

Place the orange rind in a saucepan, cover with water, bring to the boil and simmer for 15 minutes. Pour off the water.

Add more water to the pan, bring to the boil and simmer for a further 5 minutes. Strain off the water again.

Place the orange rind in a bowl, cover with cold water and leave for 12 hours.

Strain off the hot water again, cover with more cold water and leave for a further 12 hours, then drain again.

Spread the orange rinds out on kitchen paper and leave to dry for at least 2 days. Slice the rinds into small pieces and pass these through a mincer.

Put the orange paste into a saucepan, add the vinegar, salt and pepper and bring to the boil. Simmer until the mixture takes on the consistency of a thick syrup.

Pour into three 1-pint (600ml) sterilised jars, seal tightly and keep for at least 10 days.

# sauces and dressings

The most outstanding ingredient used in sauces and dressings is yoghurt – a product of the region which has now been popularised in the West. There are few sauces as *we* understand them, since many dishes are stews – or are cooked in their own juices. Yoghurt or preferably garlic-yoghurt is often stirred into a dish or spooned over food just before eating.

A fascinating sauce is Nouri Salsa – pomegranate sauce which, apart from having a beautiful colour gives a marvellous tang to a dish.

Tahina (sesame paste) also makes an excellent sauce.

# soured cream

This is also know as 'smetana' and is of East European origin being particularly popular in Poland, Hungary and the USSR. Smetana is skimmed off the milk curds before they are put to drain for making cheese. In the Middle East, soured cream is only used in two regions – Israel, due mainly to the influx of East European Jews, and in the Caucasus, due to the recent Russian influence.

Although some people still make their own soured cream the majority of housewives, especially in Israel, purchase the commercially produced smetana, which is now becoming available in supermarkets here.

Soured cream keeps well in the refrigerator and is often used instead of fresh cream.

# yoghurt

This is one of the most outstanding ingredients in Middle Eastern cuisine and it is still generally made at home. There are several methods for making it, but the one given below is the simplest and most proven.

Yoghurt can be kept in a refrigerator for several days before it starts to turn sour. When it is nearly used up, take a little as the new 'starter' to make more.

**2 pints (1.2 litres) milk**
**1 tablespoon 'live' yoghurt – called a 'starter'**

Bring the milk to the boil in a large saucepan. As the froth rises, turn off the heat, then allow the milk to cool to the point where you can dip your finger in and count up to 15 (i.e. a temperature of 100F/38C or slightly less).

Put the starter into a teacup and stir in 2–3 tablespoons of the warm milk. Beat this mixture until smooth, then pour it into the milk. Stir the milk and pour it into a bowl. Cover the top of the bowl with a large plate and wrap a teatowel around the plate and bowl.

Put in a warm place, for example, on top of a cooker or near a radiator; leave for about 8 hours or overnight without disturbing.

Transfer the bowl to the refrigerator.

# stabilised yoghurt

Certain recipes require the yoghurt to be boiled. Under normal circumstances
the yoghurt will separate and curdle, therefore it is necessary
to stabilise the yoghurt first.

This is a simple procedure and you can follow either of the following methods:

1   Stir 1 dessertspoonful of flour into a little water to form a smooth paste and then
    stir this into the yoghurt before cooking.

2   Beat 1 egg into each 1/2 pint (300ml) yoghurt before cooking.

## tan or ayran

### yoghurt drink

This is a satisfying and healthy yoghurt drink, popular throughout the Middle East
and a must on any oriental table.

The proportions given are for one person. They can be increased in proportion to
the number required.

**2 tablespoons yoghurt**
**1/2 pint (300ml) water**
**1/4 teaspoon salt**
**1/4 teaspoon dried mint**
**some ice cubes**

Spoon the yoghurt into a glass and very gradually stir in the water to make a smooth
mixture. Stir in the salt and mint. Drop in a few ice cubes and serve.

# kaymak

Kaymak is the thick cream which can literally be cut with a knife. It is usually prepared with buffalo's milk, but can also be made with cow's milk or ewe's milk.

Although often made at home it is also often brought from *kaymakjis* – small shops specialising in dairy produce. To make your own kaymak follow one of these two simple recipes.

## With double cream

Pour 2 pints (1.2 litres) double cream into a shallow enamelled saucepan. Use as wide a pan as possible to give the cream the greatest possible surface. Bring to the boil over a low heat. Using a ladle, remove some cream and then pour it back into the pan. Do this from as high a point as possible so that bubbles are formed. Continue thus for 45-60 minutes. Turn off the heat and leave to rest for 3 hours. Place the pan in the refrigerator for 15 hours or more.

## With milk

Pour 2 pints (1.2 litres) milk into a shallow enamelled saucepan. Add 1/2 pint (300ml) double cream and stir well. Bring to the boil over a low heat and simmer for 2 hours. Turn off the heat and leave the saucepan to rest for 5 hours. Place the pan in the refrigerator for 15 hours or more.

When you remove the pan from the refrigerator a thick layer of cream will have formed. Using a sharp knife free the edges of the kaymak and then cut into strips. Using a spatula remove the strips of kaymak to a large serving plate and then cut into squares or curl into rolls.

Kaymak is beautiful on its own topped with sugar, jam or honey; or served as a topping for pastries.

The nearest substitute is thick clotted cream.

# darçinli yoghurt

## cinnamon-yoghurt sauce

A delightful sauce, eaten throughout Turkey and the Caucasus, it is traditionally served as an accompaniment to roast meats, but it is also excellent with salads and vegetable stews.

1/2 pint (300ml) yoghurt
2 teaspoons sugar
1 teaspoon cinnamon

Pour the yoghurt into a serving bowl, add the sugar and mix well. Sprinkle with cinnamon and serve.

# sughtorov madzoun

## garlic-yoghurt sauce

Perhaps the most popular of all the yoghurt sauces. It is found throughout the Middle East, always accompanying vegetable dishes and stews.

1/2 pint (300ml) yoghurt
1 clove garlic, crushed
1/4 teaspoon salt
1/2 teaspoon dried mint
1 spring onion, finely chopped (optional)

Pour the yoghurt into a bowl. Mix the garlic and salt together and add to the yoghurt. Mix well.

Sprinkle the top with dried mint and serve.

# tahiniyeh

## garlic and tahina sauce

Tahina is the cream made from sesame seeds. It is *the* Arab sauce and is used extensively in Syrian and Lebanese cuisine. As well as an excellent dip, Tahiniyeh can be used as a salad dressing.

This recipe will make a substantial quantity, but it will keep for a few days in the refrigerator, so it can be re-used.

1/4 pint (150ml) tahina paste
juice of 2 lemons
1/2 pint (300ml) milk or water
2 cloves garlic, crushed
1 tablespoon finely chopped parsley
1 teaspoon salt
1/2 teaspoon chilli pepper

Pour the tahina into a bowl and stir in the lemon juice. Slowly add the milk, stirring until you have a mixture that is thick and creamy. Add the garlic, parsley, salt and pepper.

Serve as an accompaniment to salads and vegetables.

# azadkeghi salsa

## parsley sauce

This is especially good spooned over fish and boiled vegetables.
For a sauce with an extra 'bite', substitute watercress for half the parsley.

1 large bunch flat-leaf parsley
3 tablespoons fresh lemon juice
6 tablespoons olive oil
1/2 teaspoon salt

Remove the stems and rinse the parsley. Pat the leaves dry and then chop. There should be about 3 teacupsful.

Place a third of the parsley, lemon juice and oil in a blender and mix well before continuing with the next third and then the balance.

Pour the sauce into a jar, cover and refrigerate until needed. It will keep well for at least a week.

## dukkous al-tamata

### spicy tomato sauce

A strong, spicy sauce often served with pilavs.

2 tablespoons oil
8 cloves garlic, crushed
2 lb (900g) ripe tomatoes, blanched, peeled and coarsely chopped
1 tablespoon salt
1/4 teaspoon paprika
1/4 teaspoon ground cumin
1/4 teaspoon ground coriander
1/4 teaspoon black pepper
1/4 teaspoon ground nutmeg
1/4 teaspoon turmeric
1/4 teaspoon chilli pepper

Heat the oil in a saucepan, add the garlic and fry for 2 minutes, stirring constantly. Add the tomatoes and salt, lower the heat, cover the pan and simmer for 20–30 minutes.

Add all the remaining ingredients, stir thoroughly and cook for a further 5 minutes. Serve with pilavs or plain vegetables.

# lolozig

## red pepper paste

From Cilician Armenia. A strong, spicy, hot paste often just spread on bread and
eaten, but usually used in sauces or stews or as a baste for kebabs.

Will keep for several weeks in the refrigerator.

**3 lb (1.35kg) red peppers**
**1/2 lb (225g) red, hot cherry peppers – or more or less, to taste**
**2 tablespoons salt**
**olive oil**

Wipe the peppers clean and cut each one in quarters lengthways. Remove seeds, veins
and any bruised areas.

Line a large tray with kitchen paper, or a clean teatowel, and spread the pieces out skin
side down. Place in a sunny or dry, warm area and leave to dry for at least 24 hours.

Put the pieces through a mincer or chop very finely. Spoon into a shallow ovenproof
dish, sprinkle with the salt and place in an oven preheated to 350F (180C) gas 4. Bake
for 10 minutes, stirring frequently so that the paste dries uniformly.

Remove from the oven, place over a moderate heat and continue to cook, stirring
constantly. Remove and discard any paste that sticks to the sides of the pan and
becomes discoloured. After about 20 minutes the liquid should have evaporated.
Continue cooking a little longer if it hasn't. Remove from the heat and leave to cool,
stirring occasionally.

Wash and dry 2 or 3 small jars. When cold, spoon the paste into the jars and cover the
paste in each with a thin film of olive oil.

Seal and store in a cool place, or in the refrigerator.

# nouri salsa

## pomegranate sauce

This is a fabulous sauce from Kharapak, Armenia, and is extremely popular both with Armenians and Iranians. It is made from pomegranates and sugar.
It can be bought in some Middle Eastern shops as pomegranate syrup, but I believe when home-made, it is better because the commercial syrups are too thick and too expensive. If using commercial syrup then water it down a little.

juice of 24–30 fresh pomegranates
1¼ lb (560g) sugar
2 sticks cinnamon
2 spring onions, finely chopped (optional)

You can obtain pomegranate juice by cutting the pomegranates into quarters, then squeezing with any one of a number of makes of the juice extractors that are available on the market.

Heat the pomegranate juice, add the sugar and stir regularly. Add the cinnamon sticks and cook until the mixture thickens.

Remove from the heat and discard the cinnamon sticks. Allow to cool, then bottle and keep in a cool place.

When serving as a sauce, add 1 teaspoon sumak powder, a little water to dilute the syrup and some finely chopped spring onions.

# desserts

In the glorious days of Abbassid, Baghdad poets and musicians sang the praises of desserts and sherbets. Ottoman sultans paid large sums of gold to acquire concubines fattened on rahat-lokum (Turkish delight), baklava, kunafeh and other rich, sugary sweets.

No social or religious festivity was concluded until the large copper trays of sweets were emptied. During the Muslim feast of Ramadan, bakers and confectioners do a thriving trade in special cakes, bonbons and halvas. The Resurrection of our Lord is traditionally celebrated with baklava, kunafeh and basdegh, while during the Jewish Chanukah, soofganiyah-type doughnuts are consumed in abundance. In short, Middle Easterners have a sweet tooth and hence a very rich repertoire of desserts.

The recipes in this chapter do, by and large, make use of fruits, nuts and vegetables and are all related, in one form or another, to a particular social or religious event.

# baklava

## flaky pastry filled with nuts

This is by far the most popular sweet throughout the Middle East.
It appears in one version or another from Greece to Iran. Originally it was
Armenian (Bahki-Halva means Lenten sweet).

You can purchase ready-made pastry in most Middle Eastern and Continental
stores. Ask for filo or baklava or strudel pastry.

Apart from the classic walnut filling I have included two others,
pistachio and cherry.

1 packet (1 lb/450g) filo pastry
8 oz (225g) unsalted butter, melted and with froth removed
8 oz (225g) walnuts, chopped or coarsely ground

Syrup
12 oz (350g) sugar
12 fl oz (350ml) water
1 tablespoon lemon juice
2 tablespoons rosewater

First prepare the syrup by placing the sugar, water and lemon juice in a saucepan and bringing to the boil. Lower the heat and simmer for about 10 minutes or until the syrup leaves a slightly sticky film on a spoon. Add the rosewater and set aside to cool.

Most packets of filo pastry have sheets about 21 x 11in (53 x 28cm), but it is not always easy to find a tin with these dimensions. I use one 12 x 8in (30 x 20cm) and trim the sheets to make them fit. As I am loathe to waste good food I simply slip the trimmings between the sheets in such a way as to maintain an even thickness.

The one important dimension is the depth of the tin, which should be at least 1in (2.5cm).

Grease the baking tin of your choice with a little melted butter. Lay 2 sheets of the pastry on top of each other in the tray and then dribble a tablespoon of the melted butter over the second sheet. Repeat in this way until you have 6 or 8 sheets in the tray.

While you are layering the sheets, try to press on them as little as possible. This ensures that air is trapped between the layers and so enables the sweet to rise and to cook through.

Spread half the crushed nuts over the last sheet of pastry.

Continue with the layers of pastry and spoonfuls of butter until you have laid down a further 6 or 8 sheets. Spread the remaining nuts over the last sheet.

Continue layering the pastry with spoonfuls of melted butter dribbled over alternate sheets until you have used up all the pastry. Spoon any remaining butter over the last sheet, discarding the milky residue at the bottom of the pan.

Using a pastry brush, spread the butter evenly over the last sheet so that every little bit of pastry is coated. Cut the baklava into about 25 lozenge shapes, using a sharp knife, and taking care to press down as little as possible on the actual baklava pastries as you cut.

Place the tin in an oven preheated to 350F (180C) gas 4 and cook for 30 minutes. Lower the temperature to 300F (150C) gas 2 and cook for a further hour or until the pastry is pale golden. Remove and set aside until warm, then pour the cold syrup all along the cuts. Set aside until completely cold.

To serve, first run a sharp knife along the cuts to make sure that all the layers have been completely cut through.

## bahlawah-bil-fistuk halabi

### pistachio-filled baklava

Filling
**8 oz (225g) pistachio nuts, coarsely chopped**
**3–4 tablespoons caster sugar**

Mix the filling ingredients together in a small bowl.

Prepare the baklava as described above, substituting the pistachio filling for the walnut one.

# gerasov baklava

## cherry-filled baklava

### Filling
1 lb (450g) fresh, sweet cherries
4 oz (110g) caster sugar
1 teaspoon vanilla essence

Remove and discard the cherry stones; place the flesh in a liquidiser and blend. Pour the pulp into a muslin bag and squeeze out as much juice as possible. Place the pulp in a bowl, add the sugar and vanilla and mix.

Prepare the baklava as described above, only arranging about 10 sheets of pastry, with dribbles of butter between alternating layers, in the bottom of the pan. Spread all the filling over the tenth sheet. Layer the remaining sheets and cut and cook as described above.

# kunafeh

## shredded pastry with nuts

Greeks and Turks call this sweet Kataifi or Tel-Kataif. Although highly prized by the wealthy during the glorious days of Harun-el-Rashid and the tales of the *1001 Nights*, kunafeh only became the property of the masses in the Ottoman period.

There are numerous variations. The recipe below is a standard one using pistachio nuts. As with the baklava dough, you can buy the shredded pastry from most Middle Eastern shops and Continental stores. Ask for 'kataifi filo'.

1 packet (1 lb/450g) kataifi filo
3/4 lb (350g) unsalted butter, melted and with froth removed

### Filling
6 oz (175g) pistachio nuts, chopped or coarsely ground
2 tablespoons sugar
2 teaspoons ground cinnamon

**12 oz (350g) sugar**
**12 fl oz (350ml) water**
**juice of 1 lemon**
**2 tablespoons rosewater**

First prepare the syrup by placing the sugar, water and lemon juice in a saucepan and bringing to the boil. Lower the heat and simmer until the syrup begins to leave a film on the back of a spoon.

Lightly brush a baking tin, about 12 x 9in (30 x 22.5cm) or about 10in (25cm) in diameter and at least 1in (2.5cm) deep, with a little of the melted butter.

Put the pastry into a large bowl and gently ease the strands apart without breaking them. Remove any hard nodules of pastry which you may find in some brands. Pour three-quarters of the melted butter into the bowl and gently rub all the strands between your fingers until they are all well coated with the butter.

Divide the pastry into 2 equal parts and spread one part evenly over the base of the tin. Mix the filling ingredients together and spread evenly over the pastry, pressing the filling down firmly. Arrange the remaining pastry evenly over the top, tuck in any strands hanging over the sides and press the pastry down firmly. Spoon the remaining melted butter evenly over the top, discarding the white residue in the bottom of the pan.

Place in an oven preheated to 350F (180C) gas 4 for 1 hour. Lower the heat to 300F (150C) gas 2 and cook for a further 1½ hours or until golden.

Remove from the oven and pour the syrup slowly over the kunafeh, covering as much of the surface as possible. Cover with foil, place a large board over the top and add a heavy weight in order to flatten the kunafeh.

When cold, cut into squares or lozenges 1½–2in (3.5–5cm) in size.

# galatabourego

## custard-filled pastries

When fresh, galatabourego make a magnificent dessert. A Greek-Cypriot speciality, it is traditionally served like baklava, cut into squares or lozenges, but the method below is by far the most successful and attractive for it wraps the custard in the pastry – as the name suggests. Arabs call this sweet Bahlawah Osmanli.

Serve very cold with double cream or kaymak.

1 lb (450g) packet filo pastry
2–3 tablespoons clarified butter, melted

### Filling
1¹/2 pints (900ml) milk
9 oz (250g) sugar
4 oz (110g) fine semolina or rice flour
8 oz (225g) unsalted butter, cut into small pieces
1 tablespoon grated orange rind
6 eggs, separated
pinch of salt

### Syrup
6 oz (175g) sugar
3/4 pint (450ml) water
1 tablespoon lemon juice
2 tablespoons orange blossom water

First prepare the filling. Place the milk, 6 oz (175g) of the sugar and the semolina, or rice flour, in a large saucepan and cook over a low heat, stirring constantly, until the sugar and semolina have dissolved.

Add the butter and cook over a moderate heat, stirring constantly, until the butter melts and the mixture has thickened. Stir in the grated orange rind, pour into a bowl and set aside to cool.

Place the egg yolks and the remaining 3 oz (75g) sugar in a bowl and whisk until light and creamy. Fold this mixture into the filling. Now whisk the egg whites until just stiff and fold quickly into the filling.

Open the filo pastry out on a worktop and cover with a damp cloth to keep it moist. The ready-made sheets of pastry are about 21 x 11in (53 x 28cm). Take about 7 sheets and cut them crossways so that there are 14 sheets about 11 x 10¹/2in (28 x 26cm). Fold up the remaining sheets and refrigerate for later use. Stack the cut sheets on top of each other and cover with a damp cloth.

Remove one sheet, place on a worktop and place 2 tablespoons of the filling in a ridge about 2¹/₂in (6cm) from one edge and 2¹/₂in (6cm) in from each end. The filling should be about 5in (12.5cm) long, 1in (2.5cm) wide and ¹/₂in (1cm) thick. Fold and roll as shown.

Make sure that you roll the pastry up loosely so that there will be room for the filling to expand when cooking.

Brush 2 large baking trays with a little of the melted butter and place the rolls on them about 1–1¹/₂in (2.5–3.5cm) apart and with the loose end underneath. Brush the pastries all over with the melted butter and place them in an oven preheated to 350F (180C) gas 4. Bake for 30–40 minutes, or until the custard filling has puffed up and the pastry is a light golden. Remove from the oven and set aside.

Make the syrup by placing the sugar, water and lemon juice in a small pan and boiling for 5 minutes. Remove from the heat, stir in the orange blossom water and pour all over the galatabourego. Set aside until cold and then serve. **Makes 14.**

## galatabourego

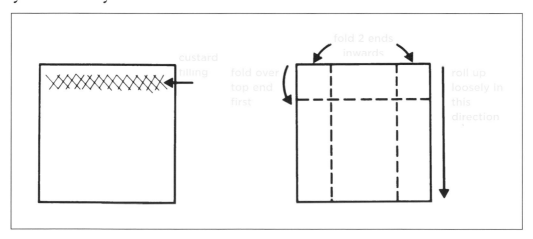

# basdegh

## fruit pastes

'Basdegh' is derived from the Armenian word *basdar* – fine linen, because a thin basdegh syrup is spread over a fine cloth and then dried. Traditionally it was prepared from pure grape juice or from apricot juice – Amardin.

The Greeks make a fine paste from quinces called Kythonopasto and indeed there is no reason why the juice of other fruits, such as peaches, apples, pears and so on, cannot be used. Here are recipes for the basic basdegh and some variations. But for the basic basdegh you need to track down some mahaleb – a Cilician spice made from the kernel of the black cherry stone. It has a sweet, spicy flavour – and can be found in good Armenian or Arab shops.

## basic basdegh

5 oz (140g) plain flour, sifted
4 oz (110g) cornflour
1 pint (600ml) cold water
4 quarts (4.5 litres) grape juice (see method)
8 fl oz (250ml) honey or corn syrup
1³/4 lb (800g) sugar
2 teaspoons ground mahaleb
2 tablespoons water

First prepare the grape juice by removing the stems from 6 lb (2.75kg) grapes. Place the grapes in a large saucepan with 4 pints (2.4 litres) water. Bring to the boil, then simmer for 15 minutes. Pass through a colander, pushing through as much of the pulp as possible. Discard what remains in the colander and place the pulp and juice in a cloth bag or jelly bag and leave it suspended over a large bowl, preferably overnight, until the last drop of moisture has been extracted.

Measure the juice you have collected and make it up to 4 quarts (4.5 litres) with water if necessary.

Mix the flour and cornflour together in a large saucepan, then very gradually stir in the cold water and mix until the mixture is smooth.

In another large pan, bring the grape juice and honey gently to the boil. Spoon a little of the grape juice mixture into the flour mixture and stir thoroughly. Repeat this several times until the mixture is diluted, then slowly pour in the remaining grape juice, stirring constantly. Bring to the boil.

Soak the mahaleb in the 2 tablespoons water for about 5 minutes, then strain the liquid into the basdegh.

When it returns to the boil it is ready to be dried. The mixture should be about as thick as double cream. If you think it is a little too thin, then mix 2–3 tablespoons of cornflour with a few tablespoons of the hot basdegh to form a smooth paste. Add a little more basdegh to thin out the paste and then stir back into the basdegh and simmer for a few minutes.

# khagoghi basdegh

## dried thin paste

Cut a fine cotton cloth into a rectangle about 30 x 50in (75 x 125cm) and spread it out on a large table. Pour the hot basdegh slowly over the cloth, spreading it out to an even layer about 1/8in (3mm) thick. Use the back of a wooden spoon. Leave it to dry. This will probably take about 2 days in summer and 4 days in winter.

When dry, turn the basdegh over and peel off the cloth. To facilitate this, soak a cloth in cold water, then rub it over the basdegh cloth until it is thoroughly wet. Now leave it for a few minutes and then try lifting a corner of the cloth. If it comes away easily, peel it off completely.

Sprinkle a little cornflour through a sieve evenly over the damp surface of the basdegh to remove any moisture. Cut the sheet of basdegh into rectangles 5 x 6in (12.5 x 15cm) and fold each one in half, floured side inside. Spread over the table and leave for 2–3 hours.

Wrap the dried pieces carefully in waxed paper and store in airtight containers.

Serve by itself, or in soups or omelettes.

# soofganiyah

## fruit doughnuts

A relatively new, but already highly popular, Israeli dessert which has replaced the Western-originated Latkes of the Chanukah (Festival of Lights) table.

The doughnuts are filled with dates, prunes or jam. They are an ideal tea-time accompaniment.

1 lb (450g) plain flour
1/2 teaspoon baking powder
1/2 teaspoon salt
1/4 teaspoon nutmeg
1/4 teaspoon cinnamon
4 oz (110g) sugar
1 egg, beaten
2–3 tablespoons oil
1/4 pint (150ml) milk
15–20 stoned dates or soaked and stoned prunes or jam of your choice
oil for deep-frying

Garnish

caster sugar

Sift the flour twice with the baking powder, salt, nutmeg and cinnamon into a large bowl. Stir in the sugar, beaten egg and oil. Begin to knead and add sufficient milk to form a soft dough. Knead until smooth and pliable, then form into walnut-sized balls.

With your finger make a depression in each ball and tuck in a date or prune or a teaspoon of jam and then close the opening and re-form the ball.

Heat enough oil in a large saucepan to deep-fry the doughnuts.

When the oil is hot, drop 2 or 3 doughnuts into it and cook over a moderate heat for about 4–5 minutes until golden all over and cooked through. Remove with a slotted spoon and drain on kitchen paper while the remaining doughnuts are being cooked.

Arrange on a serving dish and sprinkle generously with sugar. **Makes 15–20 doughnuts.**

# toot shirini

## mulberry-shaped sweets

Here is a sweet for children which is made from almonds, pistachios and sugar.
Eat them while fresh as they do not keep for long.
To give extra flavour and aroma, Iranian housewives often add a piece of vanilla
pod to the jar in which they are kept.

A most decorative and tasty sweet.

6 oz (175g) ground almonds
4 oz (110g) icing sugar, sifted
4 tablespoons rosewater
1 tablespoon vanilla essence
6 oz (175g) caster sugar
about 30 slivers of pistachio

Mix the almonds and icing sugar together in a bowl. Add the rosewater and vanilla essence and knead until the mixture holds together. Form into small, marble-sized balls (makes about 30).

Take one ball and roll between your palms to lengthen it a little to give a mulberry shape. Repeat with all the remaining balls.

Spread the sugar out on a plate and roll each 'mulberry' in it until well coated. Stick a sliver of pistachio in the end of each (this is the stem), and store in an airtight container.

# sohan asali

*'Honey or other sweets relieve faintness due to fasting.'*
Yoma 83b

Another Iranian sweet made of almonds, pistachios and honey which is very
popular with children. The most famous version comes from Qum,
which has acquired in recent years great prominence, for it is from there that the
famed Ayatollahs pontificate.

**2 oz (50g) clarified butter**
**2 tablespoons honey**
**6 oz (175g) sugar**
**6 oz (175g) slivered almonds**
**1 teaspoon powdered saffron dissolved in 2 tablespoons boiling water**

Garnish
**about 2 tablespoons halved pistachios**

Melt the butter in a large saucepan, add the honey and sugar and stir until the sugar
dissolves.

Add the almonds and cook, stirring occasionally, until the almonds turn golden brown.
Add the saffron mixture to the saucepan and stir well. Remove from the heat and allow
to cool for 5 minutes.

Thoroughly grease a shallow dish about 6in (15cm) square. Pour the mixture into the
dish and spread evenly. Arrange halved pistachio nuts at 1in (2.5cm) intervals over the
surface and set aside until cold.

Cut into 1¹/2in (3.5cm) squares with a sharp knife and store in an airtight tin.

# charoseth

## fruit and nut paste

*'Under baby's cradle
Stands a golden kid.
The kid went off to trade
With raisins and almonds
Raisins and figs
Baby will sleep, hush.'*

Jewish Folk Song

There are many variations of this symbolic Jewish sweet which is always included in the Seder – the meal served on Passover Eve.

Charoseth recalls the mortar with which the Jews were forced to make bricks when they built the cities of Pithom and Rames for the Egyptians.
Basically the sweets are a mixture of cinnamon, apples or pears and walnuts or pine kernels. The exact proportions vary from family to family.

2 oz (50g) pine kernels
1 hard-boiled egg yolk
1 apple, peeled, cored and grated
4 oz (110g) ground almonds
4 oz (110g) brown sugar
1 tablespoon grated lemon rind
1 teaspoon ground cinnamon
1 teaspoon ground mixed spice
3 tablespoons lemon juice
4 oz (110g) seedless raisins
2 oz (50g) medium matzo meal

Put all the ingredients into a large mixing bowl and mash them to a paste with a fork. Press the mixture evenly into a shallow baking tin. Mark the surface with a sharp knife, dividing it into an even number of pieces.

Place in the refrigerator and chill for at least 30 minutes before cutting it into squares and serving. **This recipe makes about 20–25 sweets.**

# hatsi-anoush

## bread pudding with fruits

*'Bread won by fraud tastes sweet to a man,*
*But afterwards his mouth will be filled with gravel.'*

Jewish Wisdom

A popular Anatolian sweet of bread and fruits; although often for the sake of economy the villagers use their stale bread for the basis of this sweet, it should really be prepared with a special dough called Kalip Ekmegi. For those of you who have an adventurous spirit – and the time – I have included the recipe for the dough. Otherwise use stale bread.

I have given two versions of this simple sweet, one Turkish, the other Armenian – to show my impartiality! As well as these, other fruits can be used, such as quinces (favoured by the Caucasians), strawberries, pears and apples.

# kalip ekmeği

## basic dough

1/2 oz (15g) fresh yeast
7 fl oz (210ml) milk
1 lb (450g) plain flour
1 teaspoon salt
2 oz (50g) icing sugar
2 oz (50g) unsalted butter
3 egg yolks

In a cup, dissolve the yeast in a few tablespoons of the milk, warmed. Set aside for about 10 minutes or until the mixture begins to froth.

Sift the flour, salt and icing sugar into a large bowl. Add the butter and rub it in until the mixture resembles fine breadcrumbs. Make a well in the centre and add the yeast mixture and egg yolks and mix with a wooden spoon. Add the milk little by little and, after mixing thoroughly, knead for about 10–15 minutes until the dough is smooth and elastic. Cover with a cloth and leave in a warm place for 30 minutes.

Lightly sprinkle a worktop with flour and divide the dough into 2 equal portions. Take one ball and roll it out to a thickness of 1/4in (1/2cm). Cut into rounds with a 3in (7.5cm) pastry cutter. Gather up the scraps, roll them out again and cut more rounds.

Repeat with the other ball of dough.

Place on greased baking sheets and bake in an oven preheated to 250F (120C) gas 1/2 for thirty minutes.

Remove and leave for 4–5 hours. These rounds are now ready to be used in a bread pudding. The ones you do not need can be stored in an airtight tin.

## visneli ekmek tatlisi

### bread pudding with cherries

This is the most popular bread pudding of Turkey. You can use canned cherries, but if they are sweetened, omit the sugar.

**8 portions of kalip ekmegi or 8 thin slices stale white bread**
**3 oz (75g) unsalted butter**
**1 lb (450g) Morello cherries, stoned or any other kind in season or canned cherries**
**8 oz (225g) icing sugar**
**8 fl oz (250ml) water**

Trim off the bread crusts and spread the slices generously with the butter. Arrange in a large shallow ovenproof dish and bake in an oven preheated to 350F (180C) gas 4 until lightly golden.

Meanwhile, place the cherries, icing sugar and water in a saucepan, mix well and bring to the boil. Boil vigorously for 2 minutes, then lower the heat and simmer for about 10 minutes or until the syrup becomes sticky and coats the back of a spoon.

Remove the bread from the oven, pour the cherries and syrup over the bread and bake until most of the syrup has been absorbed.

Remove from the oven and serve with kaymak or whipped double cream.

# dzirani hatsi-anoush

## apricot bread pudding

This is an Armenian favourite.

8 portions of kalip ekmegi or 8 thin slices stale white bread
3 oz (75g) unsalted butter
8 oz (225g) icing sugar
8 fl oz (250ml) water
2 lb (900g) firm apricots, halved and with stones removed

Trim off the bread crusts and spread the slices generously with the butter. Arrange in a large shallow ovenproof dish and bake in an oven preheated to 350F (180C) gas 4 until lightly golden.

Meanwhile, place the icing sugar and water in a saucepan and bring to the boil. Add the halved apricots and simmer, stirring occasionally, until the apricots are just tender and the syrup has thickened and will coat the back of a spoon.

Remove the bread from the oven, pour the apricots and syrup evenly over it and then bake until most of the syrup has been absorbed. Remove from the oven and serve with kaymak or whipped double cream.

# tamrieh

## date-filled sweets

Dates – the fruit of the desert folk – are understandably made much of in soups, main dishes, sauces, desserts and drinks. The love of the palm and its fruit are well expressed in the lines of the Palestinian poet Mahmoud Darwish who sings of his homeland:

*'Suspend me on the tresses of a date palm,*
*Hang me I shall not betray the palm.*
*This land is mine and long ago,*
*In good mood and in bad, I'd milk the camels . . .'*

There are many date-filled pastries and cakes in the region. The Iraqi Klaicha uses a filling of dates only. The Kurds of Iraq, as well as the people of the Gulf region, stone fresh dates and serve them in individual bowls with plain yoghurt or gibna – cheese. The Iranian Kalampeh is similar to Armavov Katah (see page 268), but contains 1/4 teaspoon ground cardamom, 1/4 teaspoon ground nutmeg and 1/4 teaspoon ground cloves in the filling.

# elmali kak

## apple cake

This is a particular favourite of the Kurds of the Dierbekir region in Turkey who grow some of the most beautiful and delicious apples known. It is a simple peasant recipe and, perhaps because of this, it is very tasty. Serve warm or cold. I prefer it warm.

8 oz (225g) clarified butter or margarine
6 oz (175g) sugar
1 egg
10 oz (275g) plain flour
1 tablespoon baking powder

Filling
6 average-sized cooking apples, peeled, cored and sliced
1 teaspoon cinnamon
4 tablespoons icing sugar

To serve
kaymak, clotted cream or whipped cream

Place the butter and sugar in a large bowl and beat until light and fluffy. Beat in the egg.

Sift the flour and baking powder together and fold into the butter mixture. Mix thoroughly to form a soft, smooth dough, then divide the dough into 2 equal parts.

Lightly flour a worktop and roll each part out into an oblong 12 x 8in (30 x 20cm) or a circle 9in (22.5cm) in diameter.

Lightly grease a baking dish 12 x 8in (30 x 20cm) or 9in (22.5cm) in diameter. Lay one sheet of dough in it and press down gently. Arrange the apple slices over the dough and sprinkle them with the cinnamon and icing sugar. Cover the apples with the other sheet of dough and press down gently.

Bake the cake in the centre of an oven preheated to 350F (180C) gas 4 for 30–40 minutes or until the cake is golden.

Remove from the oven and serve hot or cold. Serve with kaymak or cream.

# armavov katah

## date and walnut cakes

An Armenian speciality, these date rolls will enhance any tea or coffee-time.
They keep well if stored in an airtight tin when cold.

### Filling
2 oz (50g) butter
8 oz (225g) stoned dates, finely chopped
4 tablespoons milk
4 oz (110g) chopped walnuts
2 tablespoons rosewater
1$\frac{1}{2}$–2 teaspoons cinnamon

### Dough
8 oz (225g) butter
2 oz (50g) sugar
2 eggs, beaten
4 fl oz (120ml) milk
$\frac{1}{2}$ teaspoon vanilla essence
12 oz (350g) plain flour
2 teaspoons baking powder

### Glaze
1 egg, beaten

Melt the butter in a small saucepan, add the dates and cook gently. Add the milk and continue cooking until the dates form a soft pulp. Remove from the heat and stir in the walnuts, rosewater and cinnamon. Set aside.

To make the pastry, mix the butter and sugar together in a large bowl. Add the eggs, then gradually stir in the milk and vanilla.

Sift the flour and baking powder together and then add a little at a time to the butter mixture, beating continuously until it is all blended and a soft dough is formed. If the dough is still a little sticky, knead in a little more flour. Divide the mixture into 2 balls.

When the filling is cool, divide it into 6 and roll each out into a sausage.

Flour a work surface and roll out one ball of dough into a circle about 1/8in (3mm) thick. Place 1 date sausage on the pastry near the edge of the circle closest to you (a).

Roll the pastry over twice and then cut this away from the remaining pastry so that you have a pastry sausage filled with the walnuts and dates (b).

Place another date roll along the cut edge (c) and roll up to form another sausage (d).

Cut the roll from the remaining pastry and then place another date sausage along the cut edge (d) and roll up to form another sausage.

Repeat with the remaining ball of pastry and date rolls. Slice each sausage into 1–1½in (2.5–3.5cm) pieces. Place the pieces on a greased baking sheet about 1–1½in (2.5–3.5cm) apart. Brush each with a little beaten egg, and bake in an oven preheated to 350F (180C) gas 4 for about 20–30 minutes or until golden.

Remove to a wire rack and leave to cool.

## armavov katah

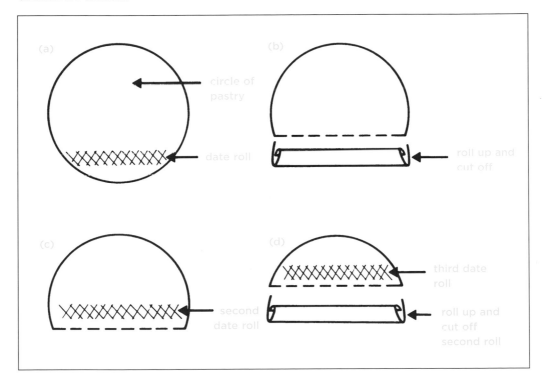

# datile

## date and almond pudding

A sweet with a history: in this case the history of oriental Jews who emigrated (to use a polite expression, but in reality escaped the vicious Spanish Inquisition) to the Ottoman Empire in the 15th and 16th centuries and brought with them most of their customs and cuisine. Datile is one of the dishes they brought and it is popular during Passover.

Serve cold, cut into slices and accompanied by a fruit sauce. It is also excellent served with tea or coffee.

4 oz (110g) sugar
3 oz (75g) medium matzo meal
3 eggs
1/4 teaspoon salt
2 oz (50g) coarsely ground almonds
4 oz (110g) dates, stoned and chopped

Mix the sugar and matzo meal together in a large bowl. Separate the eggs and add the yolks to the matzo mixture. Whisk the egg whites with the salt until stiff and fold into the mixture. Little by little, fold in the almonds and dates and mix well, but gently. Pour the mixture into a well-greased ovenproof dish about 7–8in (17.5–20cm) in diameter.

Place the dish in a large roasting tin or something similar, pour boiling water into the larger pan and place in an oven preheated to 350F (180C) gas 4.

Bake for 45–50 minutes, then remove and leave to cool.

# tahinopita

## tahina cake

This Greek cake includes tahina, orange juice, sultanas and nuts.
It is traditionally made during the forty days of Lent.

7 fl oz (210ml) tahina paste
7 oz (200g) sugar
grated rind of 1 orange
1/4 pint (150ml) strained orange juice
12 oz (350g) plain flour
1/4 teaspoon salt
3 teaspoons baking powder
1/2 teaspoon bicarbonate of soda
1 teaspoon mixed spice
3 oz (75g) finely chopped walnuts, or almonds or hazelnuts
3 oz (75g) sultanas

Place the tahina, sugar and orange rind in a large bowl and whisk until well blended. Add the orange juice and whisk thoroughly for 2–3 minutes.

Sift the flour, salt, baking powder, bicarbonate of soda and mixed spice into the bowl and fold thoroughly into the tahina mixture. Add the nuts and sultanas and mix well.

Grease a 12 x 8in (30 x 20cm) tin and spread the cake mixture evenly into it, smoothing off the top with the back of a spoon.

Bake in an oven preheated to 350F (180C) gas 4 for 40–45 minutes.

Remove, turn on to a cake rack and let it cool for 5 minutes before removing the tin. When cold cut into 1–1¹/₂in (2.5–3.5cm) squares and store in an airtight tin.

# yogurtlu çicolata kek

## yoghurt chocolate cake

This is a popular cake in Istanbul where it is often served in shops and restaurants. It is an extremely moist cake and should be eaten within 2–3 days.

❧

4 oz (110g) unsalted butter
10 oz (275g) caster sugar
2 eggs
5 oz (140g) plain chocolate
1/4 pint (150ml) natural yoghurt
2 teaspoons baking powder
1 teaspoon vanilla essence
1/2 teaspoon nutmeg
8 oz (225g) plain flour, sifted

Place the butter and sugar in a large mixing bowl and beat until soft and smooth. Add the eggs and beat into the mixture until well blended.

Place the chocolate in a heatproof bowl over a pan of simmering water and leave until just melted. Leave to cool for a few minutes and then stir into the cake mixture.

Now stir in the yoghurt, baking powder, vanilla and nutmeg. Stir in the sifted flour, a little at a time, until the mixture is smooth.

Grease and flour a cake tin about 8 1/2 in (21cm) in diameter and pour in the cake mixture. Smooth over the top and bake in an oven preheated to 350F (180C) gas 4 for 40–45 minutes or until cooked.

Remove the tin from the oven and leave to cool for 10 minutes before turning out on to a cake rack.

This cake can either be served as it is, or else slice it through horizontally, spread with cherry or apricot jam and sandwich together. If you wish, you can also serve it with cream.

# halawah min cous-cous

## cous-cous rice with sugar

An Egyptian recipe which is also very popular in Libya and, of course, throughout North Africa.

Cous-cous is a fine semolina made from wheat and although some families may still prepare their own, it is normally bought ready-made and is available here from most Continental and health food shops. The correct way to cook cous-cous is in what in France (where there are numerous North African cous-cous restaurants) is called a *couscousier*. It is a *keskes* in Arabic. However, it is possible to improvise with a steamer or a metal strainer or sieve, lined with muslin, which fits tightly over a saucepan.

This is a very simple recipe which is tasty, colourful and particularly popular with children – a definite improvement on the semolina puddings of my school days.

10 oz (275g) cous-cous
2 tablespoons rosewater
3 oz (75g) unsalted butter or ghee, melted and with froth removed
6 tablespoons icing sugar, sieved
6 tablespoons slivered almonds, toasted under the grill for 1–2 minutes until golden
6 teaspoons sultanas or raisins

Garnish
seeds of 1 small pomegranate

Spread the cous-cous over a tray or baking sheet. Pour over about 1/2 pint (300ml) warm water; work the cous-cous lightly between your fingers so that each grain is separated and moistened. Drain off excess water and set the cous-cous aside for 15 minutes for the grains to swell.

Place about 2–3 pints (1.2–1.8 litres) boiling water in the bottom of the *couscousier* or steamer or saucepan. Transfer the cous-cous to the top of the *couscousier*, or the sieve lined with muslin and then add the cous-cous. Make sure that the bottom of the steamer or sieve does not touch the water or the cous-cous will turn lumpy.

Steam for 15 minutes, then turn the cous-cous into a bowl. Stir with a fork to break up any lumps. Sprinkle with the rosewater, stir with the fork again and return to the top of the *couscousier* as before, and steam for a further 20–25 minutes.

Turn the cous-cous into a bowl and fluff up with a fork. Add the butter and stir until each grain is coated. Spoon into 6 dishes and sprinkle each with a tablespoon of the icing sugar and almonds. Top with a few sultanas or raisins and then some colourful pomegranate seeds.

# shol-e zard

## saffron pudding

A traditional Iranian pudding that is prepared for the annual observance of the martyrdom of Imam Hussein (Arba'een). On this festive day, Shol-E Zard is presented to family, friends, the poor and the orphans. Note that although traditionally made with water, you may prefer to use milk instead.

6 oz (175g) round-grain rice, washed thoroughly under cold water and drained
1 pint (600ml) water
12 oz (350g) sugar
1 teaspoon powdered saffron dissolved in 2 tablespoons hot water
1 oz (25g) butter
2 tablespoons rosewater

Garnish
1 teaspoon ground cinnamon
2 tablespoons slivered, blanched almonds
1 tablespoon chopped pistachio nuts

Place the rice and water in a saucepan and bring quickly to the boil. Lower the heat and simmer for about 20 minutes or until the rice is very tender. Add the sugar, dissolved saffron, butter and rosewater and stir constantly until the sugar has dissolved.

Continue to cook until the mixture is fairly thick, stirring from time to time. Pour the mixture into a greased baking dish and place in an oven preheated to 325F (170C) gas 3.

Bake for 30 minutes, remove and allow to cool a little.

Spoon into individual glass dishes, dust with the cinnamon and decorate with the almonds and pistachio nuts. Refrigerate until ready to serve.

# anoush gorgodabour

## christmas pudding

*'Eat a lot of anoushabour so that your child will have enough sweet milk.'*
My Grandmother's Saying

Anoush Gorgodabour, also known as Anoushabour, is a traditional Armenian Christmas pudding. Like most Middle Eastern desserts, it is a little on the sweet side, but of exquisite flavour. The skinless whole-grain wheat can be bought from most Middle Eastern shops, but you can substitute pearl barley.

3 oz (75g) skinless whole-grain wheat or pearl barley
3 pints (1.8 litres) water
4 oz (110g) raisins, soaked overnight
4 oz (110g) dried apricots, soaked overnight and quartered
6 oz (175g) sugar
1in (2.5cm) cinnamon stick
1 tablespoon rosewater

Garnish
blanched walnuts and almonds
ground cinnamon

Wash the wheat grains or pearl barley and drain. Place in a large saucepan with the water, bring to the boil and cook for about 10 minutes. Remove from the heat and set aside for 3–5 hours in a warm place.

Return the pan to a low heat for 1½ hours, stirring occasionally. Stir in the raisins, apricots, sugar and cinnamon stick and simmer for a further 30 minutes. Remove from the heat, discard the cinnamon stick and stir in the rosewater.

Pour into individual dishes or a large bowl and decorate with the walnuts and almonds and dust lightly with the cinnamon. Serve chilled.

# dessert-e miveh

## fresh fruit dessert

This is a popular fruit salad from Tehran, Iran, where large bowls of mixed fruits
piled with cream are served at banquets and in expensive restaurants.
It is very decorative and will make a fine finish to a meal.

1 large honeydew melon
8 strawberries, halved
8 Morello-type cherries, stoned
2 large, ripe apricots, sliced
1 tangerine, peeled and segmented
8 grapes, halved and seeded
6 tablespoons icing sugar
2 teaspoons orange blossom water
1/2 pint (300ml) double or whipping cream

### Garnish
1 small pomegranate, peeled and seeded
2 tablespoons finely chopped pistachio nuts

Cut the melon in half and scoop out and discard the seeds. Using a small scoop, cut
out as many balls of flesh as possible. Place in a large glass serving bowl and add the
remaining prepared fruits.

Sprinkle over half the icing sugar and the orange blossom water and toss gently.
Refrigerate for 3–4 hours.

Just before serving, pour the cream into a bowl and whisk until stiff. Fold in the
remaining icing sugar.

When ready to serve, pile half the cream over the fruit and serve the rest in a separate
bowl. Sprinkle the cream and fruit with the pomegranate seeds and chopped pistachio
nuts.

# moz bi laban

## banana yoghurt

'Heavy bars of gold, or swaying
or slow ripened in our presses,
Flasks of scent with window praying,
Windows dreaming of caresses.'

1001 Nights

A charmingly simple dessert from Lebanon and Palestine.

**1 pint (600ml) yoghurt**
**4 large, ripe bananas**
**sugar to taste**

Garnish
**1 teaspoon cinnamon**

Pour the yoghurt into a bowl and beat until creamy. Slice the bananas thinly and stir very gently into the yoghurt. Stir in a little sugar at a time until it suits your taste. Pour the sweet into a large serving bowl or into individual dishes, dust lightly with the cinnamon and serve.

# seghi baghbaghag

## melon ice cream

An Armenian recipe for 8–10 people that is simply delicious and is easy to prepare.

1 large, ripe melon, e.g. ogen or honeydew
5 oz (140g) caster sugar
4 egg yolks
2 tablespoons lemon juice
2 tablespoons orange blossom water
1 tablespoon rosewater
3/4 pint (450ml) double cream

Garnish
2 tablespoons finely chopped pistachio nuts

Cut the melon in half and remove and discard the seeds. Remove the flesh and cut into 1in (2.5cm) pieces. Place the flesh in a saucepan, add the sugar and cook over a low heat, stirring constantly until the sugar dissolves and the mixture is reduced to a pulp.

Beat the egg yolks until light and creamy, then add them to the saucepan and cook for 2–3 minutes over a very low heat, stirring constantly until the mixture thickens. Do not let the eggs curdle. Pour the mixture into a bowl and leave to cool.

Stir in the lemon juice, orange blossom water and rosewater. Whisk the cream until stiff and fold into the mixture. Chill for 1 hour, then transfer to 1 or 2 freezing trays and freeze for 1–2 hours.

Remove from the freezer, transfer to a large bowl and beat lightly with a fork. Return to the freezer trays and freeze.

Repeat this procedure once more, then freeze until needed. Serve sprinkled with chopped pistachio nuts.

# dondurma bil-moz

## banana ice cream

A Lebanese speciality which is absolutely delightful.

1 teaspoon sahleb or 1<sup>1</sup>/2 tablespoons cornflour
1 pint (600ml) milk
3 fairly ripe bananas, peeled and thinly sliced
1/2 pint (300ml) single cream
5 oz (140g) sugar
1 tablespoon orange blossom water
1/2 teaspoon yellow food colouring (optional)
3 tablespoons coarsely chopped pistachio nuts
2 tablespoons sultanas

Dissolve the sahleb or cornflour in a little of the milk and set aside. Reduce the banana slices to a pulp in a blender or mash with a fork.

Put the rest of the milk in a saucepan with the cream and sugar and bring to the boil, stirring constantly until the sugar dissolves. Stir a few tablespoons into the sahleb or cornflour mixture and then stir into the saucepan. Add the banana pulp and remaining ingredients, stir well and simmer until the mixture thickens slightly.

Remove from the heat, beat thoroughly and pour the mixture into freezing trays. Set aside and, when cool, place in a freezer for 1–2 hours.

Remove the trays, scoop the mixture into a large bowl and beat for 1 minute with a fork. Return to the trays and re-freeze.

Repeat this process once more.

Thirty minutes before serving remove from the freezer to the fridge. **Serves 8–10.**

# serferjel

## quince spread with honey

*'She is slim, tender and of a delicate taste.*
*She is as straight as a lance but has*
*not a lance's sharpness.*
*Her sweetness is useful on an evening of Ramadan.*
*What is it?'*
*–sugar cane.*

Arab Wisdom

An Egyptian recipe also popular throughout North Africa, where quinces are regarded as having almost magical qualities. This makes a delightful spread for bread or biscuits.

If quinces are not available, use cooking apples or firm, green pears.

2 lb (900g) quinces, quartered – do not peel or core
6 tablespoons honey – or more depending on taste
1 teaspoon cinnamon
1/4 teaspoon ground nutmeg
2 tablespoons ground almonds
1 teaspoon oil

Garnish
1 tablespoon finely chopped walnuts or pistachio nuts

Half-fill a large saucepan with water and bring to the boil. Drop in the quartered quinces and simmer for 5–10 minutes, or until the fruit is just tender. Remove with a slotted spoon and leave to cool and drain a little.

Push the fruit through a sieve, collecting the pulp in a bowl. Add the remaining ingredients and mix well. Taste and add more honey if necessary. Transfer to a shallow serving dish and sprinkle with the chopped nuts. This spread will keep for 1–2 weeks if covered and refrigerated.

# vartanoush

## rose petal jam

The greatest jam in the world!
Most exquisite and fragrant – and one of the great delicacies of the East.
I have tried to prepare this jam with petals from my garden, but there is little
fragrance and I have therefore added rosewater for extra fragrance.

**1 lb (450g) fresh rose petals, red and with as strong a fragrance as possible**
**juice of 2 large lemons**
**1 pint (600ml) water**
**1 lb (450g) sugar**
**3–4 tablespoons rosewater, depending on the strength**

Rinse the petals and drain well. Put them in a large glass bowl, pour half the lemon juice over them and leave for 10 minutes.

You can cook the petals whole, but because they might be tough I suggest you pass them through a mincer. (My mother used to knead them by hand but this took her ages.)

Put the petals into a large saucepan, with any juices left in the bowl. Add the water, bring to the boil and then lower the heat and simmer until the petals are tender. This may take anything from 10 minutes to 1 hour depending on the petals.

Add the sugar and remaining lemon juice and bring to the boil, stirring constantly until the sugar dissolves. Simmer, stirring frequently, until the syrup thickens – about 10 minutes. Remove from the heat and stir in the rosewater. Leave to stand for a few minutes and then skim off any scum on the surface.

After about 15 minutes pour into warm, sterilised jars. Seal when cold.

# loligi mourapa

## green tomato preserve

A classic preserve from Armenia. Use small green tomatoes
no more than 1in (2.5cm) in diameter.

2 lb (900g) small, green, unblemished tomatoes, washed and drained
2¹/2 lb (1.2kg) sugar
³/4 pint (450ml) water
1 tablespoon lemon juice
5 cloves
2in (5cm) stick of cinnamon
seeds from 3 cardamom pods

Bring some water to the boil in a large saucepan. Drop in the tomatoes and simmer for 10 minutes. Drain them and leave to cool.

Meanwhile, prepare the syrup by placing the sugar, water and lemon juice in a large saucepan and bringing to the boil, stirring constantly until the sugar dissolves. Drop the cooled tomatoes into the syrup, remove from the heat and set aside for 2 hours.

Place the cloves, cinnamon and cardamom seeds in a small muslin bag, tie tightly and hang by a piece of string into the syrup. Return the saucepan to the heat and simmer very gently for 30 minutes. Remove from the heat and set aside for a further 2 hours.

Repeat this process once more.

After the 6 hours, return the pan to the heat and cook over a low heat until the syrup is thick. Remove from the heat and set aside until cool. Discard the spice bag. Carefully drop the tomatoes into sterilised jars with a slotted spoon. Pour the syrup over the tomatoes until the jars are filled to the top. Seal tightly and store in a cool place.

# fig jam

*'Figs white, oh black, oh welcome to my plate,*
*White girls of Greece, hot Ethiopian girls*
*Though pampered feeders not appreciate,*
*So sure of my desire, experienced figs . . .'*

1001 Nights

**2 lb (900g) fresh green figs, unpeeled, washed and with stems trimmed**
**1¹/2 lb (675g) sugar**
**3/4 pint (450ml) water**
**juice of ¹/2 lemon**
**thinly peeled rind of 1 lemon**
**1 teaspoon vanilla essence**

Place the figs in a large saucepan and cover with boiling water. Simmer for 15 minutes, drain and rinse with hot water. Return the figs to the pan and cover again with boiling water. Repeat this boiling and draining process 4 times.

The fourth time, cook the figs until tender. Drain, rinse under cold water and spread them out to dry on kitchen paper.

Meanwhile, prepare the syrup by placing the sugar and water in a saucepan and bringing to the boil. Add the lemon juice and rind and simmer for 10 minutes, stirring until the sugar dissolves. Add the figs and simmer for a further 10 minutes. Remove from the heat, cover the pan and set aside for 18–24 hours.

Bring them slowly back to the boil, check the syrup and if it clings thickly to the back of a spoon, the preserve is ready.

Remove from the heat, stir in the vanilla and set aside to cool. Spoon into warm, sterilised jars and seal when completely cold.

# index

Ab Dough Khiar, 30
Ab-Goosht-e-Sib, 34
Adas Pollo, 27
Aginares Oma, 53
Almond(s),
    and Date (Pudding),
    270
    with Pilav, 125-6
    Soup, 15
    Sweets, 262
Anoush Gorgodabour,
    275
Appetisers (Mezzeh),
    35-60:
Apple(s):
    Cake, 267
    and Cherry Soup, 34
Apricot(s):
    Bread Pudding, 266
    Dried Apricot Pickle,
    238
    with Okra, 192
    with Pumpkins and
    Rice, 191
Armavov Katah, 268
Armenian Borsch, 24
Armyanski Borsch, 24
Artichokes:
    Pickled, 225
    Raw, 53
    Stuffed, 140
Ashe Lubi Kharmez-Ba-
    Esfanaj, 21
Aubergine(s),
    and Avocado Dip, 46
    Borek Filling, 198
    with Cheese, 57
    in Olive Oil, 161
    Purée with Tahina, 41
    with Scrambled Eggs
    and Tomatoes, 92
    Stews, 180
    Stuffed Pickled, 231
Avocado(s),
    and Aubergine Dip,
    46
    with Walnuts, 65
    in Wine, 60
    Wine and Mushroom
    Pilav, 122
Avocado Im Egozim, 65
Avocado In Yin, 60
Ayran, 243
Azadkeghi Salsa, 246
Badem Çorbasi, 15
Bahlawah-Bil-Fistuck
    Halabi, 253
Baki Kufta, 176
    Miss Hatz, 200
    Sini Kufte, 172
Baklali Havuçi, 187
    Ve Tereotu Pilavi, 119
Baklava, 252

Cherry-filled, 254
    Pistachio-filled, 253
Bami Titvash, 230
Bamia-Bil-Beid, 93
Bamyi-Bil-Zayt, 157
Banana
    Ice Cream, 279
    Yoghurt, 277
Banirov
    Arsha, 166
    Borek, 205
    Pilav, 113
    Tzvazegh, 104
Barbunya Fasulya Yagli,
    164
Barley and Yoghurt
    Soup, 18
Basdegh, 258
    Khagoghi, 259
Batata-Bil-Tahina, 190
Batatat Charp, 154
Bean(s):
    Black-eyed Bean
    Salad, 49
    Broad Bean and Rice
    Pilav, 119, 120
    Broad Bean Eggeh,
    90
    Broad Beans with
    Carrots, 187
    Eggeh, 91
    Egyptian Brown, 40
    Green, with Eggs and
    Cheese, 101
    Green, in Yoghurt and
    Tomato Sauce, 54
    Haricot, in Oil, 158
    Red Bean and
    Spinach Soup, 21
    Red Beans in Oil, 164
    Spicy Red Bean Balls,
    50
    White Bean Salad, 81
Bedoughi Titvash, 239
Beetroot:
    Armenian Borsch, 24
    Milchik Borsch, 25
    Pickled, 228
    Salad with Dill, 75
    Spicy Beetroot Salad,
    76
    and Yoghurt Salad, 74
Beid Bil Khal, 86
Betingan, 198
Black-eyed Bean Salad,
    49
Borani-Ye-Gharch, 55
Borek(s),
    Baked, 209
    Deep-Fried, 209
    Filo Pastry for, 207
    Savoury Fillings, 198-9
Boreki Hamuru, 197

Borsch, 24, 25
Bras Yahni, 160
Brasi-Tahinabour, 22
Bread(s)
    Cicilian, 218
    and Courgette
    Eggeh, 97
    and Cucumber Dip,
    44
    'Fortune', 221
    Lavash, 214
    Onion, 216
    Persian, 217
    Pita, 215
    Pudding with
    Cherries, 265
    Pudding with Fruits,
    264
    Salad, 78
    Spiced, 222
    Thyme, 220
Broad Beans see Beans
Buckwheat Pilav (Kasha)
    with Mushrooms and
    Onions, 138
Burghul (Cracked
    Wheat), 130 35
    Balls in Tomato
    Sauce, 178
    with Eggs, 106
    in Kufta, 173
    and Nut Soup, 14
    and Nuts in the Tray,
    172
    with Salad
    Vegetables, 79
    Vine Leaves Stuffed
    with, 152-53
Burghul-Bi-Spanikh, 132
Burghul Pilav, 130
    with Basil, 131
    with Chickpeas, 135
    with Fruit and Nuts,
    133
    with Lentils, 173
    with Spinach, 132
    with Tahina Sauce,
    134
Cabbage:
    with Milk and Eggs,
    94
    with Sesame Seeds
    and Walnuts, 51
    Stuffed Leaves, 148
    and Tomatoes, 186
Cacik, 73
Carrot(s):
    with Broad Beans, 187
    and Celery, 188
    Green Peppers
    Stuffed with, 146
    with Lentil Salad, 83
    and Nuts, 196

and Orange Salad, 64
    Salad, 68
Cauliflower:
    and Pear Pie, 95
    Pickles, 229
    in Tomato Sauce, 56
Celery Bundles, 189
    and Carrots, 188
Çevisli Nokhud Çorbasi,
    13
Charoseth, 263
Chatzilim Im Avocado
    Amol, 46
    Im Gvina, 57
Cheese,
    with Aubergines, 57
    with Courgettes and
    Egg, 100
    and Cucumber Salad,
    77
    Fried, 47, 48
    with Green Beans
    and Eggs, 101
    Grilled, 47
    with Macaroni, 166
    Omelettes, 103, 104
    Pancakes, 105
    Pilav, 113
    with Savoury Pastry,
    205
Chelo, 109
    Sabzamini, 121
Cherry(ies):
    and Apple Soup, 34
    in Baklava, 254
    Bread Pudding, 265
    Pickled, 235
Chickpeas:
    Courgettes Stuffed
    with, 143
    with Cracked Wheat,
    135
    Paste with Tahina, 38
    Salads, 62, 84
    Soup with Tahina, 12
    Spicy Fried Chickpea
    Balls, 39
    and Spinach Salad,
    80
    and Walnut Soup, 13
Chirov Burghul Pilav, 133
Chocolate-Yoghurt Cake,
    272
Chourba Adas Wa
    Isbanekh, 20
Chourba-Bi-Kousa, 27
Christmas Pudding, 275
Cicilian Thick Bread, 218
Cinnamon-Yoghurt
    Sauce, 245
Çoban Salatasi, 67
Corn Soup, 26
Courgette(s),

and Bread Eggeh, 97
with Egg and Cheese, 100
with Lentils, 195
and Milk Soup, 27
with Parsley, 185
and Rice Pilav, 117
Stuffed, 142, 143
Yoghurt Pastry Stuffed with, 206
Cous-Cous Rice with Sugar, 273
Cracked Wheat, see Burghul
Cucumber:
 and Bread Dip, 44
 and Cheese Salad, 77
 Pickles, 227
 and Yoghurt Salad, 73
Dabanabour, 23
Dampokht, 120
Darçinli Yoghurt, 245
Date(s),
 and Almond Pudding, 270
 Pickled, 237
 with Pilav and Almonds, 126
 Sweets, 266
 and Walnut Cakes, 268
Datile, 270
Derevi Blor, 150
Dessert-e-Miveh, 276
Dolmas see Stuffed Vegetables
Dondurma Bil-Moz, 279
Doughnuts, Fruit, 260
Dukkous Al-Tamata, 247
Dzedzadzi Pilav, 136
Dzirani Hatsi-Anoush, 266
Easter Omelette, 88
Egg(s),
 Boiled, with Spaghetti, 168
 with Burghul, 106
 with Cabbage and Milk, 94
 Cauliflower and Pear Pie, 95
 with Courgettes and Cheese, 100
 with Green Beans and Cheese, 101
 with Okra, 93
 Onion Cake, 96
 with Aubergines, 92
 with Spinach, 89
 with Vinegar, 86
 see also Omelettes
Eggeh,
 Bean, 91

Bread and Courgette, 97
Broad Bean, 90
Leek and Walnut, 99
Potato, 98
Spinach, 89
Eggeh Bi Khubz Wa Kousa, 97
Bi Sabanah, 89
Egyptian Brown Beans, 40
El Ful (Ful Medames), 40
Elmali Kak, 267
Enginar Dolmasi, 140
Turşusi, 225
Etsis turlu, 182
Falafel, 39
Fasulya Piyazi, 158
Fattoush, 78
Fig Jam, 283
Filo Pastry:
 Baklava, 252
 Borek, 207
 Kataifi, 254
'Fortune' Bread, 221
Fruit,
 with Bread Pudding, 264
 Doughnuts, 260
 Dried, with Burghul Pilav, 124, 133
 Fresh Fruit Dessert, 276
 and Nut Paste, 263
 Pastes, 258
 Pickles, 239
 and Vegetable Soup, 32
Gaghamp Shoushmayov, 51
Gakhosi Drtzak, 189
Galatabourego, 256
Ganachi Borek, 199
Gananchi Porani, 180
Gardofilov Aghtsan, 70
Garlic-Yoghurt Sauce, 245
Garlic Tahina Sauce, 246
Gerosov Baklava, 254
Ghalieh Esfanaj, 183
Ghalieh-Ye Kadoo, 195
Grape(s):
 Basdegh, 258
 Pickled, 236
 Soup, 33
Green Peppers, Stuffed, 146
Gvina Pancake, 105
Hadigi Pilav, 137
Halawah Min Cous-Cous, 273
Harem Pilav, 122

Hasd Hats, 218
Hatsi-Anoush, 264
Havgtov Tzavar, 106
Herb(s),
 Bowl of, 36
 Rice, 111
Herishde, 16
Hiyar Turşusi, 227
Hummus-Bi-Tahina, 38
Ice Cream, 278-9
Imam Bayildi, 161
 Kabakli, 142
İncir Reçeli, 283
Iranian Plain Rice with Butter, 109
 Vegetable Stew, 179
Iraqi Stuffed Potato Balls, 154
Jajig, 73
Kabak Pilavi, 117
Kabakli Imam Bayildi, 142
Kahtzer Tzavabour, 14
Kalip Ekmegi, 264
Kapuska, 186
Karnabahar Turşusi, 229
Kasha with Mushrooms and Onions, 138
Kasmag Pilav, 115
Kataifi, 254
Kaymak, 244
Khagoghi Basdegh, 259
 Titvash, 236
Kharapaki Lobi, 54
Kharnabit Emforakeh, 56
Kharperti Gakhos, 188
Khorak-e Kadoo Ba Ja'Fari, 185
Khubz Arabi, 215
 Basali, 216
Kibbeh, 176
 Hali, 178
Kilisi Kufta, 171
Kishuyim Memulaim, 143
Kitry, 128
Kizi-Inzi, 144
Kookoo Sibzamini, 98
Kookoo-Ye Baghala, 90
Kookoo-Ye Loobia, 91
Kookoo-Ye Tareh Ba Gerdoo, 99
Kufta,
 Lenten, 174
 Lentil and Burghul, 173
 Sumak-flavoured, 171
Kunafeh, 254
Kythonopasto, 258
Labaneya, 29
Labna, 45
Lahana Dolmasi, 148
Lavash Bread, 214
Leeks(s):

with Olive Oil, 160
and Rice Pilav, 118
and Tahina Soup, 22
and Walnut Eggeh, 99
Lemons in Oil, 233
Lemoun Makbouss, 233
Lent Pizza, 200
Lentil(s):
 and Burghul Kufta, 173
 and Carrot Salad, 83
 with Courgettes, 195
 Dip, 43
 and Pasta, 170
 with Pumpkin, 194
 and Rice, 127-9
 and Rice Soup, 17
 Salads, 82-3
 Soup, 19
 and Spinach Soup, 20
 Vine Leaves Stuffed with, 153
Letzonadz Dakdegh, 146
Lobi Aghtsan, 81
Lobou Kuntig, 50
Loligi Mourapa, 282
Loligov Bamia, 181
Lolozig, 248
Lubyi Msallat, 49
Macaroni with Cheese, 166
 with Tahiniyeh Sauce, 169
 in Olive Oil 167
Makaruni, 167
 -Bil-Beid, 168
 -Bil-Tarator, 169
Makhlouta, 17
Mannaeesh, 220
Marak Anavim, 33
 Tapouzim Im Limon, 30
 Tiras, 26
 Yerakot Ou Perot, 32
Melokhia Leaf Soup, 28
Melon Ice Cream, 278
Menemen, 103
Milchik Borsch, 25
Mirkov Soongabour, 31
Miveh Pollo-Ba-Sabz, 124
Moz Bi Laban, 277
Mujaddarah, 129
Mushosh, 82
Mushroom(s):
 Avocado and Wine Pilav, 122
 Braised, 162
 and Fruit Soup, 31
 with Kasha, 138
 with Pilav, 116, 138
 with Yoghurt, 55

Mutabbal, 41
Nan-e Barbari, 217
Nazug, 222
Nor Bayazidi Lobi, 101
Nouri Salsa, 249
Noushov Pilav, 125
Nuts and Burghul in the
    Tray, 172
    and Carrots, 196
    Lenten Kufte Stuffed
    with, 174
    and Spices Dip, 37
    and Wheat Soup, 14
Nvig, 80
Okra(s),
    with Apricots, 192
    with Eggs, 93
    in Oil, 157
    Pickled, 230
    with Tomatoes, 181
Olive(s):
    Spiced, 224
    and Walnut Salad, 52
Omelettes:
    Cheese, 104
    Easter, 88
    Egg and Cheese, 103
    Rice and Omelette
    Pilav, 114
    Sephardic, 102
    Yoghurt, 87
Onion(s):
    Bread, 216
    Cake, 96
    Pickled, 226
Orange:
    and Carrot Salad, 64
    and Lemon Soup, 30
    Pickled Orange Rinds,
    240
    Salad, 63-4
Ougat Agas, 95
Pakhtakata, 221
Pancakes, Cheese, 105
Pancar Salatasi, 74
    Tursusi, 228
Parsley Sauce, 246
Pasta,
    Home-made (Rishta),
    165
    with Lentils, 170
    Macaroni, 166-7, 169
    Spaghetti, 168
    and Tahina Soup, 16
Pastry(ies) and Pies,
    Baklava, 252
    Filo Pastry (Boreks),
    197-207
    Galatabourego, 256
    Kalip Ekmegi dough,
    264
    Kunafeh, 254
    Lent Pizza, 200

Savoury Pastry with
    Cheese, 205
    Spinach Patties, 202
    Spinach Pie, 211
    Stuffed with Spinach,
    210
    Water, 204
    Yoghurt, Stuffed with
    Courgettes, 206
Patates Köftesi, 58
    Plakisi, 163
    Salatasi, 70
Peaches, Pickled, 234
Pear and Cauliflower
    Pie, 95
Persian Bread, 217
Peynir Kagiti, 47
Pickles, 224-40
Pilav(s),
    Buckwheat (Kasha),
    138
    Cracked Wheat
    (Burghul), 130-5
    Rice, 108
    Wheat, 136
Pistachio(s),
    Baklava, 253
    Kunafeh, 254
Pita Bread, 215
Pizza, Lent, 200
Plov Shashandaz, 114
Pomegranate(s),
    Sauce, 249
    Spinach in Juice of,
    182
    and Wheat Pilav, 137
Pooreh-Ye-Adas, 43
Portakal Salatasi, 63
Potato(es):
    Eggeh, 98
    Fingers, 58
    Iraqi Stuffed Balls,
    154
    Mashed, with Tahina,
    190
    Peas and Pickles, 69
    and Rice Pilav, 121
    and Soured Cream
    Salad, 70
    Stuffed with Spinach,
    156
    and Tomato Salad, 70
    Plaki, 163
Prasifuci, 102
Pumpkin(s),
    with apricots and
    Rice, 191
    Filling for Borek, 198
    Glazed, 193
    with Lentils, 194
    with Rice, 123
Quince(s),
    Kythonopasto, 258

Spread with Honey,
    280
Rasic Agvaniot, 59
Red Pepper Paste, 248
Rehanov-Tzavari Pilav,
    131
Rice (Pilav),
    with Almonds, 125-6
    Avocado, Wine and
    Mushroom, 122
    with Broad Beans,
    119-20
    Cheese Pilav, 113
    and Courgette Pilav,
    117
    and Dough Pilav, 115
    Herb, 111
    Iranian Plain, 109
    and Leek Pilav, 118
    and Lentils, 127-9
    and Lentil Soup, 17
    with Mushrooms, 116
    and Omelette Pilav,
    114
    Plain, 108
    and Potato Pilav, 121
    with Pumpkin, 123
    with Pumpkin and
    Apricots, 191
    Saffron, 110
    with Sauce, 112
    Vegetable and Fruit
    Pollo, 124
Rishta, 165
Rishta-Bil-Adas, 170
Rose Petal Jam, 281
Roz, 108
    -Bil-Tamar, 126
    -Ou-Hamond, 112
    -Wa-Kurrath, 118
Sabzi Pollo, 111
Saffron,
    Pudding, 274
    Rice, 110
Saganaki Haloumi, 48
Salad(s),
    Avocado, with
    Walnuts, 65
    Beetroot and Dill, 75
    Beetroot and
    Yoghurt, 74
    Black-eyed Bean, 49
    Bread, 78
    Burghul with Salad
    Vegetables, 79
    Carrot, 68
    Chickpea, 84
    Chickpea, with Tahina
    Dressing, 62
    Cucumber and
    Cheese, 77
    Lentil, 82
    Lentil and Carrot, 83

Mixed Vegetable, 66
Olive and Walnut, 52
Orange, 63
Orange and Carrot,
    64
Potato and Soured
    Cream, 70
Potato and Tomato,
    70
Potatoes, Peas and
    Pickles, 69
Shepherd's, 67
Spicy Beetroot, 76
Spinach and
    Chickpea, 80
Spinach, with Cream,
    72
Tahina, 42
Tomato, 71
White Bean, 81
Yoghurt and
    Cucumber, 73
Salad-e-Havij, 68
Salad-e-Nokhod, 84
Salad-e-Sabz, 69
Salat-e Panir Ve Khiar,
    77
Salat Gezer-Hai, 64
Salata Al-Banadora, 71
    -Al-Khadar, 66
    Bi Hummus Wa
    Tahiniyeh, 62
    Bil Adas Wa Jazar, 83
    Min Shawandar, 76
Sauces (and Dressings),
    Cinnamon-Yoghurt,
    245
    Garlic-Yoghurt, 245
    Parsley, 246
    Pomegranate, 249
    Red Pepper Paste,
    248
    with Rice, 112
    Tahiniyeh, 169
    Tomato, 56, 178, 247
    Yoghurt and Tomato,
    54
Seghi Baghbaghag, 278
Sephardic Omelette, 102
Serferjel, 280
Sesame Seeds with
    Cabbage, 51
Shakarov Tutum, 193
Shepherd's Salad, 67
Shertzazoon, 88
Shesh Havij, 196
Shol-e Zard, 274
Siserov Tzavari Pilav, 135
Sogan Tursusi, 226
Sohan Asali, 262
Soofganiyah, 260
Soong Yahni, 162
Soongov Pilav, 116

Sou Boreki, 204
Soup(s),
    Apple and Cherry, 34
    Almond, 15
    Armenian Borsht, 24
    Beetroot, 25
    Chickpea with Tahina,
    12
    Cold Yoghurt, 30
    Corn, 26
    Courgette and Milk,
    27
    Fruit and Vegetable,
    32
    Grape, 33
    Leek and Tahina, 22
    Lentil, 19
    Lentil and Spinach,
    20
    Melokhia Leaf, 28
    Mushroom and Fruit,
    31
    Orange and Lemon,
    30
    Pasta and Tahina, 16
    Red Beans and
    Spinach, 21
    Rice and Lentil, 17
    Vegetable, 23
    Walnut and Chickpea,
    13
    Wheat and Nut, 14
    Yoghurt and Barley,
    18
    Yoghurt and Spinach,
    29
Soured Cream
    (Smetana), 242
    with Green Beans
    and Tomatoes, 54
    and Potato Salad, 70
Spaghetti with Boiled
    Eggs, 168
Spanak Salatasi, 72
Spanakh Boregi, 210
Spanaki Me Ladi Eyas
    Key Domates, 184
Spanakopita, 211
Spas, 18
Spiced Bread, 222
Spiced Olives, 224
Spices,
    in Lenten Kufte, 174
    and Nuts Dip, 37
Spicy Beetroot Salad, 76
Spicy Fried Chickpea
    Balls, 39
Spicy Red Bean Balls,
    50
Spicy Tomato Sauce,
    247
Spinach:
    with Burghul Pilav,
    132

and Chickpea Salad,
    80
Egg, 89
and Lentil Soup, 20
with Olive Oil and
    Tomatoes, 184
Pastry stuffed with,
    210
Patties, 202
Pie, 211
in Pomegranate
    Juice, 182
Potatoes Stuffed
    with, 156
and Red Bean Soup,
    21
Salad with Cream, 72
and Yoghurt Soup, 29
Stuffed Vegetables
    (Dolmas),
    Artichokes, 140
    Cabbage Leaves, 148
    Courgettes, 142-3
    Green Peppers, 146
    Potato Balls, 150
    Tomatoes, 59
Stuffed Aubergine
    Pickles, 231
Vine Leaves, 150
Sughtorov Madzoun,
    245
Sumak, 171
Sumpoogi Titvash, 231
Sweets,
    Date-filled, 266
    Mulberry-shaped, 261
Tá amia, 39
Tabouleh, 79
Tahina,
    with Aubergine
    Purée, 41
    Cake, 271
    with Chickpea Paste,
    38
    with Chickpea Soup,
    12
    Dressing, with
    Chickpea Salad, 62
    and Leek Soup, 22
    with Mashed
    Potatoes, 190
    and Pasta Soup, 16
    Salad, 42
    Sauce, with Burghul
    Pilav, 134
    with Shepherd's
    Salad, 67
Tahina Tarator, 42
Tahiniyeh, 246
Tahinopita, 271
Tahinov-Abour, 12
Tahinov Tzavari
    Yeghintz, 134
Tamrieh, 266

Tan or Ayran, 243
Tapooz Im Salat-Zeytim,
    64
Tapoukhai Adama im
    Tered, 156
Tereotuli Pancar
    Salatasi, 75
Tetumi Lidsk, 198
Tfihat Kishurim, 100
Thyme Bread, 220
Titvash, 232
Tomato(es):
    with Aubergines and
    Scrambled Eggs, 92
    and Cabbage, 186
    Green Tomato
    Preserve, 282
    with Okra, 181
    and Potato Salad, 70
    Salad, 71
    Sauce, 56
    with Spinach and
    Olive Oil, 184
    Stuffed, 59
    and Yoghurt Sauce,
    54
Toot Shirini, 261
Topig, 174
Torsh-e Tareh, 179
Torshi-ye Barg-e Holoo,
    234
    -ye-Gheysi, 238
    -ye-Gilas, 235
    -ye-Khorma, 237
    -ye-Piaz, 226
    -ye-Poost-e
    Porteghal, 240
Toureto, 44
Tsitblig, 52
Turnips in Olive Oil, 159
Tutum Pilav, 123
    Printzov, 191
Tzavarov-Shomini Borek,
    202
Tzibbele Kugel, 96
Tziranov Bami, 192
Vartanoush, 281
Vegetable(s),
    Burghul with Salad,
    79
    and Fruit Pollo, 124
    and Fruit Soup, 32
    and Herb Filling for
    Borek, 199
    Iranian Stew, 179
    Mixed Vegetable
    Salad, 66
    Pickles, 69, 224-40
    Rich Stew, 182
    Soup, 23
    Stuffed, 144
Vine Leaves, Stuffed,
    150-53
Visneli Ekmek Tatlisi,

265
Vorpi Jash, 87
Vospabour, 19
Vospov Kufta, 173
    Litsk, 153
    Tutum, 194
Walnut(s),
    with Avocado, 65
    with Cabbage and
    Sesame Seeds, 51
    and Chickpea Soup,
    13
    and Date Cake, 268
    and Leek Eggeh, 99
    and Olive Salad, 52
Wheat:
    Lenten Stuffed Balls,
    176
    and Nut Soup, 14
    Pilav, 136
    and Pomegranate
    Pilav, 137
    Whole-grain, in
    Lenten Kufte, 174
Yarma Dolmasi, 152
Yazarf Sabzi, 36
Yoghov Shogham, 159
Yoghurt, 242
    Ayran, 243
    Banana, 277
    and Barley Soup, 18
    and Beetroot Salad,
    74
    Chocolate Cake, 272
    Cold Soup, 30
    and Cucumber Salad,
    73
    Dip, 45
    Garlic-Yoghurt Sauce,
    245
    with Mushrooms, 55
    Omelette, 87
    Pastry Stuffed with
    Courgettes, 206
    and Spinach Soup,
    29
    Stabilised, 243
    and Tomato Sauce,
    54
Yogurtlu Çicolata Kek,
    272
Yogurtlu Kabak Boregi,
    206
Yumourtali Batrijan, 92
Yumourtali Lahana, 94
Zaffron Pollo, 110
Zahtar, 37
Zeytun Msabbah, 224